Music from the Age of Shakespeare

A CULTURAL HISTORY

Suzanne Lord

David Brinkman, Advisory Editor

GREENWOOD PRESS
Westport, Connecticut • London

Library of Congress Cataloging-in-Publication Data

Lord, Suzanne, 1946–
    Music from the age of Shakespeare : a cultural history / by Suzanne Lord.
        p.   cm.
    Includes bibliographical references and index.
    ISBN 0–313–31713–5 (alk. paper)
    1. Music—England—16th century—History and criticism.   2. Music—Social
aspects—England—16th century.   I. Lord, Suzanne.   II. Title.
ML286.2.L67   2003
780'.942'09031—dc21   2002028441

British Library Cataloguing in Publication Data is available.

Library of Congress Catalog Card Number: 2002028441
ISBN: 0–313–31713–5

First published in 2003

Greenwood Press, 88 Post Road West, Westport, CT 06881
An imprint of Greenwood Publishing Group, Inc.
www.greenwood.com

Printed in the United States of America

The paper used in this book complies with the
Permanent Paper Standard issued by the National
Information Standards Organization (Z39.48–1984).

10 9 8 7 6 5 4 3 2 1

Copyright Acknowledgment

Every reasonable effort has been made to trace the owners of copyright materials in
this book, but in some instances this has proven impossible. The author and publisher
will be glad to receive information leading to more complete acknowledgments in
subsequent printings of the book and in the meantime extend their apologies for any
omissions.

Contents

Introduction

Music does not exist in a vacuum. Social, economic, and political situations affect the arts in concrete ways. Class divisions, economic resources of patrons and citizens, and the stability or instability of government may have affected what Elizabethan musicians wrote and for whom they were writing. It may also have affected how they supported themselves, with what frequency their works were published, and whether they were repressed in any way because of their political views or religious beliefs.

In turn, musicians tend to reflect the society in which they live. What languages did Elizabethan musicians use in their vocal works? Could they expect to find a patron or a buying public? Were citizens able to afford instruments or music so that a musician would have a market for his works? What sort of music did aristocrats want to hear? What types of music did people dance to? What styles of music did religious institutions prefer? Musicians were attuned to their times and wrote their music to fit the society in which they lived.

This book is concerned with the ways in which music fit into the lives of English people living during the reign of Queen Elizabeth I. Queen Elizabeth's reign (1558–1603) began after a turbulent era of religious and political upheaval. Because of her relative religious tolerance and her diplomacy, Queen Elizabeth created a sense of stability for her citizens that they had never known. After the defeat of the Spanish Armada in 1588, England blossomed, entering into a "Golden Age" of culture in which music played a major part.

This book introduces the world of Elizabethan music to the lay reader.

For the musically inclined, it is hoped that this book may spark further interest in this or a related topic. Research methods for this book consisted of casting a wide net to find book, journal, and Internet sources relating to Elizabethan musicians and music-related aspects of Elizabethan life. Several non-English sources were included because they were resources that an English person of the time would have consulted; one of these sources was Thoinot Arbeau's French-language dance instruction book, *Orchesography*.

Inclusion of composers in this book depended largely on the amount of work they did during Queen Elizabeth's reign. Some composers commonly referred to as "Elizabethan," such as Orlando Gibbons and John Bull, were either quite young when the queen died or did more actual work for her successors. Thus, they were not included in this volume.

Bibliographies at the end of each chapter provide sources for further reading on the subjects included in those chapters. If material is used from a source but is not directly quoted, the source will be listed in the bibliography but not necessarily in the chapter's notes.

Elizabethan society and its music is part of a rich, varied, complex world that can sometimes be overwhelming to an uninitiated reader. It is the author's hope that this book will provide a clearly marked path through this fascinating time, pointing out its most interesting and important aspects along the way. It is also hoped that the reader will be sparked to an active interest in seeking out, listening to, and perhaps playing music of the Elizabethan era.

THE ELIZABETHAN WORLD

If a present-day person were to step into the England of Queen Elizabeth's time, there would be more things different than just clothing. Society in Elizabethan England was stratified. Everyone was *not* equal. A rigid class system defined Elizabethan citizens as lower class, middle class, or upper class. These divisions might be economic—lower-class people tended to be poorer than middle-class people, who in turn tended to be poorer than upper-class people. But class divisions were not always economic. Some farmers of the lower class lived quite comfortably, and some nobles were constantly in debt. Class divisions were more than simple economics. The class that Elizabethans belonged to had to do with the way they lived, what they wore and ate, their education, the kinds of jobs available to them, and even their speech patterns.

When reading Elizabethan writing, present-day readers must realize that spelling was not universal. Spelling depended on the writer. An unmarried female might be spelled "maid," "maide," or "mayde." As long as a word could be read aloud, its spelling was considered correct.

ELIZABETH'S HERITAGE

Before considering Elizabeth I's reign, or Elizabethan music, it is worth taking some time to look at the cultural and social forces that shaped her and her tastes. Those same forces also shaped the citizenry Elizabeth would inherit when she became queen in 1558.

Henry VIII (1491–1547) (reigned 1509–1547)

The first and most important influence on Elizabeth's life was her father, Henry VIII. Henry Tudor was not supposed to be king. That honor was to be reserved for his older brother, Arthur. While Arthur was groomed for statehood, Henry spent his time hawking and hunting. While Arthur was marrying Katharine of Aragon, a daughter of King Ferdinand and Queen Isabella of Spain, to increase his future kingdom's power base, Henry was learning music, poetry, swordplay, wrestling, and jousting skills. In fact, Henry was getting the well-rounded education of a well-born younger son—that of a future gentleman. His possible occupations ranged from a soldier to a church cleric.

Then, in 1503, Arthur died.

Suddenly, Henry found himself named Prince of Wales and future king. Moreover, because Arthur's widow could not be returned to Spain without causing a nasty international incident, Pope Julius II himself gave permission for the young Henry (age 18) to marry his brother's widow (age 24) when Henry ascended the throne in 1509.

As soon as Henry began his reign, it was clear that music, art, and poetry were to have a prominent place in court life. His main musician, William Cornysh, staged music revels and pageants for court functions and festivities. He arranged the music for Henry and Katharine's wedding, just as he had for Arthur and Katharine's wedding.[1] Henry made sure that he had music wherever he went—even on military campaigns. An Italian visitor described the singing of the king's royal chapel musicians as "more divine than human."[2]

Henry's own private chapel was supplied with musicians of his own choosing, known as "Gentlemen of the Chapel." And naturally, these musicians would be the best he could find. Henry was especially ruthless in securing choirboys of talent. In many cases, he would simply demand that one or another highly placed cleric or establishment hand over a boy he had heard about.[3] One boy "obtained" from a cardinal's private chapel (Wolsey) was so well-trained that the king eventually also acquired the trainer—Richard Pyggott—who ended up training boys in the King's Chapel throughout Henry's reign as well as Henry's son's reign.

Henry not only enjoyed music but he also played it. Contemporary accounts tell of the king playing various keyboard instruments such as the organ, the virginal (a small, legless harpsichord), and the lute. A psalter (Protestant hymn book) belonging to Henry VIII includes a miniature (small-sized painting) by John Mallard of Henry playing a harp. Besides playing instruments, the king was "much delighted to sing." Not only did he sing alone, or accompanied by a lute, but he occasionally sang in consort with favored courtiers. One, Sir Peter Carew, had the honor of singing duets of "certain songs they called fremen [sic] songs, as namely 'By the bank as I lay' and 'As I walked the wood so wild' and etc."[4]

Henry VIII's love of music is reflected in the following statistic. In the time of Edward IV, there had been five permanent musicians on the court payroll. By the time Henry's reign was at an end, that number had grown to 58. These were permanent musicians and did not include part-time musicians, guest artists' visits, or extra musicians hired for special occasions. Henry also had an enormous number of instruments collected for his musicians' use. By the time of his death, he had 77 recorders alone.[5] He also owned 26 lutes and multiples of trumpets, viols, fifes, drums, keyboards, and sackbuts (an early type of trombone).[6] Clearly, he was musically ready for any occasion. And as a practicing musician himself, he had a keen appreciation of others' talents.

A fascinating document made available through most university libraries is *The King's Musick* by Henry Cart De Lafontaine. This document shows the published account books of the British royals' music expenses from 1549 to 1660. Of course, this includes Henry VIII's court as well as his father's and his children's courts. This collection of accounts contains the names, salaries, and job descriptions of all the musicians in the Tudor courts. This is how a great deal of information was gleaned about the various Tudors' musical tastes. Historians have the names of singers, composers, instrumentalists, and even the names of the boys who provided the high voices in the king's chapel choir. From this listing we see how the number and variety of musicians grew from Henry VII's to Henry VIII's court. We see when certain musicians were hired and when others died and were replaced. We see that the court paid for the "liveries," or uniforms worn by court musicians.[7]

Although as king of England Henry naturally hired many English musicians, he also hired quite a number of foreigners—particularly Italian, French, and Dutch musicians. Among the Italians were violist Ambrose Lupo and organists de Opitiis and Dionisius Memo (who had formerly been organist at St. Mark's Cathedral in Venice). Lutenist Philip van Wilder came to England from the Netherlands. These musicians brought music styles from their own homelands to meld with English music, bringing new styles into being from the cross-pollination. Between the years 1519 and 1528, Henry personally collected many manuscripts of music from France and the Netherlands, which made their styles available at court for performance and study.[8]

Henry also composed music himself. Thirty-four of his works are known to have survived. One is a sacred work, a motet entitled "O Lord, the maker of all thing."[9] Thirteen are instrumental, and 20 are vocal works. For most of the vocal works, Henry's "composition" was to add an extra line to an already existing work. For instance, he would take a three-part work and without changing any of those lines, he would add a fourth line of his own composition to be sung along with the other three lines. In that way he was said to have "composed" vocal works, even though he actually wrote only one of the lines.

As Henry's reign progressed, his personal troubles began intruding into his political life. His wife became pregnant time and time again, and contrary to popular belief, she did give birth to at least one male child. That child, also named Henry, was so welcome that Henry had a tournament held in honor of the occasion. (A woven tapestry depicting this tournament survives.) Sadly, however, the baby died at seven weeks of age. The other children either died in childbirth or shortly after. Only one child seemed likely to survive, and unfortunately for the realm, it was a daughter—Mary. Worse, as the years passed, Henry was well aware that he would be fertile for many years yet, while his wife was nearing the end of her childbearing years.

Having a boy was vital to Henry. Traditionally, the English crown went through the male line from father to son. Henry was only the second king in his line. His father, Henry VII, had taken the crown by force from another line of kings. Thus, the lack of a son might touch off a civil war among several powerful families, leaving the rest of his family out of power and in danger. Only a son would guarantee that the crown would stay in Henry's family.

By 1525, Henry's queen had turned 40. Henry had been abroad in a war with France off-and-on for some years. This put him in contact with the Boleyn family. Though English, the Boleyn children had spent much of their childhoods in France. The Boleyn's oldest daughter became Henry's mistress for a time, but his attention soon settled on a younger sibling—Anne Boleyn. Anne, unlike her older sister, refused to become Henry's mistress.[10] Henry was smitten. He was so overcome with love for Anne that some people at the time believed that she had actually used witchcraft to ensnare the lovesick monarch. Henry began to think of divorcing the now-menopausal Katharine and marrying Anne.

At that time England, as most of Europe, was part of the Roman Catholic Church. Accordingly, Henry approached the Pope in Rome (head of the Catholic Church) to declare his marriage to Katharine invalid. Pope Clement VII refused. Years before, Henry had been granted a special dispensation from the papacy in order to marry his brother's bride. Now Henry wanted the Pope to invalidate that dispensation, making his marriage to Katharine illegal and leaving him free to marry Anne Boleyn. He declared that the Bible itself frowned upon the marriage, citing two texts from Leviticus: (1) "Thou shalt not uncover the nakedness of thy brother's wife" and "If a man shall take his brother's wife, it is an impurity: he hath uncovered his brother's nakedness; they shall be childless." Since his marriage to Katharine had failed to produce a male heir, Henry considered his marriage "childless."

The Pope ordered a commission to decide the case in England, but Katharine would not recognize an English commission. Henry tried to force the issue by having his new minister, Thomas Cromwell, draw up a long list of grievances against the church in Rome. The English parliament passed a resolution that anything having to do with church legislation had to be passed by the crown. England stopped sending any money to the church in Rome.[11] The Pope threatened to excommunicate (cast out from the church) the English king and his entire country. According to Catholicism, an excommunicated person could not get into heaven.

At any other time, the Pope's threat would have terrified every citizen in England. This, though, was the time of the Protestant Reformation. In 1517, only a few years before Henry's decision to divorce Katharine, a Catholic monk named Martin Luther had protested many of the Catholic Church's practices. He had put his 95 points ("theses") onto a sheet of paper that he nailed to the door of the cathedral in Wittenberg, Germany, where he was a university teacher. Luther's intention had been to reform the Catholic Church from within. But when he was excommunicated, he and his followers, wanting to reform Catholic practices, began a movement called the Reformation. They were part of a movement of people protesting and thus became known as Protestants. And since the earliest Protestant church followed the teachings of Luther, they were called Lutherans.

Henry VIII knew of this Protestant movement. He realized that if a lowly monk could start a new religion, a king certainly could, too. Pope Clement still refused to grant the divorce, but in 1533 he let Henry have his choice of the next archbishop of Canterbury, the highest church office in England. Henry selected Thomas Cranmer, who immediately declared Henry's first marriage void, blessed Henry's marriage with Anne (whom he had already secretly married in private on January 25, 1533), and crowned her queen.[12]

Pope Clement excommunicated Henry. In 1534, Henry declared that he was the head of his own church—the Church of England, a Protestant religion. He declared the archbishop of Canterbury the highest church authority in the land but still under the crown's authority. He then had smaller monasteries put under the authority of the crown and dissolved the larger monasteries, giving their lands to his supporters in the gentry and taking their treasuries for the defense of the realm.

Meanwhile, Henry had his Anne. And Anne had their child on August 7, 1533—a girl named Elizabeth. A royal christening went forward, but one person was conspicuously absent—the bitterly disappointed Henry did not attend. Anne did become pregnant a second time. But on January 21, 1536, Henry had a bad fall from a horse. Anne was so frightened that the king might die that she miscarried her child on January 27—the day of her rival Katharine's funeral. By then, Henry had had enough of his marriage and had already been seeing Jane Seymour. To eliminate Anne, Henry had Anne and several of her favorite courtiers convicted of adultery. Anne was beheaded on May 19, 1536. Henry's next wife was Jane Seymour, who did manage to give birth to a boy, Edward (who became King Edward VI after Henry died), but Lady Jane died during childbirth.

Henry married three more times before he died but produced no more living children. He did, however, solidify the Church of England, annexed lands formerly owned by the Catholic Church, and oversaw his new church's music as well as the music of his court. For a while (1537–1538), Henry thought of allying his new church with the Lutherans, an idea that eventually came to nothing. Within 10 years, an English litany had been set up in place of Latin, many saint's days had been discontinued, images and relics were destroyed, and both Catholic and Lutheran books were banned.[13]

Henry's decision to break away from the Roman Catholic Church had an enormous effect on English religious music. At least 50 large monasteries were "dissolved" during Henry's Protestant reign, including such famous abbeys as Westminster Abbey, Glastonbury Abbey, Winchester Abbey, and Coventry. All the larger abbeys had annual incomes of anywhere from 500 to 3,400 pounds annually[14] and all had skilled choirs.

When Catholicism fell in England, so did all the English church music up to that time. All of England's choirs now found themselves out of work. The church organists, instrumental musicians, and chanting monks—all had to literally change their tunes.

At first, music was adapted wholesale from the Catholic Church. The archbishop of Canterbury, Thomas Cranmer, actually wrote some new tunes to English words, which have been lost.[15] He called them "plain-songs" because they were sung without harmony. At other times, Catholic melodies were simply supplied with new English words, a practice known as *contrafactum*. Cranmer's efforts are described in this letter to Henry VIII:

> I have travailed to make the verses in English, and have put the Latin note unto the same. Nevertheless, they that be cunning in singing can make a much more solemn note thereto. I made them only for a proof, to see how English would do in song. But because my English verses lack the grace and facility I would wish they had, your majesty may cause some other to make them again, that can do the same in more pleasant English and phrase.[16]

One of Henry's favorite composers, William Cornysh, died before the religious upheavals hit the church in England. Others saw their lives and careers buffeted in the upcoming religious storms. John Taverner, for instance, was caught in the confusion just as his career was starting. Taverner got his first large post as instructor of the Choristers of Cardinal College Choir (now Christ Church) in early 1526—just at the time Henry was defying the Pope over his marriage to Katharine. Taverner lost his next job in Lincolnshire when the Guild supporting his choir was no longer able to pay him, due to the 1534–1535 split with the Roman Church. He seems to have turned with the tide, however. Later, he actually supervised the tearing down and burning of parts of his former church—which were seen as "Popish."

Edward VI (1537–1553) (reigned 1547–1553)

Edward's formal education began at age six, when he left the care of the various women in whose charge he had been up to that time. Apparently, his education was not entirely solitary. Sons of highly placed nobles learned along with him. Accounts of his studies indicate that he was bright and a fast learner. Emphasis was given to Greek and Latin classics and Scripture, but he also learned French and English grammar, mathematics, geography, government, sports, and music. It is known that Edward played the lute, and it is assumed that he played other instruments as well. His lute teacher was one of Henry VIII's best musicians and one of the foreigners at the court—a Netherlander, Philip van der Wilder.[17]

When Henry VIII died in 1547, he left his nine-year-old son, Edward, to rule the kingdom. (Edward VI was the basis of the prince in Mark Twain's novel *The Prince and the Pauper*.) Edward VI was in no condition to run a country filled with ambitious nobles, a restless lower class, and a confused religious situation. Before dying, Henry VIII had appointed a Council of Regents to guide his son. But the council voted to appoint a lord protector, who soon set England's path as though he were the king himself. Once the lord protector even tried to arrange a marriage between Edward and Mary Queen of Scots.[18] An anti-Catholic, the lord protector pushed the Church of England forward.

Edward VI did not object inasmuch as he had been born and reared in his father's Church of England and had never been Catholic. So two years into his brief reign, the crown passed the Act of Uniformity, which insisted on the Church of England's Book of Common Prayer as the proper instrument for worship. If Catholics worshiped using the Catholic ceremony (including its music), they did so in private with the knowledge that they could be arrested for doing so.

Edward's enjoyment of music did not abate during his reign. Given pocket money by the lord protector, he spent some of it for lessons in playing the virginal. He was also given viols as a gift during his reign, which indicates that he must have had some interest in stringed instruments other than the lute. The musical establishment built by Henry VIII was kept up by Edward and even expanded. As Jennifer Loach wrote in her book, *Edward VI*:

> Edward, in the first years of his reign, paid wages to a harper, two lute-players, a flautist, two singing-men, one bagpipe-player, eight minstrels, a virginals player, John Heywood, one rebec player [a stringed instrument],

viol and sackbut [an early trombone] players, a drummer, and the musicians of the chapel royal. . . . By 1552 he had two harpers instead of one, two extra drummers and virginal players, and another flautist.[19]

Edward also took an active part in court entertainments such as "masques"—diversions that included poetry, singing, acting, instrumental music, and dancing music. Participants wore masks to conceal their identities. In this way the nobility and even royalty could feel free to participate in the activity.

In February 1553, the young king contracted a cold. Usually Edward could throw off an illness, but this time he did not. Historians have pored over the symptoms of his illness, suggesting everything from tuberculosis to poison. On July 6, Edward died at the age of 15, after months of suffering.[20]

Queen Jane (1537–1554) (reigned July 10–19, 1553)

Protestant leaders were horrified at the prospect of Edward's eldest sister inheriting the crown. Mary was the daughter of Henry VIII and Katharine of Aragon, and was a firm Catholic.

The dying king had been pressured by his advisors to name a Protestant successor, and Edward's religious councilors implied that he would burn in eternal hellfire if his Catholic sister, Mary, came to the throne after his death. Partly due to these influences, Edward chose Lady Jane Grey, a favorite relative with strong blood ties to the royal family, to succeed him. The royal council reluctantly consented to crown the 15-year-old, a devout follower of the Church of England, because the Protestant council also feared Mary's succession. But the council never actively supported Lady Jane's rule. Because of this internal strife and lack of military support, Lady Jane was queen for only nine days before being overthrown by forces supporting the older, more politically savvy Mary. Mary was in favor of sparing Lady Jane her life, but after Jane's father joined a rebellion the entire family's fate was sealed, and so Lady Jane, her husband, and her father were beheaded. Mary ascended the throne in 1553.

Mary Tudor (1516–1558) (reigned 1553–1558)

Throughout her childhood, Mary was seen as a political pawn—someone to marry off for political ends. Several matches were proposed and dropped. In 1527 Henry began trying to divorce Mary's mother, Katharine, in favor of Anne Boleyn. Mary's teenage years were dominated by her mother's fight through the courts and through the church to retain her position—and her daughter's legitimacy.

Even so, Mary was not a direct target of her father's displeasure. She was allowed to visit her mother, and she was also welcome at court where her father treated her well. Every Christmas she received 20 pounds "for to disporte her wt [with]."[21] This situation continued through Christmas of 1530, after which Henry banished Katharine from court. By 1533, Henry's marriage to Katharine had been declared annulled and Henry had married Anne Boleyn, and in September of that year, Anne gave birth to a daughter, Elizabeth.

Mary, declared a bastard and stripped of her title of princess, was indignant and defiant, attitudes that hardly helped relations with her father. Having battled Mary's mother for years, Henry was not inclined to battle his daughter. Mary was therefore sent to live with her sister, the infant Elizabeth, officially as Elizabeth's lady-in-waiting. She lived there under a form of house arrest for two-and-a-half years. Mary increasingly took her mother's side—a dangerous decision, for it put her under suspicion of treason. Not surprisingly, her social life and her education were halted.

Then, in 1536, Mary's mother died, and Anne Boleyn miscarried a boy child, after which Anne was accused of adultery, treason, and of poisoning Mary's mother. She was beheaded. Mary's life became a roller-coaster of being in and out of favor at court. At one time she would be required to give up her Catholic faith in order to secure her father's love. At another she would be standing godmother to her baby brother Edward. She was one of only 18 people invited to her father's last wedding, to Catherine Parr, with whom she became good friends.[22]

In 1547, Henry died and Mary's little brother, Edward, became king. During Edward's short reign, Mary kept private Catholic religious ceremonies in defiance of the Order of Conformity. Edward worried about her safety as a Catholic in a Protestant nation. "If you are troubled or molested," he told her, "it is against my will, and I will see you made contented."[23] Unfortunately, Mary was painfully aware how little weight this promise had, from a nine-year-old king under the influence of powerful Protestant nobles. During most of Edward's reign, Mary played a cat-and-mouse game between her religious convictions and the court.

Edward died in 1553, but instead of declaring his older sister Mary to be queen, he chose his Protestant cousin, Lady Jane Grey. Mary's overthrow of Lady's Jane's reign took less than two weeks. Mary received her crown in September, in a lavish coronation ceremony, accompanied by her younger sister Elizabeth. By the end of December, Protestant services had been declared illegal.

Mary had two aims: she wanted to marry Philip (later Philip II) of Spain, and she wanted to put England back under papal authority.[24] Both aims proved to be very unpopular. English nobility and commoners alike were afraid that if Mary married a Spanish ruler, England would in effect become a part of Spain. And when Mary tried to take back the church property that her father had given away during the dissolution of the abbeys, the gentry refused to give it up. Though Mary had been rather mild in her initial treatment of Protestants, she would soon earn the name she is most commonly known by: Bloody Mary.

In 1555 Mary repealed all the anti-Catholic laws passed by her father Henry and restored not only the church courts but the heresy laws of the Catholic Church as well. Under those laws, many Protestants faced jail, confiscation of their property, or worse. At least 300 people were burned at the stake during her reign, including Thomas Cranmer, Henry VIII's archbishop of Canterbury.

Mary's new husband didn't help her situation when he tried to bring England into a war between Spain and France. More unpopular than ever, Mary now had only one hope: to produce an heir. Mary did show signs of pregnancy in 1554–1555 that heartened her and her followers. Unfortunately, as the months dragged on, it was clear that Mary was not pregnant. Cribs and other nursery equipment were quietly put away by August 1555. Mary's "pregnancy" is a medical mystery still unsolved. She may have had a phantom ("hysterical") pregnancy, or she may have had a cyst or tumor. A rumor spread that she had delivered a "shapeless mass of flesh" but nothing was ever proved.[25] Philip clearly did not regard Mary as a love object, but for her part she was hopelessly in love with Philip. As time went on, the nature of their relationship became painfully clear to the embarrassed court. Again, at Christmas time in 1557, the queen announced that she was pregnant and this time waited to make sure. Over the next year her health declined in a harrowing up-and-down situation that kept her court, her husband, and her country constantly unnerved. She died on November 17, 1558, childless and with her husband absent overseas.

Mary's court was not a light-hearted place. She was serious and devout. However, Mary did have a musical side inherited from her musical father. When she was a toddler Henry VIII had hired one of Europe's best organists for his own court. Dionysius Memo brought his own organ and apparently taught Mary keyboard. She was playing the virginal for visitors at the age of three or four and she knew Memo from all the other courtiers, because she would call out to him from across a room and ask him to play. As Mary grew, so did her keyboard skills. She had a reputation for being able to play rapid, intricate passagework. When she acquired a household of her own as a young woman, she amused herself by teaching the women and girls in her household to play.[26]

But Mary's most surprising love was that of dancing. This was surprising because dance was thought to stir up too much passion in a young lady and both her tutors and religious instructors advised against it. She was precocious and, when she was six she danced before a Spanish Ambassador, twirling "so prettily that no woman could do better" and "acquitting herself marvellously well."[27] Mary charmed the court when, at age 11, she danced with her father.[28]

During Mary's processional to be crowned Queen of England, a special musical trick amazed the gaping crowd. A mechanical angel was rigged to hold a trumpet. When the trumpet was mechanically raised to the angel's lips, a hidden living trumpeter played a flourish. To the crowd, the angel seemed to be magically playing the trumpet.[29]

When Philip II arrived in England to wed Mary, they could converse because Mary spoke Spanish. But Mary's courtiers did not, and Philip's courtiers spoke no English. The attempt to bring the two sides together failed even in dance because neither side knew the others' dances. Mary and Philip compromised by dancing German dances—and everyone agreed that Mary was by far the better dancer.[30]

During her reign, quite a bit of continental music, primarily French and Italian, came into England. As far as church music is concerned, Philip brought his favorite composer with him—Antonio de Cabezon, who was in charge of all Philip's musicians. The English church musician Thomas Tallis is the most well-known musical name in Mary's time. His life reflects the changing fortunes of the times. As the *Development of Western Music* states:

> A list of Tallis's music reflects ecclesiastical changes in England. He composed Masses and votive antiphons during Henry VIII's reign, Anglican Services and anthems while Edward VI ruled, Latin hymns and a Mass when Mary was Queen, and both Latin and English music after Elizabeth I was crowned.[31]

When Mary lay dying, unloved by her husband and childless, she was cheered by a vision of children, playing in front of her and singing, that promised more comfort in heaven than she had found on earth. Music, one of her earliest pleasures, became her last.[32]

Elizabeth (1533–1603) (reigned 1558–1603)

Upon her older sister's death, Elizabeth, Henry VIII's last child, ascended the throne. Elizabeth's new kingdom was reeling from its recent events, the people having been through five monarchs in eleven years (including one queen for nine days). The country had been Catholic, then Protestant, then Protestant again, Catholic again, and with Elizabeth's accession was now Protestant again. Some feared that Elizabeth would counter the bloodbath started by her sister Mary with a purging of Catholics.

Elizabeth's childhood had not been easy. Her father was so disappointed at her birth, when she failed to be a son, that he didn't even attend her christening.[33] Before Elizabeth was three years old, her mother had been beheaded. Like Mary, she was declared illegitimate—a stain not removed until she was 11 years old, in 1544.

For obvious reasons, Elizabeth and Mary were never close. Elizabeth's mother, after all, was the reason Mary's mother had lost her throne. And having been her baby sister's lady-in-waiting may have grated on Mary throughout their growing up. In contrast, Elizabeth and Edward were particularly close. Both had grown up motherless, both were Protestants while Mary was adamantly Catholic, and they were closer in age.

Elizabeth's bad luck in parentage was repeated with her father's fifth marriage to Katherine Howard. The young Elizabeth formed an attachment to Katherine, who responded with kindness; unfortunately, however, Katherine was accused of adultery and beheaded. Elizabeth was eight years old at the time. Soon afterward, Elizabeth told one of her father's courtiers, Lord Leicester, during a conversation, "I will never marry."[34] It made an impression that Leicester never forgot. And Elizabeth never did marry.

Unlike Mary, Elizabeth seems to have been treated well by her father throughout her entire childhood. Elizabeth had a good education, which included instruction in music. Later, relations with her father became strained—particularly during his latter days. When Elizabeth was 12, she committed an unknown offense and was actually banned from court by her father. It took a year of apologies and help from her father's last wife, Catherine Parr, to put Elizabeth back into her father's good graces.[35] But when Henry died, Elizabeth and Edward clung to one another, sobbing so hysterically for such a length of time that on-lookers were amazed.[36]

When Edward ascended the throne, Elizabeth was still too young to live alone, so she continued to live with her stepmother, Catherine Parr. The ex-queen had married again, to the lord admiral of the English Navy, Thomas Seymour. Seymour took a very personal interest in his young ward, which made the now 14-year-old Elizabeth uncomfortable enough to rise early so that she would already be dressed when he arrived at her bedchamber.[37]

After Catherine Parr's death, Seymour proposed to Elizabeth, but she declined. Secretly he had hoped to force Edward to marry Lady Jane Grey while he himself married Elizabeth. He planned to replace Edward's uncle as lord protector and thus effectively take over the kingdom. Seymour was found in the king's chambers about to enter his room, apparently planning to kidnap the young king. This was treason. Seymour's marriage proposal implicated Elizabeth in the plot and caused a rift between herself and her brother. Elizabeth trod softly until she was cleared of all complicity.[38]

Under Mary's rule, Elizabeth was entreated to change her religion to Catholicism. Mary worried that Elizabeth was plotting against her, and Elizabeth was again implicated in a plot in which she had no active part. This time Elizabeth was imprisoned in the Tower and then placed under house arrest for a year. The location was remote enough that Elizabeth could have been assassinated at any time without intervention. Most people would have broken down under such a situation, but Elizabeth managed to walk the fine line between Mary's favor and disfavor.

When Mary finally realized that her "pregnancy" was nothing of the sort and that her life was at an end, she was persuaded by her husband Philip to declare Elizabeth her heir. Elizabeth was eating an apple under a tree at her childhood home, Hatfield, when she received the news that her sister had died and she was now queen of England.

Elizabeth was 25 years old. Her country had been ripped apart by civil strife for a generation. She inherited a confused, frightened, dispirited nation. Powerful lords drew together to take over management of her affairs, just as they had taken over for the nine-year-old Edward. Everyone wanted the young queen to marry and bear an heir right away. But this woman was her father's daughter, and nobody was going to manage Elizabeth, except Elizabeth herself.

CONCLUSION

Elizabeth had the best education available at the time. Intelligent and sensitive, Elizabeth was exposed to the arts through her education and through her father's court. Having survived several political crises that brought her close to death, and having watched her father's wives and her sister mistreated by their spouses, Elizabeth was determined to steer her own course in life. Although in her youth, Elizabeth entertained thoughts of a political marriage, she was never able to accept the fact of anyone sharing the reins of power with her, and so she remained single—the "Virgin Queen."

For Elizabeth, relaxation and rest lay in the arts. Her lavish clothing and jewelry, her support of visual arts, her love of dance, and her active interest in both sacred and secular music opened her court to these pleasurable activities. And the stability of her government, relative religious tolerance, and encouragement of music publishing helped all levels of English citizenry become prosperous enough to partake in more musical activities than ever before.

NOTES

1. D. Greer, *The New Grove Dictionary of Music and Musicians*, Vol. 4 (S. Sadie, ed.) (London: Macmillan, 1980), p. 795.

2. J.J. Scarisbrick, *Henry VIII* (Berkeley: University of California Press, 1968), p. 15.

3. H. Raynor, *Music in England* (Plymouth: Clarke, Doble & Brendon, 1980), p. 46.

4. Greer, *The New Grove Dictionary of Music and Musicians*, Vol. 8, p. 486.

5. D. Stevens, *Tudor Church Music* (New York: W.W. Norton, 1966), p. 278.

6. Scarisbrick, p. 15.

7. H.C. de Lafontaine (ed.), *The King's Musick* (London: Novello and Company, n.d.).

8. Scarisbrick, p. 15.

9. Ibid., p. 16.

10. W.H. Harris and J.S. Levey (eds.), *The New Columbia Encyclopedia* (New York: Columbia University Press, 1975), p. 325.

11. Ibid., p. 1226.

12. Ibid.

13. P. Le Huray, *Music and the Reformation in England, 1549–1660* (New York: Oxford University Press, 1967), pp. 2–4.

14. Ibid., p. 3.
15. Ibid., p. 5.
16. Ibid., p. 7.
17. J. Loach, *Edward VI* (New Haven, CT: Yale University Press, 1999), p. 15.
18. Harris and Levey, p. 835.
19. Loach, p. 148.
20. Ibid., p. 167.
21. D. Loades, *Mary Tudor: A Life* (Cambridge, MA: Basil Blackwell, 1989), p. 60.
22. Ibid., p. 117.
23. H.W. Chapman, *The Last Tudor King* (Oxford: Alden Press, 1958), p. 196.
24. Harris and Levey, p. 1709.
25. Loades, p. 251.
26. C. Erickson, *Bloody Mary* (Garden City, NY: Doubleday & Company, 1978), p. 41.
27. Ibid., p. 54.
28. Ibid., p. 67.
29. Ibid., pp. 319–320.
30. Ibid., p. 378.
31. K.M. Stolba, *The Development of Western Music* (Dubuque, IA: William C. Brown Publishers, 1990), p. 249.
32. Erickson, p. 481.
33. "Christening of Ladie Elizabeth," http://www.elizabethi.org/christening.htm, July 2, 2000, p. 2.
34. E. Jenkins, *Elizabeth the Great* (New York: Coward-McCann, 1959), p. 17.
35. Ibid., p. 19.
36. Ibid., p. 23.
37. "The Lady Elizabeth," http://www.elizabethi.org/ladyelizabeth.htm, July 2, 2000, p. 6.
38. Jenkins, pp. 30–31.

REFERENCES

Chapman, H.W. *The Last Tudor King*. Oxford: Alden Press, 1958.
"Christening of Ladie Elizabeth." http://www.elizabethi.org/christening.htm, July 2, 2000.
Erickson, C. *Bloody Mary*. Garden City, NY: Doubleday & Company, 1978.
Harris, W.H., and Levey, J.S. (eds.). *The New Columbia Encyclopedia*. New York: Columbia University Press, 1975.
Jenkins, E. *Elizabeth the Great*. New York: Coward-McCann, 1959.
"The Lady Elizabeth." http://www.elizabethi.org/ladyelizabeth.htm, July 2, 2000.

Lafontaine, H.C. de (ed.). *The King's Musick*. London: Novello and Company, n.d.

Le Huray, P. *Music and the Reformation in England, 1549–1660*. New York: Oxford University Press, 1967.

Loach, J. *Edward VI*. New Haven, CT: Yale University Press, 1999.

Loades, D. *Mary Tudor: A Life*. Cambridge, MA: Basil Blackwell, 1989.

Raynor, H. *Music in England*. Plymouth: Clarke, Doble & Brendon, 1980.

Sadie, S. (ed.). *The New Grove Dictionary of Music and Musicians*. London: Macmillan, 1980.

Scarisbrick, J.J. *Henry VIII*. Berkeley: University of California Press, 1968.

Stevens, D. *Tudor Church Music*. New York: W.W. Norton, 1966.

Stolba, K.M. *The Development of Western Music*. Dubuque, IA: William C. Brown Publishers, 1990.

Music from the
Age of Shakespeare

Chapter 1

Music of the Nobility

Being a gentleman or a gentlewoman in Elizabethan times meant that you had a certain education and certain standards of conduct. Music was a big part of both, as is evident in Henry Peacham's "how-to" book for noble conduct, *The Compleat Gentleman* (1622), in which he wrote: "Whom God loves not, that man loves not Musicke: but I am verily persuaded, they are by nature very ill disposed, and of such a brutish stupiditie, that scarce any thing else that is good and favoureth of vertue, is to be found in them."[1] He answers those who say that music is frivolous with examples of music in the Bible, and continues:

> The Physitians will tell you, that the exercise of Musicke is a great lengthner of life. . . . the exercise of singing openeth the breast and pipes; it is an enemy of melancholy. . . . Yea, a curer of some diseases. . . . Beside, the aforesaid benefit of singing, it is a most ready helpe for a bad pronunciation, and distinct speaking . . . yea, I my selfe have knowne many Children to have ben holpen of their stammering in speech, onely by it."[2]

Peacham defined nobility in this way:

> Nobilitie then (taken in the general sence) is nothing else then a certain eminency, or notice taken of some one above the rest. . . . More particularly, and in the genuine sence, Nobilitie is the Honour of blood in a Race or Linage, conferred formerly upon some one or more of that Family, either by the Prince, the Lawes, customes of that Land or Place, whereby either out of knowledge, culture of the mind, or by some glorious Action per-

formed, they have beene usefull and beneficiall to the Common-wealths and places where they live."[3]

Upper-class Elizabethans acquired their status through service or relationship to the crown. Relatives of reigning heads were accorded certain titles, lands, and privileges. Other members of the upper class had been rewarded with land, which might include entire villages. Rents provided a money base on which the upper class built vast wealth and holdings of both land and businesses. They grew their wealth up through investments and intermarriage. Marriages were arranged for business advantage and social status, rarely for love.

STRATA OF ELIZABETHAN NOBILITY

The Elizabethan upper class was split into several subcategories. The gentry (gentlemen) were royally created "knights," though no one actually expected them to put on armor as a real knight would. It was an honor bestowed for serving the crown in some way, and it came with an income and the title of "Sir." During her reign, Queen Elizabeth created 878 new knights. Titles of the gentry were generally for the holder only and were not passed on to their offspring. Their offspring were known as "Esquires"—and with permission from the crown, that title might be hereditary throughout following generations. The father would sign, "Sir John Doe," the son would be "John Doe, II, Esq.," and so on.

The peerage—a rank of nobility—was a step up from the gentry and a step closer to the royal court. There were only 57 peers in all of England when Queen Elizabeth began her reign, and in her long rule only 18 peerages were created or restored. These were, in descending order: dukes (one rank below the rank of prince), marquises, earls, viscounts, or barons (the lowest order of hereditary titles), and they served in the House of Lords. These titles were supposed to come with land, but Elizabeth was outstandingly stingy in this respect.

Courtiers were at the top of the heap, closest to the crown. This did not mean that they all had to live in London, however. The court moved to different areas of the kingdom during its summer "Progresses," and anything within a 10-mile radius of the monarch was considered the "customary precincts" of the court. When the court moved, it came with about 400 people—and some of those had household servants of their own! Of the more powerful offices, the lord high steward was responsible for 25 "below-stairs" departments of servants who kept the royal household running day to day and also oversaw the treasury department.

The lord great chamberlain headed the "above-stairs" servants such as the Privy Chamber and Bedchamber servants. These were personal servants to the royal body and were scrupulously screened. Any of them would be close enough to assassinate a monarch, if they were so inclined. Another important office was master of the horse; this person was responsible for the care of the royal stables and kennels. Although classed as "servants," these were upper-class people. Monarchs weren't dressed by commoners.

During Elizabeth's time, the Privy Chamber lost its status. These close advisors could only be men, and men were not going to be helping Elizabeth get dressed. Queen Elizabeth's personal servants usually included four "ladies of the Bedchamber," seven or eight "gentlewomen of the Privy Chamber," six to eight maids of honor, three or four "chamberers," and a number of unpaid "ladies of honor" who stood with the queen during ceremonies.

NOBLE ATTITUDES TOWARD MUSIC

The Elizabethan Court

The best example of Elizabethan music appreciation came from the crown—Queen Elizabeth herself. Besides playing the virginals and the lute and singing, she had even composed music in her youth. And best of all, her lively interest in music kept her aware of, and open to, new music trends. The musicians (composers, singers, and instrumentalists) at court knew how musical she was and appreciated that she understood what they were doing. Between the secular music at court and the sacred music in her chapel, Elizabeth employed about 60 musicians at any one time. In fact, through the records of payment, known as the Old Chequebook, it is possible to see when particular musicians were hired and when they left or died.

Ambassadors and other important court visitors were treated to England's best music, either at court or at any estate at which they might be staying. When a Spanish ambassador visited the Elizabethan court in 1576, he declared, "in all my travel of France, Italy, and Spain, I never heard the like [of] a concert of music, so excellent and sweet as cannot be expressed."[4]

Elizabethan court accounts show changes in music over her 40-year reign. For instance, the first year of her reign—1558—is the last time a "rebec" (a stringed instrument more medieval than Renaissance) is listed as being bought. It was also the year that the last court bagpipe player died. He was not replaced. Over the years, Elizabeth hired fewer viol players and more violin players—a clear indication that the newer, more superior instrument was overtaking its ancestor. There were also an increasing number of foreign musicians on the court payroll—particularly from the Bassano, Ferrabosco, and Lanier families.

The Courtiers and Other Nobles

The queen's example encouraged her courtiers and other nobles to have some knowledge of music and, if they did not personally play or sing, to encourage those who could by means of patronage. It did not mean that the gentlefolk had to perform like professionals or display their talents in public. As Peacham put it, "I desire no more in you then to sing your part sure, and at the first sight, withall, to play the same upon your Violl, or the exercise of the Lute, *privately to your selfe*."[5]

Mention of musical ability in Elizabethan courtiers is fairly common. One of Elizabeth's ladies-in-waiting sang and played the lute. The earl of Oxford was so musical that "using the science as a recreation, your Lordship has overgone most of them that make it a profession."[6] The groom of the Privy Chamber studied music with Thomas Tallis. When the first earl of Essex lay dying in Dublin, he asked his musician to play on the virginal while he, the dying man, sang.

Elizabeth's father, Henry VIII, had unwittingly set the stage for all this musicality among the nobility when he dissolved the monasteries and put hundreds of Catholic church-supported musicians out of work. Somebody had to pick up the tab, and it was largely the noble class. Of course, the Church of England also hired musicians. But the Protestant church never used as many musicians as the Catholics had. Part of the reason was the rise of Puritanism throughout Elizabeth's reign. Puritans saw little use for music, except within the strictest religious boundaries. So instead of the Protestant church taking up music from the Catholic Church, it was the nobility who hired musicians for their private courts or commissioned works, in imitation of the court. Many talented musicians jostled among themselves from Henry's reign to Elizabeth's for a spot either in the court or in a well-established private household.

Elizabeth's reign itself had a direct effect on musicians and other artists. Particularly after the defeat of the Spanish Armada, England exploded

with self-confidence. The arts—particularly the literary and musical arts—
were one of its major manifestations. The Elizabethan Age was one of
the rare times in history when the arts, the patrons, and the audience
coalesced. The creative artist could "fulfill himself within the general
tradition, which [was] wide enough and inclusive enough to allow space
for development in every direction."[7] Although Elizabethan England did
not invent many new types of music, it took other preexisting forms of
music such as the ballad and madrigal to their highest point of development.

MUSIC EDUCATION

Nobly born children learned musicianship at home. For example, in
the Petre family, Sir William—a politician and member of the Royal
Privy Council—gave his housekeeper extra money to teach his daughters
how to play the virginals. Little Lord Petre had his own virginals and a
lute made in Cologne by the time he was nine years old. The Kytson
family hired a musician to teach their children to play the virginals. The
earl of Rutland paid a lutenist to teach his children, as well as a personal
servant to play the lute, so that his children's musical education would
not be interrupted when the regular teacher was away. Some lucky children had very highly placed music teachers. In 1579 the daughter of the
earl of Northumberland had William Byrd as her music tutor. Other families had servants who did double duty as musicians. One household had
six servants who played treble lute, treble viol, bass viol, bandora, cithern,
and flute. Since they do not show up in the financial records as a privately
supported professional sextet, scholars conclude that they had other duties
to perform at other times.

Noble boys and girls did not attend petty (public grammar) schools;
instead, they were taught by a governess in their earliest years. After that,
the vast majority of children undergoing formal education were boys.
Many went to public (boarding) school, which only meant that they were
not being taught at home by a tutor. Parents paid tuition and boarding
fees if the child lived at the school, which many children did. Schools
were designed to breed unquestioning obedience, courage, self-control,
and an appreciation for serving country and crown. School hours were
6:00 to 11:00 A.M., lunch, and 1:00 to 5:00 P.M.

Some public grammar schools offered music instruction in their cur-
riculum. The Merchant Taylors' School, geared more toward the gentry
than the upper nobility, taught both instrumental music and singing. Its

headmaster wrote that teaching instrumental music was good "to get the use of our small joints before they be knit, to have them the nimbler, and to put musicians in mind that they [students] be no brawlers, lest by some swash of a sword they chance to lose a joint." Singing was good "by way of physic, to spread the voice instruments within the body, while they be yet young."[8] This headmaster also had pupils learn a certain amount of composition and counterpoint, just as a student might be required to write a poem or try to paint, "so that his criticism of these arts would be more informed and intelligent."[9]

One type of school that taught music was the Choir School. Many future music professionals got their start in these Choir schools. One of the best of them was Magdalen College School which ended at what an American would call a high school level (about age 18). The Magdalen School was founded in 1480 as a Catholic school. It was meant to be a "feeder" school to prepare boys for later education at Magdalen College. Among its more famous early pupils was St. Thomas More. All boys received an excellent education, but only the most musically talented were trained to become choristers. The school became Anglican later, but its training of choristers remained steady. Both the Magdalen School and Magdalen College are still in existence, and still train talented boys to serve as College Choristers.[10]

The colleges offered more music opportunities than the grammar schools had. Trinity College had a set of instruments on hand for their members to use either for their own amusement or to learn. Music was so popular in St. John's College that in 1576 it had to institute a rule that instruments were not to be played during quiet study times. In 1581, the head of Caius College complained that the singing and organ playing was a constant distraction from studying.

Music in Higher Education

After college, the vast majority of well-born young gentlemen went to university. Most sons of the well-to-do went to the Inns of Court. Four legal societies comprised the Inns and were able to admit candidates to the bar: Lincoln's Inn, Gray's Inn, the Inner Temple, and the Middle Temple. It was there that young gentlemen learned governance and law. Elder sons would be governing estates in the future, whereas younger sons might go into the law or politics as a profession. Going into the law was a good way to make a living in Elizabethan times; people sued one another so often that knowledge of the law was essential.

The Inns of Court also served as the place where young gentlemen learned how to act like gentlemen. The Inns were valued "for their cultivated atmosphere and for their nearness to the Court and its manners."[11] This acquisition of "polish" included music, even as far back as Henry VIII's day when the following was written: "there is, besides a school of law, a kind of academy of all the manners that the nobles learn. There they learn to sing and to exercise themselves in every kind of harmonics. They are also taught there to practise dancing and all games proper for nobles, as those brought up in the King's household are accustomed to practise."[12]

Privately, noble students would exchange lutes with one another and lend music manuscripts out for copying by a friend. A student in 1581 asked for money from his father because his lute was substandard. If his father wanted him to learn to play better, the student wrote, he would need a better instrument. Presumably, he got the funds. Besides music, students learned to dance, and they learned something of drama, particularly at the traditional Christmas "revels." Later, these revels—the equivalent of Harvard's "Hasty Pudding" entertainments—were replaced by masques—a hodge-podge of singing, dancing, and play-making that were the forerunner of English opera. Some masques have survived and still carry the name of their Inn, such as "Gray's Inne" and "Lincoln's Inn Masque." Although these students were not going to be musicians, because of their training, they were poised to become patrons of the arts as well as enthusiastic amateurs.

Other young gentlemen went to other universities, some of which offered courses—or even degrees—in music. In universities, music courses were generally a branch of mathematics. During the Renaissance, scholars looked to ancient Greece and learned that civilization had counted music as a science. Possibly as a part of this perception of music, the bachelor of arts degree in music attained the same level of prestige as degrees in law, theology, and medicine.

Even with courses in music, it was understood that young gentlemen would continue their music education—particularly instrumental learning—with a music tutor on a private basis. These tutors, though not technically on the university staff, were readily available to students. When the future earl of Northampton went to King's College, he brought his lute to further his skill, and he hired a tutor to this end. Some professors who had musical talent also tutored music. A student in one university was taught music by his professor of Greek. Students and "dons" (professors) sometimes engaged in informal music making. It was not particularly unusual for a student and professor to take a walk and sing in parts along the way.

Singing was essential, and playing an instrument was also quite acceptable. But all instruments were not equal in Elizabethan eyes. For instance, it was considered demeaning for a gentleman to play a wind instrument because it caused one's face to be distorted. From Shakespeare's *Hamlet*, we have this assessment:

> To play on the viol with a stick, doth not alter man's favour, nor disgraceth any gentleman: but otherwise, to play on the flute, his countenance altereth and changeth so oft, that his familiar friends can scant know him. Moreover, the harp or viol doth not let him that playeth on them from speaking or singing as he playeth: where he that playeth on the flute, holdeth his mouth so hard to it, that it taketh not only his words from him but his voice.[13]

The Grand Tour

Before settling down to adult matters, yet one more experience was essential to a young gentleman's cultivation: the Grand Tour. This was an extended trip throughout Europe, which put the final shine on young men's "polish" and acquainted them with various cultures, systems of government, and styles of warfare. All this experience would be of great use for future ambassadors, political figures, and military leaders. It also afforded youth a chance to add a "European touch" to their other skills, such as fencing, horsemanship, dancing, and music. As tourists do today, these young travelers brought back souvenirs—often music and instruments. They also took lessons abroad. The twelfth earl of Arundel made so many trips to Italy that Italian composer Innocenzo Alberti dedicated a collection of madrigals to the earl in 1566. The young earl, for his part, sent a great deal of music from Italy and the Netherlands back to England. "His enormous library . . . illustrates the interest shown in European musical developments by many English musicians and patrons in the last quarter of the century."[14]

This cross-pollination worked both ways, with Europeans becoming aware of English music through the same tours. English music had actually been introduced on the Continent over 100 years before, when British composer John Dunstable's "contenance Anglois" had caused musical electricity throughout France and ultimately changed European music. After the interruption caused by England's political situation, the doors opened again in the Elizabethan Age. Italian composer Filippo di Monte and William Byrd exchanged works in a musical "show and tell" of their individual treatments of the same Psalm. John Bull was so in demand on the Continent that a nervous Queen Elizabeth ordered him back to England before another court could snatch him up. Over the years, English music gained respect: "while the Italians and the French supposed that English poetry could not exist, they knew that English music might equal or surpass their own."[15]

Women and Music Education

Although a young woman's education was less important, "it was part of every young gentlewoman's education to read and write, and play upon the virginals, lute, and cittern; and to read pricksong at first sight."[16] Since women ran the household part of the estates, they would also grow to become important patrons of music and other arts. It was lamented that, after having learned an instrument in their youth, women tended to drop it in their later lives. "We see this daily verified in our young women and wives, that they being maids took such pains to sing, play and dance, with such cost and charge to their parents to get those graceful qualities, now being married will scarce touch an instrument."[17]

FASHIONABLE MUSIC AND UPPER-CLASS PATRONAGE

Even as late as 1589 (when the queen was 56), it was said that Elizabeth's musical skill "is so well as I assure you six or seven galliards in a morning, besides music and singing is her ordinary exercise."[18] Even in her later years she still played the virginals and lute privately, and she enjoyed hearing music at festivities in London or when visiting her nobles at their manors. Heads of great houses served at court, including minors who were wards of the court. They learned the importance of music at court and spread it to their own estates.

Some nobles played music themselves, and others supported it. They hired musicians, entertained friends and guests with music, exchanged music with friends, had a musical influence in the locality, bought instruments, and had musicians write, copy out, or buy music for them. These are the nobles pictured holding their favorite instruments or with musical symbols on their family emblems. They are named in title pages, and they made lists of their personal libraries that included many music books. Modern researchers owe much to these avid collectors inasmuch as volumes in their libraries were sometimes the only way that certain works have survived. The music list for one gentleman's private library included music by Dowland, Byrd, Robert Jones, Philip Rosseter, Michael Cavendish, Thomas Morley, John Farmer, John Bennett, Giles Farnaby, Nicholas Yonge, Thomas Robinson, John Wilbye, and Henry Youll—as well as other manuscript books privately copied. Without private library collections, much of Elizabethan music—particularly that of lesser composers—would have been lost.

Noble Elizabethan families did not hire house musicians only to teach their children how to sing or play an instrument. They also served as agents, ever on the lookout for good music. If the lord's estate was in an outlying area of England and they didn't have a family member serving at court, their house musician might make frequent trips to London, the seat of English power, where the best English musicians could be found. It was in London where the wealth of English trade centered, where powerful and wealthy courtiers lived, and where music was brought for publication. It was also where foreign musicians tended to live and where foreign music publications were imported. The British nobility especially favored Italian music of the Renaissance. In fact, a book of Italian madrigals brought that form to England and caused a madrigal "boom" after 1588. The Ferrabosco family in particular had been a fixture in Elizabeth's court for years. "These men and their families established their own dynasties of royal musicians and were of as great importance to the flowering of the English madrigal and lute songs as were the Italian musical publications themselves."[19] Library records and the wills of noble families point to their collections of foreign works. Edward Paston's will cited "many printed and manuscript setts of Lattin, French and Italian songs."[20]

A musicial agent might hear of a good work through court circles or connections through his lord's family and would look through a manuscript or hear it to judge its worthiness. If it were suitable, the musician would recommend that his lord purchase it or arrange for the manuscript to be copied. Household accounts of the Petre family show that even a person of William Byrd's stature was not beneath checking out and recommending music books for the Petre household's children.

Queen Elizabeth was an active participant in this hunt for good music. In one specific instance, the queen heard that her secretary had some good "older" verses. She had them sung before her and found them to her liking. Once that happened, a musical agent who had heard of the queen's favor had the same songs copied and recommended them to his lord. In a letter accompanying copies of the manuscript, this agent wrote, "It was told her Majesty that Mr. Secretary had rare musicke and songes. She wold needs hear [them] and so this ditty was soung which ye see first."[21] The queen was not above "drafting" good musicians—either composers or performers—from her subjects' courts to her own. Nobles who had musicians of quality often found them hired away by the court. The family had no choice in the matter except to give up their musician.

THE QUEEN'S MUSICK

The orchestra as we know it today was unknown in Elizabethan times. A stringed orchestra described by Praetorius in the early 1600s consisted of a spinet (a keyboard instrument), plucked stringed instruments such as theorboes, lutes, bandores, orpharions, citterns, or a large bass lyra, and possibly a bowed stringed instrument such as a bass viol. The equivalent of a court orchestra in Elizabethan times was a group called the "Queen's Musick," instrumentalists who were gathered from all over the world for their playing skill and were hired to provide instrumental music for the queen. About 30 in all, anywhere from half to two-thirds of the musicians were foreign born. Most of those were from Italy, and many were Jewish. The English court was very attractive to Italian Jews, providing greater chance for a life in a court that was at least officially anti-Catholic and anti-Lutheran. It also got them out of the ghettos, which had been recently established in Italy. Elizabeth's court was more paranoid about its Catholic members, who might plot to put the Catholic Mary Queen of Scots on the throne, than it was about any Jewish people at court.[22]

Foreign or native, Jewish or Christian, the Queen's Musick musicians were paid more than any other musicians at court—including the musicians in the Chapel Royal. The average wage for playing in the Queen's Musick was 46 pounds per year, as opposed to 30 pounds for a Chapel Royal singer. And if the queen really wanted a particular musician, she was not stingy about offering more. Alfonso Ferrabosco was paid 66 pounds a year when he first arrived at court from his native Italy. By the time he returned to the Continent five years later, he had become one of the queen's favorite instrumentalists, and she offered him the unheard of wage of 100 pounds per year to come back.[23] Scholars regard this as a sign of Elizabeth's respect for instrumental music making and as a catalyst for the rest of her country to follow her lead.

Musicians of the Queen's Musick played for court occasions, festivities, and for the queen's pleasure. If Elizabeth entertained an ambassador from

France or the Netherlands, the Queen's Musick stood ready to play for their entertainment. If a theater production were put on at court, they might play whatever music was required for the performance. If the queen held a ball, the Queen's Musick would play for the dancers. And if the queen wanted music while she ate, or to lull her to sleep, they provided that as well.

GENTLEMAN COMPOSERS

With the surge in music literacy, some nobles themselves became as good as professionals either in their playing or composing. The talented Fernando Heybourne was a trusted courtier, and the musical William Stanley was a peer of the realm. It was not a gentleman's place, however, either to perform in public or to have works put on public display—for instance, having them published. In a 1570 behavior manual, young gentlemen are urged to "singe and playe of instrumentes cunnyngly."[24] On the other hand, they are cautioned that the "over much studie" of some "sciences"—one of which is music—could mar a person's character.

Since being in the public eye as a professional was not part of the gentlemanly code, most gentlemen with a musical bent made excuses for having a work in publication. Some, for example, used initials rather than their full names. Heybourne wrote under the name of Richardson. Others insisted that the work was a very old one that they had recently discovered and had put a few improvements on—not something that they had in fact written. Often they wrote that the only reason the work was published was because their friends insisted on it. One ruse for allowing a work to be published was to claim that some unscrupulous person had put out a bad print of the same piece under another name, and therefore the true composer was printing his work only to straighten things out. This made the printing of a work more of a moral duty than an act of purpose. Philip Rosseter used both excuses, writing that his 1601 *Book of Ayres* was "made at his vacant houres, and privately emparted to his friends, whereby they grew both publicke, and (as coine cract [cracked] in exchange) corrupted; some of them both words and notes unrespectively challenged by others."[25] Another common excuse was that the poetry was so wonderful that the composer couldn't help putting it to music. As one dedication stated, "The language they speake you provided them. I onely furnished them with Tongues to utter the same." Whatever the excuse, the upper class did dabble in music composition. One of Thomas Whythorne's first jobs was to copy out "diverse songs and sonnets that were made by the Earl of Surrey, Sir Thomas Wyatt the Elder and Mr. Moor the excellent Harper besides certain Psalms that were made by the said Mr. Wyatt and also Mr. Sternold, the which be also in my book."[26]

PROFESSIONAL MUSICIANS AND THE NOBILITY

Professional musicians—and particularly composers—were anxious to make it known that they were people of quality. If they did not have knighted status, they would at least put "Gent.", for "gentleman" after their names, and then they would list every degree they had ever earned. Whythorne was so sensitive about the issue that he published his lineage along with his music. Morley made the same excuse for his published work as a nobleman. One book, he wrote, was "Newly set forth at the coast (cost) and charges of a Gentleman, for his private pleasure, and for divers his friendes which delight in Musicke."[27] In other words, he wasn't really doing this himself, and it certainly wasn't done for money—it was practically an accident. Lutenist Robert Jones said his ayres were set to music at the insistence of certain gentlemen, and

> which though intended for their private recreation, never meaning they should come into the light, were yet content upon intreaty to make the incouragements of this my first adventure, whereupon I was almost glad to make my small skill knowne to the world: presumng that if my cunning failed me in the Musicke: yet the words might speake for themselves.[28]

Even though Elizabethan music composers knew they were at the mercy of their patron—be it noble, church, or court—their service tended to be treated as a gift and was repaid as such. The pose worked this way: a composer would write a work and dedicate it to a worthy noble. Sometimes the composer would mention that the noble insisted that the composer do the work and sometimes the dedication was worded as a gift to the noble, always in the most flattering terms. Then the noble would give a gift to the composer for the honor of the dedication. In this way any sense that the work was bought and paid for was avoided—it was a gift, with a gift given back. It pleased everyone. The noble was honored, and the musician did not feel servile. One way to increase the possibility of gifts was to dedicate a work to more than one patron. Thomas Morley, for instance, dedicated his 1599 *Firste Booke of Consort Lessons* to the lord mayor and all the aldermen of the city of London. Altogether, that was quite a few possible patrons. Another ploy was to publish a collection and dedicate single works to one patron each. Dowland's *Lachrimae* (1605) had 14 out of 21 pieces dedicated to individuals—all of whom were expected to reciprocate with a "gift." By using the patronage system, adding benefits from private, court, and church patronage, and whatever profits might occur from publication, musicians managed to tilt the system in their favor and gain a small amount of artistic freedom.

The drawback for the nobility, was of course, that once they had been identified as a "soft touch" a flood of dedications would arrive at their door from every sort of artist. Apparently, Sir Philip Sidney was especially vulnerable.

> The Universities abroad, and at home . . . dedicated their Books to him; and communicated every Invention, or Improvement of Knowledge with him. . . . His heart and capacity were so large, that there was not a cunning Painter, skilful Engineer, an excellent Musician, or any other Artificer of Extraordinary fame, that made not himself known to this famous spirit.[29]

Part Singing and the Nobility

All classes of Elizabethan citizens enjoyed singing. The lower class had its catches, the middle class its broadsheet ballads, and the upper classes their part-songs and ballades. Part-songs were polyphonic works (works in which several melodies of equal importance were sung simultaneously) in which all four (or sometimes five or even six) parts could be sung, or some parts could be sung while others were played on instruments. Part-song books were printed so that when the book lay open, everyone could see his own individual part. Obviously, with up to three parts per page (one upside-down, one right-side up, and one sideways facing out), these were not going to be long works. This was a popular home entertainment, and everyone among the upper classes was expected to be able to join in. Thomas Morley describes an embarrassing moment for anyone of gentle birth in his 1597 book A *Plaine and Easie Introduction to Practicall Musicke*.

> . . . supper being ended, and Musicke bookes, according to the custome being brought to the table: the mistresse of the house presented mee with a part, earnestly requesting mee to sing. But when after manie excuses, I protested unfainedly [honestly] that I could not: everie one began to won-der. Yea, some whispered to others, demaunding how I was brought up: so that upon shame of mine ignorance I go nowe to seeke out mine olde frinde master Gnorimus, to make my selfe his scholler.[30]

Just as with the middle class (and the lower class for that matter), upper-class ballads were poems set to music. The difference was that the nobility picked more refined literary sources. Ballads became a "good news–bad news" form of music in Elizabethan times. The good news was that many people—both professional musicians and amateurs—wrote ballads. The bad news was that many were so awful that the form developed a bad name. The bad news traveled both ways. Sometimes a lovely poem was put to an uninspired tune. Other times tunes from such composers as John Dowland were set with hack-work poems. Popular poetic works were set to many different tunes. One of the most popular, set several times, was the following:

> How can the tree but waste and wither awaie,
> That hath not sometime comfort of the sunne?
> Howe can the flower but fade and soone decaie,
> That allwaies is with darke cloudes overrun?
> Is this a life?
> Nay death you may it call,
> That feeles each paine
> And knowes noe joye att all.[31]

Ballads found a second life as instrumental consort music, each of the formerly sung parts being played on an instrument. Works specifically written to be played on instruments were drafted into the service of poetry and made into ballads. Surprised composers sometimes heard their works sung when they themselves had never set the music to words.

ELIZABETHAN UPPER-CLASS ENTERTAINMENT

Tournaments

Tournaments, primarily a medieval spectacle, were still held during some Elizabethan festivals. This entertainment was only for the upper class, basically because participation involved a lot of money. Preliminaries to a tournament practically equaled a pageant. Each contestant paraded into the tournament arena with retainers and accompanying trumpet fanfares with everyone dressed in their finest matching colors and presenting compliments to the queen.[32] Elizabethan knights engaged in "jousts" or "tilts" in which two horsemen tried to knock one another off their mounts using a long wooden lance. They also fought in "tourneys" in which two combatants fought with swords on foot. In "running

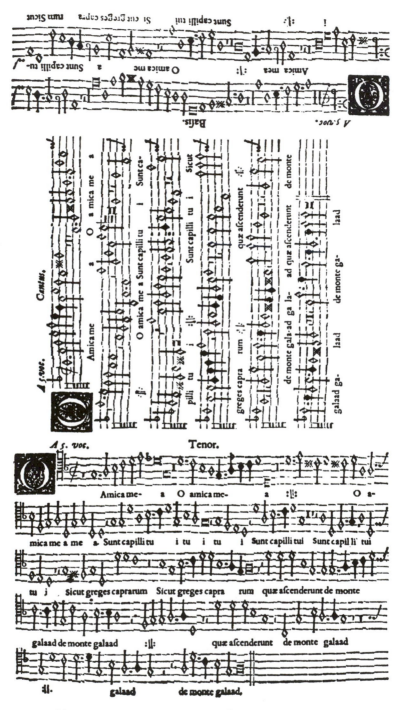

Figure 1. "Tabletop" part-song arrangement for six people.

16

17

Figure 2. First page of Thomas Morley's book, A *Plaine and Easie Introduction to Practicall Musicke*.

at the ring," horsemen tried to secure a rather small ring on the end of their lance while riding a galloping mount. The "quintain" required a horseman to hit a dummy target and gallop past it before the dummy's weapon smacked them in the back.[33]

Music underscored the excitement of a tournament. Trumpet fanfares accompanied the knights as they entered the arena. When combatants presented their compliments to the queen before the actual games began, trumpeters gave each knight a musical flourish. More trumpet fanfares made sure that everybody knew a combat was about to begin. Musicians with less strident instruments, such as a singer with a lute, strolled through the crowds taking requests and being repaid with coinage. Also, musicians were hired to play music as evening entertainment for the feasting and dancing after a long day of watching or participating in a tournament.

Masques

The upper classes enjoyed masques to the virtual exclusion of other classes. In this particularly English institution, "disguised guests bearing presents would break into a festival and then join with their hosts in a ceremonial dance." Later, this evolved into a presentation in which actors mingled with guests (wearing masks to conceal their identity), putting on allegorical plays complete with costumes and stage designs—and including a great deal of dancing and music. Because everyone was in disguise, anyone could join in without the slightest embarrassment—including royalty, if they were so inclined. Although these entertainments became quite elaborate in later years, the masques of Queen Elizabeth's day were not. For instance, the masque put on for a visit Queen Elizabeth made to a noble estate in 1578 only contained music by recorders and cornets. Still, masques were outlets for private music making among the aristocracy—funded by it and put on for their own amusements.

The Waits

The "waits" was a band of musicians hired by the governors of a town. If you lived in London or Norwich, you might have gone to regular public concerts played by those cities' "waits." On Sundays from Lady Day (March 25) to Michaelmas (September 29), and on every holiday, the London waits played a public concert at the Royal Exchange. These concerts started in 1571 and continued until 1642. In Norwich, the waits of the city shall have liberty and licence, every Sunday at night and other holidays at night betwixt this and Michaelmas next coming, to come to the Guildhall, and . . . shall betwixt the hours of seven and eight of the clock at night blow and play upon their instruments the space of half an hour, to the rejoicing and comfort of the hearers thereof.[34]

Musicians from town waits were used for public ceremonies and were paid by the town fathers. Although the public concerts and public ceremonies might not have been attended by many nobles, the waits musicians were also available for private hire. When the queen visited Sir Nicholas Bacon in 1587, he hired waits musicians to play for her entertainment. In 1589, Sir Francis Drake took five Norwich waits with him on a voyage.

CONCLUSION

The Elizabethan nobility furthered the music of their time through their peer connections and cultural leanings. In addition, because of their financial resources, they underwrote much of England's musical renaissance. They advanced musicians' careers by hiring them to instruct their children in the musical arts. Buying instruments either for themselves or their children encouraged instrument craftsmen in their business. It also set an example of instrument ownership that the middle class would emulate, within their means. Some of the wealthier families had household musicians to supply them with music in their private chapels or for secular entertainments; the nobility commissioned composers to write music; and the noble class spread the knowledge and availability of music by making international purchases during their trips overseas, loans during which they might have private copies made, and through outright exchange of manuscripts among peers. And in a time before public libraries, the nobility preserved both published music and unpublished manuscripts in their extensive libraries, making those works available to future generations.

NOTES

1. H. Peacham, *The Compleat Gentleman* (Amsterdam: Da Capo Press, 1968 [originally published in 1622]), pp. 96–97.
   2. Ibid., pp. 97–98.
   3. Ibid., p. 2.

4. J. Buxton, *Elizabethan Taste* (New York: St. Martin's Press, 1964), p. 195.

5. Peacham, p. 98.

6. K.L. Emerson, *The Writer's Guide to Everyday Life in Renaissance England from 1485–1649* (Cincinnati, OH: Writer's Digest Books, 1996), p. 108.

7. H. Raynor, *Music in England* (Plymouth: Clarke, Doble & Brendon, 1980), p. 59.

8. Buxton, p. 192.

9. Ibid.

10. Magdalen College School, Oxford, http://www.mcsoxford.org/index.php, 2003.

11. D.C. Price, *Patrons and Musicians of the English Renaissance* (Cambridge: Cambridge University Press, 1981), p. 27.

12. Ibid.

13. Buxton, pp. 214–215.

14. Ibid., p. 32.

15. Ibid., p. 172.

16. F. Keel, *Music in the Time of Queen Elizabeth* (February 24, 1914), pp. 11–12.

17. Price, p. 40.

18. Ibid., p. 16.

19. Ibid., pp. 67–142.

20. Ibid., p. 33.

21. Ibid., p. 17.

22. H.M. Brown and L.K. Stein, *Music in the Renaissance* (2nd ed.) (Englewood Cliffs, NJ: Prentice Hall, 1999), p. 85.

23. Ibid., p. 86.

24. Ibid., p. 6.

25. Ibid., p. 192.

26. T. Whythorne, *The Autobiography of Thomas Whythorne* (J.M. Osborne, ed.) (Oxford: Clarendon Press, 1961), p. 14.

27. Price, p. 191.

28. B. Pattison, *Music and Poetry of the English Renaissance* (London: Methuen & Co., 1948), p. 35.

29. Price, p. 195.

30. T. Morley, *A Plaine and Easie Introduction to Practicall Musicke* (New York: Da Capo Press, 1969 [originally published in 1597]), p. 1.

31. Pattison, p. 168.

32. F. Laroque, *Shakespeare's Festive World* (J. Lloyd, trans.) (Cambridge: Cambridge University Press, 1991), p. 66.

33. Ibid., pp. 66–67.

34. Ibid., p. 217.

REFERENCES

Brown, H.M., and Stein, L.K. *Music in the Renaissance* (2nd ed.). Englewood Cliffs, NJ: Prentice Hall, 1999.

Buxton, J. *Elizabethan Taste*. New York: St. Martin's Press, 1964.

Emerson, K.L. *The Writer's Guide to Everyday Life in Renaissance England from 1485–1649*. Cincinnati, OH: Writer's Digest Books, 1996.

Harris, W.H., and Levey, J.S. (eds.). *The New Columbia Encyclopedia*. New York and London: Columbia University Press, 1975.

Keel, F. *Music in the Time of Queen Elizabeth*. A paper read before ye sette of odd volumes February 24th, 1914. Presented to the sette by Brother John Lane bibliographer: at the 341st meeting, Tuesday, May 26th 1914.

Laroque, F. *Shakespeare's Festive World* (J. Lloyd, trans.). Cambridge: Cambridge University Press, 1991.

Magdalen College School, Oxford. http://www.mcsoxford.org/index.php, 2003.

Morley, T. *A Plaine and Easie Introduction to Practicall Musicke*. New York: Da Capo Press, 1969 [originally published in 1597].

Pattison, B. *Music and Poetry of the English Renaissance*. London: Methuen & Co., 1948.

Peacham, H. *The Compleat Gentleman*. Amsterdam: Da Capo Press, 1968 [originally published in 1622].

Price, D.C. *Patrons and Musicians of the English Renaissance*. Cambridge: Cambridge University Press, 1981.

Raynor, H. *Music in England*. Plymouth: Clarke, Doble & Brendon, 1980.

Rimbault, E.F. (ed.). *The Old Cheque-Book*. New York: Da Capo Press, 1966.

Whythorne, T. *The Autobiography of Thomas Whythorne* (J.M. Osborne, ed.). Oxford: Clarendon Press, 1961.

Chapter 2

Life and Music
of the Middle Class

Because of their success, the Elizabethan middle class had some spending money and even some leisure time. Music was a major component of both. "Although diligence and industry were cardinal points in the trades-man's creed, he took time for honest pleasure, of which music was a favorite . . . the Elizabethan tradesman sang himself, either at his work or in the evening with his household."[1] As one writer put it:

> Tinkers sang catches; milkmaids sang ballads; carters whistled; each trade, and even the beggars, had their special songs; the bass-viol hung in the drawing room for the amusement of waiting visitors; and the lute, cittern, and virginals, for the amusement of waiting customers, were the necessary furniture of the barber's shop. They had music at dinner; music at supper; music at weddings; music at funerals; music at night; music at dawn; music at work; and music at play.[2]

The Elizabethan middle class fueled the English Renaissance. This am-bitious group, hungry for improvement of all kinds, equated being godly with being financially successful. It was this group that formulated the "Protestant work ethic," that equated a good education with getting ahead in life, and that made thrift and industry virtues with religious overtones. It was a largely conservative group, constantly debating the merits of what was socially proper or morally correct. The interrelation of church and state, characteristic in all classes of Elizabethan society, was especially evident in middle-class life.

Middle-class workers included craftsmen such as cobblers who made shoes, coopers who made barrels, farriers who made horses' shoes, goldsmiths who made jewelry, shipwrights who built ships, millers who ground flour, and bakers who made it into baked goods. The middle class also included the retail dealers who sold goods, notably tailors, grocers, and milliners (who sold hats). It included the services of local ministers, clerks who balanced financial ledgers, ink-stained printers who operated presses, and barbers who kept their customers looking neat and trim. In short, the middle class was the oil that made Elizabethan commerce and society run smoothly.

The middle class, seeking riches through trade, initiated England's Golden Age of Exploration. Corporations sent ships out to find other lands, other peoples—and to find out what those peoples had and what they needed. If their industry and thrift brought financial success, a middle-class person might put some of his money into speculation on the import trade. Many middle-class Elizabethans had become wealthy by speculating on a ship which, if it made the journey to far-flung ports and back safely, could bring a fabulous return on an investment. Investors scrambled to share in potential profits from the latest venture. Eventually, even the upper class—all the way to the crown—invested in trade schemes. But control remained in the middle class.

The Elizabethan middle class was education-minded and supported schools with their own purses. They supported petty schools (grade school) and grammar schools (high school), and they provided scholarships to universities. Almost all middle-class children received at least the rudiments of reading, writing, and "ciphering" (mathematics). The middle class had a vested interest in these fields, since they would have to read and write contracts and keep their accounts. In most families, the eldest son was expected to go into the family business. That child might leave after grammar school to begin apprenticing at the family trade. But a younger male sibling might go on to university and perhaps bring honor to his family by becoming a preacher or taking on another worthy profession. By providing scholarships, the middle class ensured that poverty as well as social status would not keep a deserving student from an education.

Some middle-class tradesmen became wealthy enough to endow a school. In 1555, Sir Thomas White founded St. John's College in Oxford, England, from money he made as a merchant tailor. The school was dedicated to St. John the Baptist—the patron saint of the Merchant Taylor's Company. He also remembered his own formal education at

Reading Grammar School with two scholarships to that school in his name.

Other schools and scholarships were funded by middle-class guilds. The Company of Ironmongers put up money for five poor scholars at Oxford University and another five at Cambridge University to go into divinity studies and become ministers. The Guild of Saddlers, the Pewterers Guild, and the Cutler's Company all supported poor scholars with trust funds. Others, such as the Haberdashers (men's clothing) Guild, used company funds to support their poor scholars.

Girls were not left out of education. They attended the "petty" (public grammar) schools to learn basic literacy, and after that, middle-class girls learned from private teachers rather than going to grammar school. The literacy of Elizabethan women was a source of general pride. In 1581, a publication entitled *Positions* stated:

> We see yong maidens be taught to read and write and can do both passing well; we know that they learne the best, and finest of our learned languages, to the admiration of all men. I dare be bould therefore to admit yong maidens to learne, seeing my countrie gives me leave. . . . To learne to read is very common . . . and writing is not refused, where opportunitie will yield it.[3]

Literacy for women should be encouraged, the publication continued, for reading religious matter, instructional matter in housewifery, and moral discourses toward the goal of leading a model life. Since women were not only housekeepers, but often the family doctor, surgeon, and pharmaceutical dispenser, they needed medicinal "how-to" books as well as cookbooks and needlework books. After all this, if women wanted to indulge in sentimental romances, so much the better for publishers.

The obvious result of all this education was a literate middle class with a thirst for learning. Publishing burst into life with unheard-of vigor. There were open book stalls in London where reading matter could be perused and purchased for as little as a penny, similar to the magazine sections of bookstores today. Intense competition drove the prices down. The Stationers' Company had licensed 97 printers during Elizabethan times, and all wanted to lure readers. Booksellers hawked an amazing variety of wares—from the most serious works to frivolous trifles—which were sold in stores, book stalls, and were sent out with salesmen to small towns and rural provincial fairs all over England.

WOMEN, COURTSHIP, AND MUSIC

With the country ruled by an obviously capable, intelligent, and literate woman in Queen Elizabeth, other women began to assert themselves. This increasing freedom resulted in several ballads about women. Some spoke in praise of women; others were horrified at women's extravagance in dress, in application of "paint" (makeup) to enhance what heaven had endowed her with—or falsify what was missing. Satirists made fun of May-December marriages, of the race to gain access to rich widows, and of deceived husbands.

The following are two verses from "A Warning to London Dames," which both praise and warn the women of London:

> (1) You London dames, whose passyng fames
>   Through out the world is spread,
>   In to the skye, ascendying hye
>   To every place is fled:
>   For thorow each land and place,
>   For beauties kyndely grace:
>   You are renowmed over all,
>   You have the prayse and ever shall.
>   What wight on earth that can beholde
>   More dearer and fayrer dames than you?
>   Therefore to extoll you I may be bolde,
>   Your pace and graces so gay to view.
>
> (4) And learne to know, as grasse doth grow
>   And withereth in to haye,
>   Remember therfore, kepe vertue in store
>   For so you shall decaye:
>   And pitie on the poore
>   With some parte of your store,
>   Loke that your lampes may ready bee
>   The dreadfull day approcheth nye:
>   When Christ shall come to judge our deeds
>   No faireness nor clerenes can helpe you then,
>   The corne to separate from the weeds
>   Fayre dames, when cometh the day of dome.[4]

Courting was a popular ballad subject. There were ballads of young men persuading young women into lovemaking, of jilted lovers, faithful lovers, and of the "game of love" itself. In "The Panges of Love and Lovers

Fittes," a young man slyly uses historical and biblical samples to persuade his lady to yield to his attentions:

(1)   Was not good Kyng Salamon (Solomon)
       Ravished in sondry wyse
       With every livelie Paragone
       That glistered before his eyes?
       If this be true as trewe it was
       Lady lady.
       Why should I not serve you alas
       My deare lady.

(9)   Besides these matters marveilous
       Good Lady yet I can tell thee more
       The Gods have ben full amourous
       As Jupiter by lerned lore
       Who changed his shape as fame hath spred
       Lady ladye
       To come to Alcumenaes' bed
       My deare ladye.[5]

TRADE SONGS

Every tradesman was expected to know something of music—either sung or played on an instrument of some sort. And every trade had its own melody. In a 1598 book about shoemaking entitled *History of the gentle Craft*, a person was trying to pass himself off as a shoemaker. He was caught not because he didn't know shoemaking terms, but because he could neither "sing, sound the trumpet, play upon the flute, nor reckon up his tools in rhyme."[6] (Apparently, his lack of singing and instrument playing might have been overlooked, but his inability to make up an Elizabethan "rap" about the tools of his trade was a dead giveaway that this person was a fake!)

Some trade songs are quite charming. A tune called "Paddington's Pound" was used with many different words, but one interesting version praises dairy products:

> In the virtues of milk there is more to be muster'd
> The charming delights both of cheese-cake and custard.[7]

Just as with the lower class, rounds or "catches" were a favorite form of amateur singing among the middle class. "Tinkers, tailors, blacksmiths, servants, clowns, and others are so constantly mentioned as singing music in parts, and by so many writers, as to leave no doubt of the ability of at least many among them to do so."[8] The tendency of middle-class workers to get together and entertain themselves by singing rounds or part-songs is recorded in many literary references. For instance:

(1) Peele, "This (black)smith leads a life as merry as a king. Sirrah Frolic, I am sure you are not without some Round or other. . . ."

(2) Jonson, "We got this cold sitting up late and singing Catches with cloth-workers."

(3) Shakespeare, "Do you make an ale-house of my lady's house that ye squeak out your cozier's (i.e., tailor's) Catches, without any mitigation or remorse of voice?"[9]

A favorite tune in Elizabethan times was "The Carman's Whistle." A carman was something like a taxicab driver and was famous for his musical abilities—especially his ability to whistle his tunes. This was intended to give his tired horse renewed vigor for the rest of his shift, as well as to keep him awake late at night. The tendency to whistle a happy tune late at night when everything was quiet caused one Elizabethan physician to write: "A carman's whistle . . . many times alters, revives, recreates a restless patient that cannot sleep"[10]

BARBERSHOP MUSIC

One middle-class occupation specifically known for its music-making was the barbershop. Nowadays customers at a barbershop or hair-styling salon are accustomed to having some reading material, such as magazines, to read while waiting for their turn to be shaved or shorn. Some places might also have a radio, or even a television to help the customer while away the waiting time. In Elizabethan England, barbers had musical instruments hanging on the walls which customers were allowed to use.

Barbers plucked out tunes on stringed or keyboard instruments when business was slow. Waiting customers might also strum a tune or engage in instrumental and vocal part-singing. Barbers were also known for a particular cracking of their fingers, knocking them together and making a rhythmic sound that customers expected. This was called "knacking," probably from the term for medieval percussion instruments known as "nackers." The usual instruments available in the shop were the virginal, the lute, and the cittern.

The virginal was a type of keyboard instrument, similar to a harpsichord but more portable. The lute was a stringed instrument that was as popular in Elizabethan England as the guitar is today. The cittern, variously known as a cittern, gittern, cister, cither, cithara, cetera, cistola, or citole, was a member of the guitar family and had four sets of double strings. These strings have been described as gut by some sources and as wire by other sources. A particular feature of citterns was that the "head" or top of the neck of the instrument was often elaborately carved. They were tuned to the intervals g, b, d, and e, but there were no real rules for the absolute pitch. Generally, the highest string would be tightened as much as possible without breaking it, and then the other strings would be adjusted by interval to the first.

Elizabethan plays occasionally made allusions to barbershop music. An angry character in a Ben Jonson play hoped that a barber might pull his own teeth and add them to his lute-string. Anyone who came into the barbershop could stroll over to the cittern, which was hung by its tuning pegs on the wall, take it down, and play with it. The cittern therefore became a way of alluding to an unfaithful woman. In one play a character who suspects that his wife—the barber's daughter—is unfaithful, moans, "That cursed barber! I have married his cittern, that is common to all men!"[11] Although barbershops no longer keep instruments handy for barbers and their customers, the musical barber tradition lives on in so-called barbershop quartet music.

SEAFARING MERCHANTS

Commercial vessels sailed worldwide, hauling a variety of cargoes. Everything from spices to coal sailed the seas as various trade corporations carved out their special territories. The Muscovy Company opened trade with Russia, bringing England to the attention of Ivan the Terrible (who once sent a letter to Queen Elizabeth proposing a marriage of convenience!). The East India Company traded in spices from the Far East. The Levant Company traded with Turkey, Syria, and Egypt. The men who sailed those ships, known as merchant seamen to differentiate them from military seamen, were proud of their abilities. The following sea song—"We be Three Poor Mariners"—pitted working on a merchant ship against working on a warship:

(1)   We be three poor mariners,
       Newly come from the seas

We spend our lives in jeopardy,
While others live at ease.
Shall we go dance the round?
Shall we go dance the round?
And he that is a jolly boy,
Come pledge me on this ground.

(2)   We care not for those martial men
That do our states disdain;
But we care for the merchantmen
Who do our states maintain
To them we dance this round
To them we dance this round.
And he that is a jolly boy,
Come pledge me on this ground.[12]

TRAVELOGUES AND ROMANCES

In the Age of Exploration, stories and songs about faraway places had a natural appeal. This is one area in which translations of texts from other countries were popular. English readers would even buy books translated from Spanish, if the subject were enticing enough. Some titles of translated travel books were: "Joyfull Newes Out Of the Newe Founde Worlde" (1577), "The Strange and delectable History of the discoverie and Conquest of the Provinces of Peru" (1581), and "The Pleasant Historie of the Conquest of the West India, now called new Spayne" (1578).[13]

Stories of heroic deeds were a popular diversion and could be seen as instructive or inspirational. One Elizabethan wrote, "As bees out of the bitterest flowers, and sharpest thornes, doe gather the sweetest hony: so out of obscene and wicked fables some profit may be extracted."[14] Most popular were stories of middle-class heroes such as the *Nine Worthies of London* (1592), a chronicle of tradesmen who had done something abnormally brave or wonderful. Middle-class Elizabethans loved reading about someone of common birth who saved the kingdom or became worthy of a royal person's favor. They could be from any country, but English heroes were best. A favorite fictional romance figure was *Tom a Lincoln*. Tom was supposedly a bastard son of King Arthur, brought up as a commoner. Readers followed his adventures breathlessly, which eventually culminated in his becoming a knight of the Round Table and a wealthy landowner.[15] Another hero, Guy of Warwick, rose from humble circumstances to fight all manner of enemies with equal aplomb. Guy's exploits entertained a rapt middle-class public for years.[16]

LEISURE READING AND THE BALLAD

The middle-class enthusiasm for reading tied into music by way of the ballad—a song of many verses that told a popular story, sung to well-known tunes. Any theme a middle-class person might be interested in reading could also be turned into a sung ballad. Ballads could be about politics, history, travel and adventure, crime, love, or any topic of current popularity.

While sharing a taste for the lurid with the lower class, middle-class buyers were able to afford more variety in their reading and singing matter. Elizabethans had a wide variety of venues for their reading material: tearsheets, broadsides and broadsheets, pamphlets, chapbooks, and pocket manuals as well as books. The Elizabethan middle class could indulge almost any interest—from moral guidance and the latest scientific invention to joke books. Tearsheets were literally torn off a roll and were a cheap source of information, including advertisements. Pamphlets were made up of several pages cheaply sewn together and sold much as paperback books are sold today. Pamphlets normally contained prose narratives, not poetry, and might contain subjects taken up by ballads, or plays, sermons, or novelettes. Chapbooks were much the same, only with more pages. They were, however, smaller than a regular, hardbound book. A pocket manual was a small booklet meant to be carried in one's pocket or used as a handy reference guide in one's place of business.

When middle-class persons bought a ballad, they got a sheet of paper with only the words printed on it. The sheet printed only the name of the tune that the words were supposed to be sung to. A single tune, in some cases, might have many sets of words to it. A case in point is "Greensleeves." This tune is first mentioned in print in 1580, when the Stationers' Company issued a license to print "A new Northern Dittye of the Lady Greene Sleeves." This is not to say that the ballad was new—only when it was finally put into print. The words of "Greensleeves" have changed many times over the years from its early 18-verse version. Apparently, the words weren't very good; it was the tune that captivated everyone. Even today, the tune is also known as the beloved Christmas tune, "What Child is This." In Elizabethan times different words were already being put to this tune—one of which was another religious treatment: "Greene Sleves moralised to the Scripture, declaring the manifold benefites and blessings of God bestowed on sinful man."[17] This particular tune was so popular that it turns up in Shakespeare's play, *The Merry Wives of Windsor*, where Falstaff says, "Let the sky rain potatoes! Let it thunder to the tune of Green Sleeves."[18]

A NEW COURTLY SONET OF THE LADY GREENSLEEVES.

To the new Tune of—' *Greensleeves.*'

Greensleeves was all my ioy,
Greensleeves was my delight;
Greensleeves was my hart of gold;
And who but Ladie Greensleeves.

ALAS! my Love, ye do me wrong,
    to cast me off discurteously;
And I have loved you so long,
    Delighting in your companie.

    Greensleeves was all my ioy,
    Greensleeves was my delight;
    Greensleeves was my heart of gold;
    And who but Ladie Greensleeves.

I have been readie at your hand,
    to grant what ever you would crave;
I have both waged life and land,
    your love and good will for to have.
    Greensleeves was all my ioy, &c.

I bought thee kerchers to thy head,
    that were wrought fine and gallantly;
I kept thee both at boord and bed,
    which cost my purse well favouredly.
    Greensleeves was all my joie, &c.

Figure 3. Ballad sheet, tune indicated under the title "Greensleeves" (from an 1814 reprint).

Another ballad tune popular in Elizabethan times was called "Wal-singham." Although the tune was apparently sung, whistled, and played on a daily basis, the words indicate that this ballad was passed down from times past. Walsingham was a Catholic place of pilgrimage in which a famous shrine was kept. Pilgrims flocked to the shrine for hundreds of years not only because the shrine was a holy place, but because miracle cures supposedly took place there.

Middle-class professionals often wrote broadside ballads. Writers of a higher class heaped the same kind of scorn on broadside ballad writers that we heap today on tabloid reporters and paparazzi. Known commonly as "pot-poets," they pandered to readers' basest instincts just as tabloid reporters do today. Elizabethans were drawn to descriptions of physical deformity. As L.B. Wright notes, "Descriptive ballads of two-headed calves and malformed children (were) a regular item in the stock of the ballad vendors."[19] They also lapped up vivid descriptions of horrible crimes—justified as moral deterrents—and the criminals' confessions. No ballad was complete without details of their executions and their pitiful last words. The Elizabethan middle class also enjoyed reading about the lives and punishment of traitors. Since many readers had lived through four monarchs and religious persecution on all sides, there was plenty of paranoia regarding people plotting to overthrow the queen or sell state secrets to foreign powers.

Not all broadside ballads were composed by professionals; this was one form where anyone who was literate could find self-expression. There were many "citizen-writers" such as Thomas Deloney and Lawrence Price who wrote ballads on a wide variety of subjects. Sometimes ballad writers would answer one another. For instance, the following two ballads appeared on the same broadside. The first was entitled "Harvest Home" and sang the glories of England's farmers reaping their crops, reacting to un-invited, mooching religious guests, and toasting England with home brew:

(1) Our Oats they are how'd (hoed) and our Barley's reap'd
     Our Hay it is mow'd, and our Hovel's heap'd;
     Harvest home, Harvest, home, We'll merrily roar out our Harvest home.

(2) We cheated the Parson, we'll cheat him again;
     For why shou'd the Vicar have One in Ten?
     For staying while Dinner is cold and hot, and Pudding and Dump-ling's burnt to pot?

(3)   We'll drink off our Liquor while we can stand,
       And hey for the Honour of Old England!

The second was entitled "An Answer to Harvest Home or, A true Character of such Country-men who Glory in cheating the Vicar, & prefer Bag-pudding & Dumpling before Religion and Learning." In part, its words were:

(1)   The Country store up Hay, Oats, and Wheat,
       And glory how they can the Parson cheat,
       The Country Bumpkin may speak with shame,
       That ever he cheated, for he's to blame.

(2)   Degrading of Learning do's (does) plainly show,
       They never knew nothing but Hi, ji, ho,
       Their hungry Appetite to suffice,
       Bag-pudding and Dumpling they Idolize

(3)   Religion and Learning they all contemn,
       A lusty Bag-pudding is more to them.
       Tell them of going to Church to pray,
       They'd rather hear Robin the Piper play.[20]

Broadside ballads were sold in both the city and country, and broadside writers often wrote about the rivalries between city dwellers and country folk. City writers poured venom on what they saw as greedy farmers driving up prices through withholding goods until they got what they wanted, or fencing off land that was supposed to be used by the community of farmers. One thinly disguised ballad was entitled "News from Antwerp," but its subtitle was "or, a Glass (i.e., Looking glass) for greedy Farmers and God's Judgement showed upon a covetous Encloser of common pasture in Germany (sic), who was strangely trodden to death by his own Cattle."[21]

Similarly, country balladeers sang with great relish of the sins and evils of city life. To them, city people were extravagant and idle, their children were ill-mannered brats, the merchants cheated their customers, and those who rented out rooms or apartments drove up the prices and profiteered on rents. Then, as now, crime and moral looseness were two evils of city life about which middle-class Elizabethans had an almost morbid curiosity. One can almost hear vengeful cackling in the title of a ballad entitled, "A Warning to Youth, shewing the lewd life of a Marchant's Sonne of London, and the userie (money borrowing) that at the last he sustained by his riotousnesse. This youth squandered his fortune, seduced a maide after making her drunk, and came to a miserable end."[22]

CRIME BALLADS

The middle class had an unending fascination with life in the underground. An entire literature of pamphlets described the terrible lives of rogues and vagabonds. A few of these were entitled: "A manifest detection of the most vyle and detestable use of Diceplay" (1552), "The Fraternitye of Vacabondes" (1561), and "A Caveat or Warening For Common Curestors Vulgarely Called Vagabonds" (1567). These offerings were known as "rogue-books," and the king of all their authors was Thomas Greene. He claimed to be writing so that the average citizen could learn how to avoid the snares of "conny-catchers," or con-men. But the titles, such as "Discovering the Secret Villanies of Alluring Strumpets," promised a delectable dip into the gutter with no more danger than the loss of a shilling to buy the book.

Of course, there were ballads outlining lives of crime, and, as expected, those on the other side of the law ended up badly. One Elizabethan ballad entitled "News from the Tower Hill" is subtitled "A gentle warning to Peg and Kate, To walk no more abroad so late." This, sung to the tune of "The North Country Lass," was a warning to loose young women against streetwalking and luring innocent young men into sin. Notably, there is no ballad scolding young men on the prowl looking for their favors.

The ballad has 22 verses in all. A very short version of the story is told in the following excerpts:

(1)   A pretty jest I'll tell, which was performed of late.
      Let lasses all in general be warned, Peg and Kate.

(6)   As they walked forth one night, as twas their custom still,
      A young man kind did chance to find them upon Tower Hill

(7)   And finding them so free, and easy to go down,
      He got them both, they were not loath, with him to Greenwich Town.

The young man took them to a tavern where he ordered food and drink for all three—himself and the two women. While the women were downing a hearty meal and plenty of wine, the young man slipped out and left them with the bill. They had no money, and the tavern owner threatened to have them arrested. Peg had to get them out of trouble in a most embarrassing way.

(17) All night they tarried there, in morning Peg did send
      To her mother dear, who came to her as did become a friend.
      Her husband came with her, and he did (give) his word, At a certain
      day, the (bill) to pay which they (i.e., Peg and Kate) had scored.

(18) The young man I commend, and wish that others would
      Him imitate, then Peg and Kate would no more be so bold.[23]

"Wonder stories" were also popular with the middle class. Chapbooks (cheaply sold reading matter) described the terrible fates of those who dabbled in witchcraft and magic. The *Historie of the damnable life, and deserved death of Doctor John Faustus* was a favorite, even with Puritans. Dr. Faustus (better known as Faust to present-day readers) was an old man whose bargain with Mephistopheles, a devil figure, brings him 24 years of pleasure, followed by an eternity of torture. The following is part of a 20-verse ballad entitled "Judgement of God shewed upon one John Faustus" (to the tune of "Fortune my Foe") outlining Doctor Faustus's sorrowful fate:

(1) All Christian men give ears awhile to me,
     How I am plung'd in pain but cannot dye,
     I liv'd a life the like did none before
     Forsaking Christ and I am damn'd therefore.

(4) The Divell [devil] in Fryers weeds [friar's clothing] appear'd to me,
     And soon to my request he did agree,
     That I might have all things at my desire
     I gave him soule and body for his hire.

(7) The time I past away with much delight,
     Mongst Princes, Peers, & many worthy Knight,
     I wrote such wonders by my Magick skill,
     That all the world may talk of Faustus still.

When Dr. Faustus's contract was up, he began to regret his bargain. He called in learned men to help him, but none could. He asked his students to stay close by. They did, but when they heard a dreadful cry, they rushed in.

(18) Then presently they came into the Hall,
      Whereas my brains were cast against the wall,
      Both arms and legs in pieces torn they see,
      My bowels gone, this was the end of me.

(19) You Conjurers and damned Witches all,
      Example take by my unhappy fal,
      Give not your souls and bodies unto hel,
      See that the smallest hair you doe not sell.[24]

HISTORICAL AND PATRIOTIC MUSIC

History, travel, and romance were popular subjects for books, ballads, and other forms of literature. After the defeat of the Spanish Armada, English pride knew no bounds, and histories of England were big sellers in prose and poetry for the next 50 years. Ballads described the terrible enemy and breathlessly told of the strange whips and poisons with which the Spanish ships were packed in order to force Englishmen to become Catholic.

After the Armada, middle-class readers eagerly looked for other sources of pride in their country. Reading history was neither a frivolous nor an idle diversion. To a middle-class Elizabethan—even the most conservative Puritan—reading history was seen as second only to reading the Bible. The Merchant Taylors' Company and the Grocers' Company were especially active in subsidizing the printing of historical books. While tailors bankrolled John Stow, one time tailor turned historian and antiquarian, the grocers supported Richard Grafton, a historian who was also responsible for printing some of the first religious books for the Church of England. Competition among the two subsidizing companies hit a peak when Grafton brought out a handbook entitled *A Manuell of the Chronicles of England from the creacion of the worlde, to this yere of our Lorde 1565* in the same year that Stowe published his *A Summarie of Englyshe Chronicles*, reduced to pocket size. As one historian put it, "Certainly so much history had never before been packed into so convenient a pocket manual."[25]

MARRIAGE

Marriage was a highly desirable state in Elizabethan England. About 87 percent of the Elizabethan population was or had been married, according to a 1590 census. The age of consent was fourteen for boys and seven for girls, but usually people married somewhere in their mid-twenties. The five steps to an Elizabethan marriage process were: (1) consent, (2) betrothal in front of witnesses, (3) a public proclamation in church, known as the "banns," (4) a church wedding and, (5) sexual consummation. In between one-fifth and one-third of Elizabethan weddings, the bride was pregnant. Elizabethans considered a child born between the betrothal and the marriage to be legitimate. If the bride was too far along for the wedding to wait, the couple might eliminate the "banns," with church permission.

After the wedding ceremony, there was usually a feast held at the home of the groom featuring a lot of drinking, dancing, and music. Some of the songs were rather bawdy in a joking way, upsetting many a clergyman who called the marriage feasts "publique incendiaries of all filthy lusts." Instead, they asked that a marriage feast be conducted as though Christ himself were going to be there. Of course, some ballads made fun of married life, such as the dilemma of a young man who married a woman so quiet that he thought she lacked the power of speech, "The Dumb Maid: or, The Young Gallant Trappan'd":

(1)   All you that pass along, Give ear unto my Song,
       Concerning a Youth that was young, young, young:
       And of a Maiden fair, Few with her might compare,
       But alack, and alas, she was Dumb, dumb, dumb.

(2)   She was beautious, fresh, and gay, Like the pleasant flowers in May,
       And her Cheeks was as round as a Plum, plum, plum:
       She was neat in every part, And she stole away his heart,
       But alack and alas, she was Dumb, dumb, dumb.

(8)   To the Doctor he did her bring, And he cut her chattering string,
       And he set her Tongue on the run, run, run:
       In the morning he did rise, And she fill'd his house with cries,
       And she rattled in his ears Like a drum, drum, drum.

(9)   To the Doctor he did go, With his ears well fill'd with woe
       Crying Doctor I am undone, done, done:
       Now she's turn'd a scolding Wife, And I am weary of my Life,
       Nor I cannot make her hold her tongue, tongue, tongue.

(10)   The Doctor thus did say, When she went from me away,
       She was perfectly Cured of the dumb, dumb, dumb.
       But it's beyond the Art of man, Let him do the best he can,
       For to make a scolding Woman hold her tongue, tongue, tongue.[26]

DEVOTIONAL MUSIC

Although family life was a favorite target for ballad sarcasm, most middle-class Elizabethans lived quiet, sober lives. A favorite at-home pastime for families and friends was devotional singing. Elizabethans believed that the Old Testament Book of Psalms was intended to be sung. Singing implied rhymed words and particular rhythms. The Church of England leaned away from Latin and toward the vernacular (although Queen Elizabeth never forbade Latin). So it was a "natural" for the Psalms, out of all the books of the Bible, to be translated into rhymed, metered verses. Books of these verses and tunes for them to be sung to were known as "psalters." Any tune could use any set of words that fit its particular meter. Just as a broadside ballad verse would be "sung to" the tune of another work, two or more sets of Psalm verses might fit the same psalter tune. Monophonic at first, psalters later included harmony. These works might be sung at church or at home. They were very popular, particularly with the Puritans. It is not an accident that psalters were brought to the New World along with other necessities for life, when English settlers landed. As part of this heritage, it is worth noting that—many years later—the first book printed in the New World, on a New World press, was a psalter.

ENTERTAINMENT

Dance

Then, as now, people danced to the popular tunes of the day. Since middle-class Elizabethans had access to better education and more leisure time than ever before, they were able to channel some of their energies into this form of entertainment. Young people in particular used dancing as an excuse to make one another's acquaintance in a socially acceptable manner.

Today, dancing is done to instrumental music, with or without vocals. But in Elizabethan times, people danced to a cappella vocal singing (voices alone), as well as to instruments playing, or to a combination of the two. One very popular dance tune was called "Turkeloney." This dance was referred to in print by the 1570s, when the words were printed. Apparently, the words were meant to amuse, as this verse shows:

> If ever I marry, I'll marry a maid;
> To marry a widow I'm sore afraid.

For maids they are simple and never will grudge
But widows full oft, as they say, know too much."[27]

"Watkin's Ale" was another popular dance song. Although the dance has been lost, the tune and verses have survived. The first verse outlines a young man's "pickup line" for a future seduction:

There was a maid this other day
And she would needs go forth to play;
And as she walked she sighed and said,
"I am afraid to die a maid,"
When that be-heard a lad what talk this maiden had
Thereof he was full glad and did not spare
To say, "Fair maid, I pray, whither go you to play?"
"Good sir," then did she say, "what do you care?"
"For I will without fail, Maiden, give you Watkin's Ale."
"Watkin's Ale, good sir," quoth she, "what is that? I pray, tell
    me."[28]

Pageants

Before the creation of the Church of England, pageants had been religious plays, and by Elizabethan times, they meant something on a moving platform. This moving show was a series of floats depicting representations of giants, wild men, certain saints, and animals such as unicorns, elephants, camels, or dragons—all equally fantastic to the Elizabethan population. Along with this entertainment, minstrels and traveling musicians played and sang music of various sorts. Two of the biggest days for this sort of pageantry were St. George's Day (April 23) when England's most famous saint slew its most famous dragon, and the Lord Mayor's Pageant (October 29) when the lord mayor of London was annually "enthroned."

Theatrical Music

Middle-class Elizabethans had a love-hate relationship with theater. They loved make-believe, as long as it could be justified as morally uplifting. The upper class had private theaters, but the middle class (and as many of the lower class as could afford it) went to public theaters. London responded to popular demand with several theaters which, just as movie houses do today, tended to cater to certain types of clientele. The Red

Bull, for instance, was "frankly a plain man's playhouse, where clownery, clamor, and spectacle vied with subject matter flattering to the vanity of tradesmen"[29]

Elizabethan play-going was a guilty pleasure. Although they might enjoy the play, the Elizabethan middle class did not idolize the actors. Actors were viewed with suspicion to the point that they were denied burial on church grounds. After all, actors led unsteady lives. They drank, and they swore—even onstage. Just as people say today about filmmaking, some middle-class Elizabethans felt that certain plays made heroes out of characters that seemed frivolous and morally loose. They didn't like plays in which sons and daughters defied their parents, in which the hero defies civil authority, in which a dishonest character gets the upper hand. Most of all, they didn't like plays in which tradespeople were put up for ridicule as grasping, greedy types who would come to a bad end at the hand of an upper class hero. What they flocked to were plays that included flattering descriptions of England, reminders of tradesmen's role as God's chosen to bring their country to a peak of prosperity and Protestant values, and middle-class heroes who gathered praise, riches, and honor from those of a higher station in life.

There is a great deal of evidence that plays included music. As far back as 1562, before a "mummery" or "dumb-play," a personal letter stated, "first the violins began to play." An Elizabethan foreign visitor wrote that, "for a whole hour preceding the play one listens to a delightful musical entertainment on organs, lutes, pandoras, mandoras, viols, and pipes."[30] Another wrote in 1598 that he listened to music for about half an hour after the play had ended. Grand entries of main characters called for music, and there was music between acts. Lines within plays indicate that music was being played, such as a character entering and saying "Fiddler, forbear." That means, fiddler, stop playing. This music was so much a part of the plays that it was hardly mentioned in English diaries. It is only in foreign diaries that the abundance of music within English drama is mentioned.

During the Elizabethan age, play writing was undergoing a golden age, culminating in the works of its most famous playwright—William Shakespeare. The nobility joined the middle class in its passion for going to the theater. Shakespeare's plays show evidence of including quite a bit of music. Actors were hired not only to act, but also to sing.

Some Shakespearean plays were comedies, and the audience left the theater in a good mood. But others were historical plays that made an audience serious, or tragedies which might leave an audience in tears.

Rather than put the entire audience in a depressed mood, which might cause them to avoid coming to other plays, actors added a short, cheerful play. Known as a "jigg," this extra play was a type of musical comedy. The jigg was a small affair using anywhere from two to five characters. It had a loose plot that included a lot of improvising from the actors, really bad jokes, and plenty of singing and dancing. The comedy was not only low but sometimes rather bawdy. Characters sang popular songs of the day that fit with the plot, usually accompanied by a musician playing a stringed instrument such as a fiddle. Two actors who usually played comic roles in Shakespearean plays were also famous for acting in jiggs. Their names are Richard Tarlton and William Kemp. In fact, there is an instrumental tune still heard today known as "Kemp's jig."

Shakespeare's plays themselves called for songs. For instance, there is a drinking song in *Antony and Cleopatra* performed by a boy soprano. Magical scenes, such as the witches' scenes in *Macbeth*, were also set to music. Music also set the mood, as in Desdemona's death scene in *Othello*, when she sings "The Willow Song." The original actor who played Ophelia in *Hamlet* had a good deal of singing to do. Since the parts of women were played by boys, they must have been young enough to sing soprano parts. The staff of the theater must have had some instrumental musicians play soothing music to waken King Lear from his madness. There must have also been march music, music to spur Orsino to greater lovemaking efforts in *Twelfth Night*, drum and trumpet calls in battle scenes, and dance music playing at the ball where Romeo and Juliet met. What no one knows is who those players were, how they were recruited, and exactly what music they used. It is known that musicians were seated in the "top gallery" over the balcony stage. Historians speculate that local town musicians may have been used.

Middle-Class Heritage

The Elizabethan middle class was the vibrant backbone of its time, a welter of contradictions, with a wealth of interests. It is from this class that the colonies of England inherited attitudes and their own set of contradictory actions and beliefs that live on today in the United States. Ambition in business, debates over social and moral correctness, a Protestant work ethic, an economy driven by global trade, an equation with success and moral correctness, a firm belief in the positive virtues of education, and middle-class pride came across the Atlantic on the *Mayflower*. These positive aspects live on today. So did a fascination with crime and political scandal, with disasters natural or otherwise, and a sometimes morbid curiosity about the seamier aspects of life. Although differing in form, sales of cheap literature, X-rated films, tabloid newspapers, and the rise of "reality" television continue these negative aspects of our Elizabethan middle-class inheritance.

Music infused middle-class life. Many middle-class citizens bought instruments and played them at every opportunity. These enthusiastic amateurs gave composers and publishers a reason to put out music for nonprofessionals. Middle-class workers differentiated their trades through special melodies. People waiting for a haircut and shave plucked on instruments available at the barbershop to pass the time. Sea chanteys became an entire genre of Elizabethen music; broadsides gave the words to songs about romance, adventure, patriotism, and crime; and even Puritans, who disapproved of music for entertainment, sang devotional music at home as well as at church.

NOTES

1. L.B. Wright, *Middle-Class Culture in Elizabethan England* (Ithaca, NY: Cornell University Press, 1958), p. 13.

2. H.E. Wooldridge, *Old English Popular Music* (New York: Jack Brussel, 1961), p. 59.

3. Ibid., p. 164.

4. H. Collmann, "Ballads and Broadsides chiefly of the Elizabethan Period," http://www.pbm.com/~lindahl/ballads/collmann.html, n.d., pp. 15–16.

5. Ibid., pp. 7–9.

6. Wooldridge, p. 59.

7. W. Chappell, *Popular Music of the Olden Time* (New York: Dover Publications, 1965), p. 125.

8. Wooldridge, p. 67.

9. Ibid., p. 65.

10. Ibid., p. 253.

11. Ibid., p. 65.

12. R. Baker, and A. Miall, *Everyman's Book of Sea Songs* (London: J.M. Dent & Sons, 1982), pp. 27–28.

13. Wright, p. 355.

14. Ibid., p. 376.

15. Ibid., p. 392.

16. Ibid., p. 391.

17. Wooldridge, p. 240.

18. Ibid.

19. Wright, pp. 419–420.

20. J. Holloway, *The Euing Collection of English Broadside Ballads* (Glasgow: Robert Maclehose & Company, 1971), p. 75.

21. Wright, p. 425.

22. Ibid., p. 187.

23. J.H. Marshburn and A.R. Velie, *Blood and Knavery, A Collection of English Renaissance Pamphlets and Ballads of Crime and Sin* (Rutherford, NJ: Fairleigh Dickinson University Press, 1973), pp. 155–158.

24. Holloway, pp. 226–227.

25. Wright, pp. 308–309.

26. Holloway, p. 97.

27. J.F. Millar, *Elizabethan Country Dances* (Williamsburg, VA: Thirteen Colonies Press, 1985), p. 105.

28. Ibid., p. 113.

29. Wright, p. 609.

30. J. Buxton, *Elizabethan Taste* (New York: St. Martin's Press, 1964), p. 215.

REFERENCES

Baker, R., and Miall, A. *Everyman's Book of Sea Songs.* London: J.M. Dent & Sons, 1982.

Buxton, J. *Elizabethan Taste.* New York: St. Martin's Press, 1964.

Chappell, W. *Popular Music of the Olden Time.* New York: Dover Publications, 1965.

Collmann, H. "Ballads and Broadsides Chiefly of the Elizabethan Period." http://www.pbm.com/~lindahl/ballads/collmann.html, n.d.

Emerson, K.L. *The Writer's Guide to Everyday Life in Renaissance England from 1485–1649.* Cincinnati, OH: Writer's Digest Books, 1996.

Holloway, J. *The Euing Collection of English Broadside Ballads.* Glasgow: Robert Maclehose and Company, 1971.

Marshburn, J.H., and Velie, A.R. *Blood and Knavery, A Collection of English Renaissance Pamphlets and Ballads of Crime and Sin.* Rutherford, NJ: Fairleigh Dickinson University Press, 1973.

Millar, J.F. *Elizabethan Country Dances.* Williamsburg, VA: Thirteen Colonies Press, 1985.

Springfels, M. "Music in Shakespeare's Plays," from Encyclopaedia Britannica Online. http://www.Shakespeare.eb.com/shakespeare/esa/660007.html, n.d.

Wooldridge, H.E. *Old English Popular Music.* New York: Jack Brussel, 1961.

Wright, L.B. *Middle-Class Culture in Elizabethan England.* Ithaca, NY: Cornell University Press, 1958.

Chapter 3

Life and Music
of the Lower Class

The lower class is the least known stratum of Elizabethan society. Generally, people of this class were called "peasants" if they lived in the country. Most peasants were farmers. City people of this class usually worked as servants of some sort and could be called the "servant class" or "lower orders." Access to music and musical instruments wasn't as prevalent for them as it was for the middle and upper classes. Their lack of a broad education also meant a lack of music education and lessons. However, they did find ways to enjoy music and dancing, just as the other classes did, and music still played an important role in their lives.

Life for the lower class was for the most part a life of unremitting work. Their work was usually of the dirtiest, most dangerous, or most monotonous kind.

Disease and injury were part of lower class life. In Elizabethan England, medicine and sanitation were in a rather primitive state. Flush toilets were unknown. For indoor use, chamber pots were used and emptied outside later. In urban areas, that sometimes meant heaving the contents out of an upstairs window. Nobody was sure how communicable diseases were spread or what to do about them. Plague was a recurring threat. Elizabethans believed that crowded conditions had something to do with its spread, and urban dwellers who could afford to do so usually moved out of cities when the plague appeared in urban areas. But country folk got it too. The best preventative was quarantine. Families of plague victims were locked inside their own homes, and a red-painted wooden cross was nailed to the door to warn others not to enter. For victims without families or servants, a special type of nurse could be hired to take care of plague victims.

Because they were often impoverished, crime was a temptation to the lower class. For men, organized crime was usually smuggling; for women, it usually meant prostitution. But the most common crime for the lower classes was theft. Punishment for petty theft (anything under a shilling) was a public whipping. Punishment for felony theft was death, though sympathetic juries might deliberately undervalue the worth of stolen goods to avoid having to pass a death sentence. Any person accused by the crown was considered guilty until proven innocent. A witness testifying against the crown's findings was considered a liar. Females accused of a crime could be tried by a jury, but women were not allowed to sit on a jury.

EDUCATION

Some free schools existed for both sexes, particularly in urban areas. Even girls were taught to read and write, as reading to one's mistress seems to have been an expected part of a ladies' maid's duties.[1] However, teaching methods were harsh, as we see in a scene from a morality tale of Elizabethan times, *The Miseries of Mavillia*, by Nicholas Breton. Here the heroine is "taught" by her mistress, an elderly woman:

> Oh, heere was a miserrabel metamorphosies; then got shee me a booke . . . now began a new miserie; when I woulde bee at play, either with the catte, or a little dogge, or making of a babie, of an olde ragged cloute: then woulde shee come with a rodde, Come on, you urchen, you will never come to good; pull the clout out of my hand, slap it in my face, tosse mee by the shoulders, and squatte mee downe so mischievouslie, that I had more mind to crie, then to [read].[2]

LITERACY AND MUSIC

The encouragement of literacy, which in Elizabethan times even reached to the lower classes, gave an enormous boost to the printing industry. Catering to urban peasants, street vendors peddled "broadsides" and "chapbooks" containing sensationalized news and stories. Lower and middle-class people shared a taste for this sort of information and entertainment. But broadsides were the major form of written literature for the poor. A broadside was a single sheet of paper (roughly the quality of newsprint) with words printed on only one side of the sheet. The price ranged from a halfpenny to a penny per sheet. If a sheet had words printed on both sides of the paper, it was known as a "broadsheet." The lure of reading about the latest murder, doomed romance, or current event was so great that sometimes several people from the lower class would form a loose "club"—every member contributing, say, a penny a week so that all members could share the paper.[3]

Typically, a broadside would include at least one ballad. Topics of interest—whether current events or ancient tales of heroism or romance—became the subjects of metered, rhymed verses. The verses were written so that they could be sung to older, familiar tunes. This way the broadside only had to print the words—not the music. Usually there would be a rather crude-looking woodcut of the subject matter, with a sentence such as "To the Tune of, Your Humble Servant Madame" or "The tune is Bonny Sweet Robin." Then the reader sang the verses printed underneath to the tune indicated. Most of these songs are quite long and tell involved stories of murder, broken hearts, revenge, adventure, mystery, or the latest scandal. The woodcuts illustrating these ballads did not necessarily have anything to do with its subject matter. A printer would buy, say, a woodcut of a hanging. That woodcut would show up on dozens of ballads concerned with a hanged man's last-minute confession and repentance, and might be used for decades.[4] Sellers were not always honest about what they were selling either. Sometimes a broadside advertised as "the newest horrible murther" had actually been reprinted from a long-ago crime.

A favorite subject for rural peasants was the execution of criminals. "Death-hunters" carried an advertisement of sorts—a long pole on which a canvas was attached onto cross bars. The canvas showed the picture of a crime on one side (murders were especially big sellers) and the execution on the other side. Broadsides sold on the subject included not only the crime and punishment, but a confession of guilt from the villain and a heartfelt speech imploring both human and divine pardon—and by implication a warning to all who would break the law.

DANCE AND DANCE MUSIC

Young people of the lower class found opportunities to meet socially through dancing. Some holidays involved dancing (particularly May Day—May 1), and there was also plenty of dancing at country fairs. Naturally, music was needed. Dance music generally took the name of the dance it was to fit and therefore had names such as jigs and hornpipes. There were "longways" dances in which pairs formed two long lines, "square" dances where sets of couples formed a square, and others where couples formed a circle, or round. One Elizabethan historian wrote that Country dances were marked "not only by variety but by spontaneity and dramatic quality. The dances call for kissing, shaking hands, slapping, stamping, snapping the fingers, peeping, (and) wiping the eyes."[5] Dances might be for couples or for groups of four to eight or more dancers.

> Let them take their pleasures then . . . young men and maids flourishing in their age, fair and lovely to behold, well attired and of comely carriage, dancing a . . . galliard [a type of Elizabethan dance] and as their dance required, kept their time, now turning, now tracing, now apart, now altogether, now a curtsie, then a caper. . . . and it was a pleasant sight to see those pretty knots and swimming figures.[6]

Country dancing became so popular and was the source of so much fun that the gentry took it up. When that happened, the dances were written down so that upper-class people could learn them. This is how descriptions of these dances have come down to us, although the descriptions may be from a later era.

Opinions varied as to whether these energetic dances were decent. Philip Stubbes wrote in his *Anatomy of Abuses* in 1588: "what clipping, what culling, what kissing and bussing, what smooching and slavering one of another, what filthie groping and uncleane handling is not practised in those dancings?"[7] But writer T. Arbeau justified the practice on grounds of practicality, in his *Orchesography* of the same year: "dancing is practised to reveal whether lovers are in good health and sound of limb, after which they are permitted to kiss their mistresses in order that they may touch and savour one another, thus to ascertain if they are shapely or emit an unpleasant odour as of bad meat."[8]

LOVE AND MARRIAGE

Although much was written about romantic love, in real life romance did not naturally lead to marriage. Although love matches existed, they were not necessarily the norm. Marriage was designed to help the family fortunes—even if that meant marrying a neighbor to bring the field next door into your family's home as a dowry. This may seem strange or even cruel to the present-day reader. But Elizabethan young people had a much more heightened sense of duty—duty to God and to their parents.

Most people married within their station; that is, peasants married peasants, nobility married nobility. However, this state of affairs was not universally accepted. One Elizabethan source railed against the practice, saying that society was not always reasonable on this subject:

> If I chance to settle in affection with a mayde of base condition, and by a tollerable suggestion of nature, proceede with hir in holye maryage, shall I not runne into a popular obloquie, as proclayming in me an act and example of wilfull folly? . . . But if in a greedie desire of gold and transitorie drosse, I practice a Ladie of equall place and value to my selfe, then that blind ignoraunce commendes and congratulates with me, as esteeming that for my benefite, which in deede convertes to my extreeme displeasure."[9]

Because of the complications of class and society versus love or the lack thereof, situations involving romance and social standing were ripe for ballads. One contemporary broadside ballad is described as "The Covetous-minded Parents OR, The Languishing young Gentlewoman Whose Friends would have her Marry an old Miser for the sake of his Gold, which she utterly refused to do, resolveing to be true to the first."[10] The opening verse outlines the problem (sung to the tune "Farewell my dearest Dear"):

> I Am a Damosel fair
>   Of blooming Beauty;
> Therefore I do declare
>   It is my Duty
> My Parents to obey,
>   Father and Mother;
> They'd have me Marry Gray,
>   I love another.[11]

Country peasant weddings had one foot in Christianity and another in practices of the pagan past. However, all the customs had settled into a comfortable "traditional" state by Elizabethan times. Music was an integral part of the festivities, as was dancing.

The following is a contemporary account of a country peasant wedding:

First, all the lusty lads and bold bachelors of the parish, suitable every wight
with his blue buckram bridelace upon a branch of green broom (because
rosemary is scant there) tied on his left arm, . . . and his alder pole for a
spear in his right hand, . . . and these to the number of a sixteen wight
[hardy] riding men, and well beseen: but the bridegroom foremost, in his
father's tawny worsted jacket, . . . a fair straw hat, with a capital crowne
steeple wise on his head, . . . well, sir, after these horsemen, a lively morris-
dance, according to the ancient manner, six dancers, Maid Marian, and
the fool. Then, three pretty (maidens) as bright as a breast of bacon . . .
that carried three special spice-cakes of a bushel of wheat . . . before the
bride. . . . Then followed the worshipful bride, led (after the country manner) between two ancient parishioners, honest townsmen . . . after this
bride came there, by two and two, a dozen damsels for bridesmaids.[12]

This paragraph describes a "lively morris-dance." Most traditional get-
togethers, such as weddings and fairs, featured this dance. Morris dancing
was an ancient tradition still alive during Elizabethan times. Actually,
there were two types of Morris dances—one had to do with the story of
Robin Hood, and the other had a more ancient ancestry. According to
tradition, the Morris dance came to England during the time of Edward
III (1312–1377) and may have originated in Spain where it had been
danced by Moors and "was probably a kind of Pyrrhic, or military dance."[13]
Although by Elizabethan times, Morris dancing was performed in many
venues—as in the wedding above—the dance was really associated with
May Day (May 1). Formerly, May Day had been celebrated with a King
and Queen of the May. When Morris dancing was introduced, the king
was eliminated, leaving the Queen of the May as sole sovereign. Characters in this type of Morris dance were the Lady of the May, a Fool or
Jester, a Piper, and anywhere from two to six Morris dancers. The Lady
of the May, as all the others, was male—a young boy dressed as a female.
Sometimes "she" was carried on the shoulders of the dancers in a procession. The piper provided music. But fiddlers, harpers, drummers, and other
instrumentalists might join in to play traditional tunes. The Morris-
dancers wore bells that jingled as they danced. "These worn round the
elbows and knees, were of unequal sizes, and differently denominated; as
the fore bell, the second bell, the treble, the mean or counter-tenor, the
tenor, the great bell or bass, and sometimes double bells were worn."[14]
    A variation of the Morris dance, known as the "games of Robin Hood,"
included a Robin Hood, a Maid Marian (usually a young boy dressed as
a girl), a large person playing Friar Tuck dressed in a Franciscan friar's
garb, a Little John, a Fool, "Tom Piper," a varying number of dancers,

and the hobby-horse man. "The hobby horse was a pasteboard resemblance of the head and tail of a horse on a wicker frame . . . attached to the body of a man who, with feet concealed by a . . . cloth hanging to the ground, was to imitate the ambling, the prancing, and the curvetting of the horse."[15] Often a dragon, made in the same way, made a frightening display and was attacked and vanquished by the hobby-horse knight, who in this case represented St. George the Dragonslayer—patron saint of England.

The "games of Robin Hood" were originally held to encourage the sport of archery, and the appearance of the Morris-dancers was secondary. Eventually this, too, became associated with May Day, and the Queen of the May's character became identified with Maid Marian. In Elizabethan times, Puritans began to attack the games by showing up and preaching against them, loudly making "considerable havoc among the May-games."[16] They furiously denounced Friar Tuck as obviously Popish, the hobby-horse as a pagan relic, and Maid Marian as the "whore of Babylon" for her unmarried relationship to Robin Hood.[17] Nonetheless, Morris dancing persisted and showed up at fairs, weddings, and other festive occasions.

MAGIC AND MUSIC

Although Elizabethans of all classes were superstitious, members of the lower class were especially ignorant of natural laws. As one source puts it, "people lived in their own villages and parishes more shut off from what was fifty miles away than we are now from Africa and Australia."[18] Anything out of the ordinary was considered a miracle, and people attempted to chart the course of their lives with work and prayer—but also, when needed, with spells and magic. Elizabethans believed in magic and witchcraft. Even high-minded, educated people were not above consulting a fortune-teller in times of need. And women—for whom marriage was of vital importance—relied on charms for good luck in their future lives.

Music was part of the ritual for securing good luck. English people still held to ancient traditions such as celebrating the coming of spring and the renewal of life. Elizabethans of all classes—but particularly the rural lower class—celebrated May Day. The celebration of May Day dated back to the Roman occupation of England and was associated with the festival of the Roman goddess of spring, Flora. Morris dances, as noted earlier, were an important part of May Day festivities, but so was decorating the

Maypole. The Maypole was an ancient phallic symbol, and decorating it with ribbons held by young men and women weaving among one another in a Maypole dance had once been a fertility rite. Tolerated by most people, May Day festivities made conservatives nervous, inasmuch as the ceremonies were still a pagan celebration of sex, overlaid with a thin layer of Christianity. Although not only a lower-class celebration, the lower classes in both city and country vigorously participated in May Day traditions. A 1598 description of May Day celebrations in London tells us:

> I find that in the month of May the citizens of London, of all estates, lightly in every parish, or sometimes two or three parishes joining together, had their several Mayings, and did fetch in May-poles, with divers warlike shews, with good archers, Morris-dancers, and other devices for pastime all the day long: and towards the evening they had stageplays and bonfires in the streets.[19]

Although some festivals revolved around the agricultural calendar, others had roots in pagan traditions. City people made fun of rustic country songs with their crude, unpolished poetry. As William Webbe in his *A Discourse of English Poetrie* (1586) wrote:

> popular Musickes song by these Cantabanqui upon benches and barrels heads . . . or else by blind harpers or such like taverne minstrels that give a fit of mirth for a groat, & their matters being for the most part stores of old time, as the tale of Sir Topas, the reports of Bevis of Southampton, Guy of Warwicke, and Clymme of the Clough & such other old Romances of historicall rimes, made purposely for recreation of the common people at Christmasse diners and brideales, and in tavernes & alehouses and such other places of base resort, also they be used in Carols and rounds and such light or lascivious Poemes, which are commonly more commodiously uttered by these buffons or vices in playes then by any other person.[20]

MUSIC AT HOME

Few lower-class homes contained instruments; a more popular home entertainment was singing. Friends and family gathered together to sing in parts. Part-singing was a favored hobby for the lower classes, as well as for their betters. Younger people learned from their elders and sang traditional carols, tunes, and devotional songs with no written music.

A favorite type of part-song was the "round." The tune was easy to learn because all the singers sang the same thing. The hard part was that each part came in at different specific times (a typical round of today would be "Row, Row, Row Your Boat"). These songs could also be known as a Roundelay, a Canon in Unison, Freemen's Songs, or Three Men's Songs. They were generally sung in three parts—that is, with three groups if there were more than three people singing—and were sung three times before ending. Besides being sung at home with family members, males gathering in local taverns or other venues also engaged in vigorous round singing. "The chief pastime of men at convivial gatherings, if they had no instruments was singing catches or rounds."[21] Elizabethans looked upon this activity as harmless entertainment. John Playford wrote in his *Musical Companion*:

> I recommend them; for this is a catching Age, all kinds of catches and catchers are abroad, Catch that catch can, Catch that catch may, Thine catch it and mine catch it; But these harmless catches; my wish is, those that catch them with delight to learn and for instruction may hereby reap both Pleasure and Delight.[22]

Singing carols was another popular at-home entertainment. In Elizabethan times, the word "carol" did not automatically go together with the word "Christmas." Carols could be on any subject and had actually started out as music sung to dancing. Carols had a series of verses, but instead of an English-language refrain they had a "burden"—a refrain in Latin. Many carols were religious in nature, but some dealt with secular subjects. Carols were traditional, sung from generation to generation, and some were already one or two hundred years old by Elizabethan times. (see also Chapter 5).

FARMERS AND FESTIVE MUSIC

Most members of the lower class in rural areas were tenant farmers, working land owned by a member of the nobility and paying for the privilege either in coin or with a part of their crop or livestock. The entire year was one of unrelenting work. Winter was a time for ploughing, harrowing, and spreading manure. It was also the time to prune fruit trees, chop trees for timber, "set" hedges, fill up holes in pastureland, make sure that there was enough "browse" for livestock, and thresh grain. In spring, peasant farmers plowed and harrowed fields, turning over the earth for planting. When the soil was readied, they sowed crops such as flax, hemp, barley, oats, and some wheat. In late spring, ditches were cleaned for proper drainage, and peasant women and children planted home gardens. In summer, fields were ploughed and manured for later crops, and hay was mowed after Midsummer Day (June 21).

Harvest started the first day of August. In September peasant farmers planted rye grain, and harvesting continued. Families harvested grapes and crabapples, making "verjuice," a liquid used in cooking, out of the crabapples. Apple cider and "perry" were made for drinking. In fall, peasant farmers cut wood for winter use and dug peat or turf to dry and burn for fuel. Garden beds for plants were covered over for the coming winter. (In fact, strawberries got their name from being covered with straw so they would survive over the winter.) Meanwhile, farm wives tended the household animals, made cheese, cleaned and cooked, foraged for "extras" such as mushrooms and berries, did the gardening, helped with weeding and haymaking, sewed, spun wool, and then knitted and wove it into clothing and blankets.

Livestock was a major source of revenue—especially sheep. Farmers raised sheep for their meat, their fleece or wool, their skin (which was used as leather and also as writing material—even now a diploma is commonly known as a "sheepskin"), their milk (six ewes gave the milk equivalent of one cow), and their manure, which was used as fertilizer. Other livestock included cows, pigs, and goats.

Some farmers kept bees in wicker hives covered with clay because honey was an important sweetener. Domestic poultry meant chicken as well as geese, swans, and doves—were all raised for food. Domestic animals were expected to work for their living. For example, cats killed rodents, and dogs guarded hearth and home and were also used to herd livestock. One odd household pet was the weasel, which Elizabethan farmhands trained to kill rats and mice.

Although much of the farmers' produce was for their own use, market days provided opportunities to sell livestock and the fruits of harvest. Festivals or country fairs followed these market days. The holiday known as Michaelmas (September 29) marked the official end of one farming year and the start of the next. Country fairs mixed business with pleasure. Farmers exchanged new farming techniques and looked at improved equipment on display for sale, met friends not seen in some time, talked politics, and engaged in contests such as sheep shearing and horse racing. Women bought goods at the fair's market and exchanged home remedies for improving the health of both humans and animals.

Country fairs were also a time for music and dancing. Besides the inevitable Morris dances, fairs provided the opportunity for other types of dancing and music. The "Hay" (or, "Hey") was a popular folk dance "in which the dancers, in single file, pass alternately by the right and left, half of them going one way, the rest in the opposite direction. It is one of the oldest dance figures . . . the snake being, of course, a well-known symbol in all religions."[23] The "Shepherd's Hey" was a preferred tune, and dancers accompanied it by waving handkerchiefs or sticks. Other dances were the "Jigg," the "Brawl," the "Almaine," the "Canary," and the "Hornpipe." Most of these dances were versions of upper-class dances such as the gigue, bransle, and Allemagne (see Chapter 7). The "canary," mentioned in Shakespeare, was supposedly named for the Canary Islands where the dance was rumored to have originated. The hornpipe was named for an instrument with that name but later became known as a sailor's dance instead of the instrument that had accompanied it.

Musicians played a variety of instruments at these fairs. These instruments were mostly homemade, and though old-fashioned in Elizabethan times, were still used in country celebrations. The pipe and tabor and the bagpipes were some of the most popular peasant instruments. The pipe and tabor was a two-instrument ensemble played by one person. The pipe was a whistle-like flute with two finger holes and a thumb hole, capable of making enough notes to make a merry tune—using only one hand to make all the notes. The tabor was a tom-tom drum slung over the player's shoulder with a leather strip and hit with a stick or bone. A good pipe and tabor player could be the life of a party. Bagpipes had been brought back from Eastern countries (such as Syria) during the Crusades and had been a favorite instrument of European peasants ever since. Smaller than the traditional Scottish bagpipes one thinks of nowadays, these instruments sent out enough sound to be heard over the noise of a country fair.

These instruments were often played by traveling musicians, known as "minstrels." Just as today, some musicians made a living by following fairs and celebrations in various towns and playing for tips. They sang and played music for dancing and group singing. In both city and country, wandering musicians were viewed by the law as only one step—and a small one at that—above Gypsies. In the thirty-ninth year of Queen Elizabeth's reign, "minstrels wandering abroad" were declared "rogues, vagabonds, and sturdy beggars" and could be picked up as vagrants. The term *wandering minstrels* also began to apply to freelance harpers, fiddlers, pipers, and other strolling musicians. They are described this way in a 1598 tract:

> The over busy and too speedy return of one manner of tune, doth too much annoy, and, as it were, glut the ear, unless it be in small and popular musicks . . . where they have none other audience than boys or country fellows that pass by them in the street.[24]

Apparently, many people felt that instead of being entertained, they had been musically mugged! In 1586, one Elizabethan wrote: "London is so full of unprofitable pipers and fiddlers that a man can no sooner enter a tavern, than two or three [companies] of them hang at his heels, to give him a dance before he departs."[25] The person being "entertained" in this way was expected to give a donation whether or not they asked for music.

URBAN LIFE AND MUSIC

Lower-class people who lived in the cities were most likely employed as domestic servants. Servitude began in a person's early teens and the average age was between 15 and 29 years old. A household servant received wages, room and board, and clothing. Servants were generally regarded as part of the household in the same way that fine furniture was—as "chattel."

A servant's time was entirely under his master's rule. Masters were free to punish their servants with a blow or a whipping with a horsewhip. But masters who abused this "privilege" by beating a servant severely were considered against the law, and the servant might be released from that master's service by a court order.[26] Masters were not only allowed to inflict corporal punishment on their servants, they might also levy fines on them for particular offenses.

Servants used music to lighten the hardships of their daily lives. Employers approved of servants who enjoyed music, even if their enjoyment was on a very elemental level. Elizabethans generally tended to distrust people who did not like music. It was felt that a person who had no feeling for music was less than human—and thus, not a person to be trusted. This extended to the hiring of servants from the lower class. The 1570

"Points of Huswifry United to the Comfort of Husbandry" urged employers to hire servants that sang at their work. "Such servants are oftenest painfull and good, That sing in their labour, as birds in the wood."[27]

Of course, employers preferred that their servants sing devotional songs, but the servants were more likely to be at least thinking the words from the newest broadside as they hummed a supposedly innocent tune. Wandering "hawkers" sold broadsides to urban lower-class buyers on the streets, much as a newsboy might sell newspapers. In big cities, hawkers might have an assistant—a boy or young man—who ran about shouting out things like "Terrible", "Frightening Monster," or "Horrible Event." When anyone asked what it was—the "running patterer" pointed to the broadside seller and told the person to find out by buying a broadside.

Many ballads were bawdy—with some of the lyrics more frank than those of today. Consider this ballad from an ex-virgin:

> What pleasure is there like to this,
> The Damsel then did cry.
> I've heard them talk of lovers' bliss—
> Oh, what a foole was I
> So long to live a maid, ere I
> Did this same sport begin!
> This death I now could freely die—
> I prithee thrust it in![28]

Ballads were viewed with a certain amount of distrust by the upper class and were periodically suppressed, or at least attempts were made to regulate their subject matter. When the Church of England was formed, for instance, a proclamation sought to suppress foolish "books, ballads, rhimes, and other lewd treatises in the English tongue."[29] Ballads were supposed to be licensed by Stationer's Hall, which put them under censorship laws. Printers suspected of having put out treasonous lyrics were both persecuted and prosecuted, usually with a heavy fine. If the offense was bad enough and the person who wrote it could be identified, they could be executed for treason—as a man named William Carter was in 1580.

Besides being bought and sung, ballad sheets had other, more unusual uses. Sometimes illustrated ballads were used to decorate the walls of poorer housing. They might also be hung on gravesites, presumably because the words might express the respect or grief felt by the person who hung it there.

SEA SONGS

For adventurous or desperate lads who wanted neither the life of a farmer nor a life of servitude, becoming a sailor was an option. Actually, sailors also lived a life of servitude, but along with it came opportunities for travel and adventure. Sailors saw strange sights, encountered new cultures, and ate foods they had never imagined. But this was life onshore. Life at sea was quite a different proposition.

The common sailor's plates and cups were made of wood. Since refrigeration was unknown, food was dried, salted, or pickled for the most part. Sailors had salted meat (four times a week), fish (three times a week), beer, and biscuits. These biscuits were not soft and buttered, but were "hardtack"—much closer to a dog biscuit in texture. Sailors were guaranteed biscuits and beer every day—a gallon of beer per sailor per day! Sailors also caught food from the sea such as fish, porpoises, or seals. A ship might have a hired cook, or cooking duties might be rotated among the crew. But food could only be cooked during calm seas. Building a fire in a wooden ship tossing in a storm, which was days or weeks away from land, created an obvious danger.

Lack of fresh fruits and vegetables on long sea journeys meant that a disease called scurvy was a constant threat. Lack of Vitamin C caused this disease. Even though nobody knew why, sailors did realize that citrus fruit had something to do with curing scurvy. At a much later date, the British navy distributed lime juice as part of a sailor's rations and to this day British sailors are known as "Limeys."

Below decks, common sailors slept in hammocks or on straw mats. The distance between decks was six feet, so headroom was practically non-existent. There were rats. It was dark even in daylight. There were always leaks, which kept sailors perpetually wet. Corporal punishment was common—usually a whipping with a "boatswain's rod," with a certain amount of lashes per offense. For all this, common sailors were paid 10 shillings a month.

Common sailors might end up on a royal Navy ship, a merchant ship, or a fishing ship. Singing helped them pass the time, gave vent to feelings of loneliness and homesickness, helped keep groups together during physical labor, kept up spirits, and celebrated a life at sea despite its brutalities. The same songs were sung on both war ships and merchant ships. The generic name for the common sailor was "Jack." Sea songs eventually acquired the name "Chanteys" or "Shanties," a name that may have come from the French word for song—*chanson* (pronounced "shan-son"). One of the earliest surviving shanties was probably sung during the reign of Henry VIII. A work song, it is called "Haul the Bowlin'."

Verse 1: Haul the bowlin', the skipper he's a-growlin'

Chorus: (sung after every verse) Haul the bowlin', the bowlin' haul!

Verse 2: Haul the bowlin', so early in the morning (Chorus, after each verse)

Verse 3: Haul the bowlin', the chief mate he's a-growlin'

Verse 4: Haul the bowlin', the wind it is a-howlin'

Verse 5: Haul the bowlin', the ship she is a-rollin'[30]

Some sailors found work on pirate ships. During Elizabethan times, it seems that every other ship was a pirate vessel but of course, that isn't true. Nonetheless, pirate escapades occupied quite a lot of ballad music. Pirate ships plundered merchant vessels for goods and money, raided seacoast towns (many in the New World islands), and engaged in mutually profitable smuggling ventures with onshore criminals. Though officially abhorred, the exploits of pirates and their sensationally terrible crimes were eagerly snapped up as broadside ballads by lower class Elizabethans. Unfortunately, precious few ballads of these times have survived, and many of those that have survived have no dates printed on them, so it is unclear exactly when they were printed. Most of those clearly from Elizabethan times are political or amorous in nature.

CONCLUSION

The basic level of literacy given to the lower class gave them access to printed broadsheets with words to songs that could be sung to already-known, familiar tunes. Dances at holiday celebrations and country fairs included plenty of music. Morris dancing and Maypole dances accompanied by song and rustic instruments gave the lower class ties to their pre-Christian past as well as serving as an outlet from their usual life of unrelenting work. Sailors sang and played whatever instruments were available, to bear a life of hardship, privation, and loneliness. Made fun of by their betters and living lives full of drudgery, danger, and even despair at times, the Elizabethan lower class had their music as a companion in life.

NOTES

1. G. Bradford, *Elizabethan Women* (Cambridge: Houghton Mifflin Company, 1936), p. 30.

2. Ibid.

3. M. Vicinus, *Broadsides of the Industrial North* (Newcastle Upon Tyne: Frank Graham, 1975), p. 7.

4. Ibid., p. 8.

5. Ibid., p. 168.

6. Bradford, p. 88.

7. J.F. Millar, *Elizabethan Country Dances* (Williamsburg, VA: Thirteen Colonies Press, 1985), p. 12.

8. Ibid., p. 13.

9. C. Camden, *The Elizabethan Woman* (Mamaroneck, NY: Paul P. Appel, 1975), p. 64.

10. J. Holloway, *The Euing Collection of English Broadside Ballads in the Library of the University of Glasgow* (Glasgow: Robert Maclehose and Company, 1971), p. 63.

11. Ibid.

12. Bradford, p. 52.

13. M.J. Gutch, *A Lytell Geste of Robin Hode with Other Ancient & Modern Ballads and Songs relating to this Celebrated Yeoman* (London: Longman, Brown, Green, & Longmans, 1947), p. 301.

14. H.E. Wooldridge, *Old English Popular Music* (New York: Jack Brussel, 1961), p. 244.

15. Ibid., pp. 243–244.

16. Gutch, p. 348.

17. Ibid.

18. Bradford, p. 32.

19. Wooldridge, p. 246.

20. F. Laroque, *Shakespeare's Festive World* (J. Lloyd, trans.) (Cambridge: Cambridge University Press, 1991), p. 34.

21. F. Keel, *Music in the Time of Queen Elizabeth* (February 24, 1914), p. 38.

22. Ibid., p. 39.

23. Ibid., p. 57.

24. Wooldridge, pp. 58–59.

25. Ibid.

26. Ibid.

27. Wooldridge, p. 60.

28. E. Lee, *Music of the People: A Study of Popular Music in Great Britain* (London: Barrie & Jenkins, 1970), pp. 43–44.

29. Wooldridge, p. 54.

30. R. Baker and A. Miall, *Everyman's Book of Sea Songs* (London: J.M. Dent & Sons, 1982), p. 74.

REFERENCES

Baker, R., and Miall, A. *Everyman's Book of Sea Songs*. London: J.M. Dent & Sons, 1982.

Bradford, G. *Elizabethan Women*. Cambridge: Houghton Mifflin Company, 1936.

Camden, C. *The Elizabethan Woman*. Mamaroneck, NY: Paul P. Appel, 1975.

Greene, R.L. *The Early English Carols*. Oxford: Clarendon Press, 1935.

Gutch, M.J. *A Lytell Geste of Robin Hode with Other Ancient & Modern Ballads and Songs relating to this Celebrated Yeoman*. London: Longman, Brown, Green, & Longmans, 1947.

Holloway, J. *The Euing Collection of English Broadside Ballads in the Library of the University of Glasgow*. Glasgow: Robert Maclehose and Company, 1971.

Keel, F. *Music in the Time of Queen Elizabeth*. A paper read before ye sette of odd volumes February 24th, 1914. Presented to the sette by Brother John Lane bibliographer: at the 341st meeting, Tuesday, May 26th 1914.

Laroque, F. *Shakespeare's Festive World* (J. Lloyd, trans.). Cambridge: Cambridge University Press, 1991.

Lee, E. *Music of the People: A Study of Popular Music in Great Britain*. London: Barrie & Jenkins, 1970.

Millar, J.F. *Elizabethan Country Dances*. Williamsburg, VA: Thirteen Colonies Press, 1985.

Vicinus, M. *Broadsides of the Industrial North*. Newcastle Upon Tyne: Frank Graham, 1975.

Wooldridge, H.E. *Old English Popular Music*. New York: Jack Brussel, 1961.

Chapter 4

Elizabethan Notation

Written music notation has had a long evolution. The ancient Greeks and Romans used a system of alphabetical note names, a system whose pitches have been lost over the ages. The early Christians used a variety of dashes, dots, and squiggles (known as *neumes*) over text words to indicate whether a pitch was supposed to be higher or lower than its predecessor. These marks had no way of telling a performer exactly how high or low a pitch was in relation to any other pitch, and there was no way to tell how long or short a note should be. In the Middle Ages, an unknown musician drew a horizontal line indicating where a particular pitch should be. Other pitches became marks closer to or farther away from that horizontal line. Over time, more lines were added, and neumes placed on particular lines or spaces acquired particular pitches. Gradually, systems of indicating rhythms were also developed. By the Renaissance, written musical notation had begun to resemble the system musicians use today, although it still retained some aspects from its Middle Ages roots.

Learning to read music in any age is very much like learning a foreign language. Written music has its own method of setting itself up to be understood by many people. Known as notation, it has its own vocabulary and even its own notational alphabet. Just as written language is put down in lines, music is written on a system of lines and spaces called a "staff." Notes placed on the staff are read from left to right, and every note's spot on the staff system indicates how high or low its pitch will be.

Notes placed higher on the staff will sound higher in pitch, and notes placed lower on the staff will sound lower. Notes have letter names that spell out a system known as a "scale." Note names are: a, b, c, d, e, f, and g. Music has only seven possible letter names. The eighth note is called an "octave" and is twice as high as the first note. This starts the sequence over again—a, b, c, and so on.

The length of time a note is sung or played is indicated by rhythmic signs. The first sign is whether a note has a white center or is colored in black. Black notes are shorter in duration. They will have a "stem"—a stick—coming out of each note head. If the stem has a "flag" on top, that note is even shorter. Two flags, three flags, or four flags indicate ever shorter note durations. Moments of silence have a similar system to show duration of silence between notes. These moments of silence are known as "rests."

The rhythms of the notes generally indicate a "beat"—the part of music to which we tap our feet. In most music, vertical lines on the staff, called "bar lines," put a certain amount of beats in the area between two bar lines. No matter how many notes are written between two bar lines, their rhythmic values should add up to a set amount of beats. Musicians know how many beats should be in each bar by looking at a set of numbers on the upper left-hand corner of each work known as the "time signature." There will be two numbers, one on top of the other, making the time signature look much like a fraction. The upper number indicates how many beats should be in each measure of the work. The lower number indicates what type of note will get the beat. For instance, a time signature with a "3" on top of a "4" indicates that there will be three beats in each measure, and a certain type of note known as a "quarter note" will indicate one beat.

A scale is a series of notes progressing up or down, step by step. Melodies in music are taken from the notes of scales. The smallest distance between two notes in Western music is called a "half-step." Different types of scales are made up of half- and whole-steps in different combinations. For instance, a scale made up of all half-steps is known as a "chromatic" scale. The two most common scales are the "major" scale and the "minor" scale. Sometimes other notes besides those from the scale must be used in a piece of music. Those notes will be displaced by a half-step higher or lower. To boost a note a half-step higher, a note will have a sign in front of it called a "sharp" that looks like a small tic-tac-toe board. To make a note a half-step lower, a note will have a sign in front of it called a "flat" that looks like a small letter "b." When a note has been flatted or sharped and must be returned to its original state, the note will have a sign in front of it called a "natural" that looks like a lopsided ladder. All of these signs are known as "accidentals"—even though none of them is an accident. If a work has a note (or several notes) that should *always* be flatted or sharped, there will be a "key signature" on the left-hand side of each staff line, showing one or more flats or sharps on the staff. Wherever those sharps or flats are placed, those notes in the piece will always be treated as though they have a flat or sharp in front of them, throughout the musical work.

When playing an instrument or singing, a musician will usually be dealing with mostly higher notes or lower notes. For instance, a flute will play mostly high notes, and a tuba will deal with mostly low notes. To avoid confusion, every staff line has a "clef sign" on its extreme left side, even before the key signature or time signature. A clef sign that looks like an "S" with a hooked line through it is the "treble" clef and indicates that these notes will be relatively high. A clef sign that looks like a backwards "C" followed by a colon is the "bass clef" and indicates that these notes will be relatively low. Pianists have music that uses two staff lines—one for the left hand and one for the right hand. The left hand plays mostly low notes and is in the bass clef. The right hand plays mostly high notes and is in the treble clef. Music sung by a soprano will be in the treble clef. Music sung by a baritone or bass singer will be in the bass clef.

Sometimes singers learn other names for notes besides the alphabet name. These other names are called "solfeggio." When someone sings the song "Doh, a Deer, a female deer . . ." from *The Sound of Music*, they are singing solfeggio names. The usual solfeggio names for notes are: doh, re ("ray"), mi ("mee"), fa, sol, la, and si (or ti). Then the eighth note—or "octave"—is reached and the sequence begins again, just as it does with alphabet note names. When several singers get together and sing different parts that make harmony, it is known as "part-singing." That is because everyone sings his part, and if done correctly, it will fit with all the other parts to make beautiful music.

NOTATION IN THE ELIZABETHAN AGE

At first glance, Elizabethan music looks both familiar and strange. The modern reader sees that there are black and white note heads, some with ligatures, some with flags. There is a staff of lines and spaces, and accidental markings of sharps and flats. Then one notices that the clef signs and time signatures may look strange, that the rests are odd, and that there may or may not be bar lines. Also, some of the note heads are square and many are diamond-shaped. This does not, of course, include tabla-ture—a notation system meant only for a particular instrument such as a lute or an organ!

Therefore, Elizabethan notation deserves a second look and some explanation. Fortunately for us, Thomas Morley published his book, A *Plaine and Easie Introduction to Practicall Musicke*, in 1597 and explained how to read the music of his time beginning with its most basic aspects. Morley is one of the most famous names among Elizabethan musicians. Besides being a composer in his own right, he served the queen as a Gentleman of the Chapel Royal. His very comprehensive work is divided into three parts. The first part, "Introduction to Musicke," teaches the basics of reading Elizabethan notation. The second part teaches the art of part-singing at sight. The third part teaches composition, with explanations of different vocal, instrumental, and dance forms. After all this, there are songs included for practicing one's newly found skills in duets, or in three, four, or five parts.

Morley's work was not dedicated to the queen, as one might expect. Instead it was dedicated to his old teacher, William Byrd. Morley's dedication says that after God and one's parents, a person should honor his "maisters"—the people who influenced his life in a positive way. For Morley, that person was Byrd. The dedication was meant "both to sig-nife unto the world, my thankfull mind: & also to notifie unto your selfe in some sort the entire love and unfained affection which I beare unto you."[1]

The first thing a modern reader notices when looking at Morley's explanation is that some notes seem to be missing. When naming the notes in "solfeggio," Morley does not use the usual "doh, re, mi, fa, sol, la, si (or ti), doh." He uses an older term for "doh"—the medieval term "ut." And then he adds only five more syllables—"re, mi, fa, sol, and la." The Elizabethan scale consisted of only six notes. Elizabethans thought in terms of "hexachords"—groups of six notes. They did not build major and minor scales using a series of half- and whole-steps to build an eight-note major or minor scale. When Elizabethan musicians ran out of notes, they simply switched to another hexachord with the amount of half-steps and whole-steps that they wanted. In this way, Elizabethan music sounds to our ears as though they are using major and minor scales, even though their actual system of thinking about scales was quite different.

The modern major scale is formed from the following system of whole- and half-steps: C, whole-step to D, whole-step to E, half-step to F, whole-step to G, whole-step to A, whole-step to B, half-step to C.

Morley and his readers would say instead "ut, re, mi, fa, sol, re, mi, fa," counting the steps this way: UT, whole-step to RE, whole-step to MI, half-step to FA, whole-step to SOL (also UT of the NEXT hexachord), whole-step to RE, whole-step to MI, half-step to FA.

This was no more difficult for Elizabethans than it is for the modern reader to remember key signatures. It simply needed practice, just as in our time remembering what key the modern reader is in needs practice. A minor scale, using a different set of whole- and half-steps, would use a slightly different set of syllables.

The modern reader's next problem is finding what notes to play on the staff. Fortunately, Elizabethan staff lines had normalized to the five lines and four spaces with which modern musicians are familiar. (The six staff lines of *Parthenia* was an unusual circumstance.) But modern readers might have some trouble with Elizabethan clef signs. Elizabethans built their music theory based on the human voice, which gave them three basic ranges: the bass range, the "meane" or middle range, and the treble range. Each of these ranges had its own clef sign.

The bass clef sign looks very familiar to the modern reader. It is a backwards C followed by a colon. Known as the F clef, the sign was written on the second line from the top, and the colon dots framed that line. Therefore, the Elizabethan note F corresponds to our modern bass note F—and makes the Elizabethan bass notes correspond to modern ones.

The treble clef looks like an "S" with a hooked line through it, that is, a line ending in a spiral. Though not exactly the same, the Elizabethan treble clef resembles the modern treble clef. Known as the G clef, its spiral wraps around the second line from the bottom, framing the note known as G in both Elizabethan and the modern notation. So Elizabethan treble clef notes also correspond to modern ones.

The "meane" clef is more problematic for most modern musicians. This sign looks something like a ladder—two long vertical lines connected by shorter horizontal lines. To Elizabethans, this was the C clef. A holdover from medieval times, this clef moves about on the staff. Whatever staff line was in the middle of the horizontal lines became the note C. That is, if the middle staff line was between the horizontal clef lines, then that middle line would be C—not the B that modern musicians know it as. If the staff line between the horizontal clef lines was the second line from the bottom, that line would be C instead of G. And wherever that note C might land, the note below it was still B and the note above it was still D.

Elizabethans had accidental signs. Their sign for a "flatted" note, that is, to play a note a half-step lower than usual, looked like a small letter b—just as it does now. Their sign for a "sharped" note, that is to play a note a half-step higher than usual, did not look exactly like the "tic-tac-toe" mark familiar to modern musicians. Instead, it looked like two capital Xs parallel to one another. In fact, a modern musician might mistake an Elizabethan "sharp" sign for a modern "double-sharp." Elizabethans put their key signatures in the same place where modern musicians put a key signature today. However, if this signature was in a "meane" clef, the key signature might be on different staff lines and spaces than the modern musician is used to seeing.

Time signatures were placed in the same place as they are today. And some meters look familiar. "Common" and "cut" time—4/4 and 2/4 time—are the familiar capital C and C with a slash. Triple time signs looked a little different. Actually, they look upside-down. In Elizabethan times, there would be a C on top to tell the performer that the quarter note got the beat, and the "3" was underneath to tell where the divisions should be.

After negotiating staff lines, clef signs, and time and key signatures, the modern musician might note with some horror that there may be no bar lines. Elizabethans put bar lines in scores (music that shows two or more parts at once) but not necessarily into individual parts (such as an alto part, or a bass part printed by itself). For instance, keyboard music was in score form and would have bar lines. Part-songs—vocal works printed as individual parts—would not. That is why transcribing a six-part Elizabethan song would be harder than putting out a keyboard work in modern notation.

Elizabethan music may look very slow to modern eyes because there are so many "white" notes—that is, notes not filled in. Most of these notes are now known as slow notes, such as half notes and whole notes. But the tempo of these notes is arbitrary. It is just a difference in the way music was written and had no bearing on its actual tempo (how fast or slow a piece is performed). In medieval times, "black" notes were rather unusual. Even in the early Renaissance, music written with more "black" notes was a novelty. By Morley's time this was no longer true, but a great deal of music was still written in the older, "white note" script. For modern readers, it might help to remember that modern music written in 2/2 or 4/2 is not necessarily slow, but is written mostly in "white" notes.

Modern musicians may be surprised to see square or diamond-shaped note heads instead of the round note heads used today. And instead of being on the right- or left-hand side of the note head, note stems were in the middle of the diamond-shaped note head. This makes Elizabethan music look a bit like a series of lollipops. Its essential components, however, are the same as modern notation.

A dot following a note was worth half the preceding note's value, just as it is today. In other words, a dotted Elizabethan half note would still be worth three beats. The dot, because it was "pricked" on the paper with a quill pen, was known as a "pricke." A note common to Elizabethan but not to today's manuscripts was a square white note with no note stem. This was a double whole note, worth eight beats.

Elizabethan rests correspond to the notation. A double whole rest looks like a thick line drawn vertically between the second and fourth staff lines. A whole rest is the same as today's—a short line hanging below the fourth staff line. A half rest is a short line rising up from the middle staff line. A quarter rest is a small note stem with a flag on its right side. An eighth rest is a small note stem with a flag on its left side. A sixteenth rest is a small note stem with two flags on its left side.

Elizabethans did not call their notes "whole" or "quarter" notes. The longer notes were referred to as "breves." What Americans call a quarter note, Elizabethans called a "crotchet." Smaller notes were called "quavers" or "semi-quavers." Notation names in the United Kingdom still use these terms.

MUSIC PRINTING

One of the most visible signs of music literacy in Elizabethan England was the emergence and growth of printed music. The business of music printing in England had a rocky start, although to modern eyes it doesn't seem that it should have. In 1575 Queen Elizabeth granted Thomas Tallis and William Byrd a joint crown music printing monopoly on "all Musicke bookes whatsoever, and the printing of all ruled paper, for the pricking (writing down) of any song to the lute, virginals, or other instrument."[2] This would seem to be a very profitable enterprise, but the monopoly was a bust. The monopoly system was a foreign idea, and some circles balked at supporting it for that reason. In addition, Tallis and Byrd were not the greatest businessmen in the world—and they were both Catholics. Even though Elizabeth made her religious tolerance clear, the two composers were living in a country paranoid about being seen as having "popish" leanings—despite the fact that the monopoly was backed by the crown.

There were other items that hurt this enterprise. For one thing they were not allowed to sell any imported music. "We straightly by the same forbid . . . to be brought out of any forren Realmes . . . any songe or songes made and printed in any forren countrie."[3] This created a vicious circle. Tallis and Byrd couldn't profit from the demand for music from overseas and couldn't improve their own circumstances without the profits this trade could have commanded. Moreover, the two composers may have monopolized music printing, but they didn't own the rights to music type fonts, printing patents were not under their command, and they didn't actually own a printing press. This meant that in order to put out any music, they had to pay the Stationers' Company for the copyright, the owners of the type font they wanted to use, and the printing press for doing the actual printing. Not much was left over. And when competing with penny tear sheets and broadsides that could be bought on the street by the middle class, and the private copying of manuscripts going on in the upper class—who would bother to buy an expensive piece of music from the crown monopoly? As one agent told the family he was buying music for, "This [music manuscript] paper is somewhat beneficiall. As for the musicke bookes, I would not provide necessarie furniture to have them."[4]

The crown monopoly improved somewhat after Tallis's death, when Byrd ran it alone. But the buying of preprinted English music didn't take off until Thomas Morley ran it. Much of this activity was because English lute music was in great demand, and an improved "tablature"—or notation system—made specifically for lute players was more accurate and easier to read than earlier versions. By the last decade of Elizabeth's reign, the Italian madrigal had hit England. Although the monopoly could not profit from that venture, the demand for madrigals written by Englishmen rose immensely, and quickly.

By the last decade of Elizabeth's reign, the printing of English music had taken off, and it was no longer embarrassing for nobles to purchase it and write for it, or for talented amateurs to have a work appear in a printed collection. Because at least the upper and middle classes were reading the same literature and singing the same works, and because exploration and trade had elevated some middle-class persons into the upper class, the lines between the classes blurred for a time, particularly in music. Court music adopted folk idioms from the lower classes, while middle- and lower-class music copied the forms of their betters. During festivals or celebrations, the private households of the nobility could enjoy Morris-dancers, clowns, jugglers, or bagpipes. And town waits, theater consorts, ambassadors' musical retinues, university players, and court musicians performed publicly enough for middle- and lower-class citizens to be familiar with a more refined musical experience.

NOTES

1. T. Morley, *A Plaine and Easie Introduction to Practicall Musicke* (New York: Da Capo Press, 1969 [originally published in 1597]), dedication page.

2. D.C. Price, *Patrons and Musicians of the English Renaissance* (Cambridge: Cambridge University Press, 1981), p. 181.

3. Ibid.

4. Ibid.

REFERENCES

Morley, T. *A Plaine and Easie Introduction to Practicall Musicke*. New York: Da Capo Press, 1969 [originally published in 1597].

Price, D.C. *Patrons and Musicians of the English Renaissance*. Cambridge: Cambridge University Press, 1981.

Chapter 5

Elizabethan Religious Music

THE EARLY CHURCH OF ENGLAND

In 1533, the year that Elizabeth was born, her father, Henry VIII, was excommunicated from the Roman Catholic Church by Pope Clement VII. The breaking point was Henry's divorce from his first wife and his marriage to Elizabeth's mother, Anne Boleyn. Instead of returning to the church, Henry joined the Protestant Reformation and took his entire country along. Through the Act of Supremacy passed in 1534, Henry became the supreme head of the Church of England (also known as the Anglican Church). No English monarch had ever had this kind of power over the church before.

England was immediately thrown into enormous religious confusion. Latin texts had to be translated into English, and someone had to establish a new type of religious service. Most church music had been constructed around much older music called "plainchant"—vocal music with no harmony and no set rhythmic values. Would the new church allow the older, Catholic plainchants to be used as a base for new music? Would the old chants be destroyed? And there were other, more practical concerns. Who now owned property that the Catholic Church had formerly owned in England? What would the country's religious leaders do? Who would now fund schools formerly supported by the church? What about all the organists, singers, and choirboys who were Catholic?

Some of these questions were answered with frightening speed and simplicity. In 1536, the crown began a wholesale takeover and redistribution of property formerly belonging to the church. Through what became known as the Dissolution of the Abbeys, over 800 monastic foundations disappeared in the first four years. Although many of these abbeys were small operations, some of the larger ones had skilled choirs that were also dissolved.[1]

Religious services using the Latin language ("Latin rite") were abolished everywhere except in a few schools where Latin was understood, such as Eton and Winchester, or Oxford and Cambridge colleges. Preachers had to be licensed by the crown. They were encouraged to preach sermons instead of having daily services with rites, and sermons had to be based on the new English Bible. The public suddenly found holy days discontinued, images and relics destroyed, and pilgrimages abandoned. For a while Henry thought about an alliance with the Lutheran Protestants. A delegation actually came to England for negotiations, but the idea came to nothing. In fact, Henry had a backlash reaction against Lutheranism after this alliance's failure and had anything with Lutheran leanings burned or banned. This included one of the earliest books of music written for the Church of England, Coverdale's *Goostly Psalmes*, because although it was in English, the tunes were based on popular Lutheran melodies.[2]

THE REFORMATION AND ENGLISH CHURCH MUSIC

Music had an important role in all this controversy. Henry VIII had always procured the best musicians in the country for his "Gentlemen of the Chapel." He had agents who traveled the country as talent scouts looking for singers (particularly boy singers) of talent. He was not above "impressing" (drafting) boys from another church into service for the crown. Now that the cathedral schools and monasteries had been dissolved, so were the training grounds for young musicians and the choirs, organists, and composers of church music.[3] The effect was that only the best church musicians found immediate employment in the Church of England, and even the best endured a slip in their salaries and a "temporary loss of prestige."[4] By Elizabeth's reign only about 40 cathedrals in the whole of England, Ireland, and Wales had kept their choral services. A great deal of old English religious music—mass books, song books, processionals, and antiphonal music—was lost forever.

Regrouping musically, composers began setting English text to familiar Latin melodies—in a practice called "contrafactum." Although much of the music was the same, musical style would have to change somewhat because of reforms to the liturgy. Reformers demanded that scriptures be clearly understood and insisted that sung parts should not obscure the text. "It would indeed have been most ridiculous to translate the psalms and canticles into English and then sing them so that the congregation could not tell whether they were in English or Latin."[5] So old-style polyphonic music had to tone down its points of imitation, or resort to more areas of homophony.

RELIGIOUS CONFUSION AFTER HENRY VIII

The switch from the Latin rite to English services was neither clean nor swift. Following Henry VIII's death, Edward VI was crowned with a Latin rite. Two months later, however, the Chapel Royal choir was singing services in English. Changes came with lightning speed but were sometimes haphazardly applied, occasionally contradictory, and seemingly without official guidance.

During Edward VI's reign of six years, warnings, or "injunctions," spelled out new rules for music as well as liturgy. Polyphony (music made up of several simultaneous parts of equal importance) was now an endangered species in church music. For instance, a 1552 injunction in York decreed that its anthems would be in English and syllabic (sung with one note per syllable of text) with no discernible polyphony. It said there should be "none other note sung or used . . . saving square note plain, so that every syllable may be plainly and distinctly pronounced, and without any reports or repeatings which may induce any obscureness to the hearers."[6]

Mary's succession to the throne in 1553 following Edward's death marked a violent return to Catholicism. During her short reign, a large number of foreign musicians worked at her court. When Philip of Spain came to court, he and his entourage were invited to hear High Mass in the cathedral at Winchester. In Philip's entourage was Antonio de Cabezon, an excellent organist and composer. But English organists were actually ahead of Spain in "virtuosity, experiment, and ideas," so Cabezon had little influence on English music.[7]

ANGLICAN SERVICES

When Elizabeth I ascended the throne in 1558, the country braced itself for yet another violent reversal. But Elizabeth abhorred religious strife. She demonstrated her religious leniency quite clearly with the choice of musicians in her private chapel, many of whom were Catholics. Under her reign services for the Anglican Church settled into specific types.

The Anglican liturgy had three services: a morning service (or Matins), Communion (in which worshippers received Eucharist—bread and wine commemorating Christ), and Evensong (or Vespers). The Matins service included Psalm 95 ("Venite exultemus") sung as "O come let us sing unto the Lord," a Te Deum sung as "We praise thee, O God," and a Benedictus (blessing of the congregation before leaving services) sung as "Blessed be the Lord, God of Israel." The Catholic Church had five sung parts to its Ordinary masses. (1) The Gloria is also known as the Doxology and glorifies the Trinity (God the Father, Son, and Holy Ghost). (2) The Credo is a statement of beliefs. (3) The Kyrie is a plea for mercy ("Christ have Mercy, Lord have Mercy, Christ have Mercy") and is the only part of the Mass not in Latin—it is in Greek. (4) The Sanctus praises God ("Holy, holy, holy"). (5) Agnus Dei means "Lamb of God" and asks for peace. The Anglican Communion service was much like a Mass, but with only a Gloria, Credo, Kyrie, and Sanctus—no Agnus Dei—and these were usually (but not always) sung in English. In Anglican services, the Gloria came after the actual act of taking Communion and could be either sung or recited. Evensong services included a Magnificat sung as "My soul doth magnify the Lord" and a Nunc Dimittis sung as "Lord, now lettest thou thy servant depart in peace."

In the Catholic Church all the sung works of the Matins and Evensong services would have been known as motets; in the Anglican Church, they were known as anthems. The difference between the two was (1) anthems were in English instead of Latin and (2) anthems were an integral part of the Anglican liturgy, whereas motets were not required parts of the Catholic liturgy. There were two sorts of anthem: full and verse. A full anthem implied a choir singing without accompaniment, although an organ might be used. A verse anthem alternated a soloist and a choir. But this is not what made them an innovative form of church music. It was the use of obbligato instrumental accompaniment that made them fundamentally different from former styles. The Anglican verse anthem includes musical instruments as an integral part of the music. Older music might have had instruments playing along, but if you took the instruments away the works would still be whole. If you were to take the instruments out of a late 1500s verse anthem, the music would become "hopelessly incomplete."[8]

At first, anthems were adapted wholesale from Latin motets; the Latin tunes were simply refitted with English words. Later, English composers gave the Anglican Church and the rest of the world some of the most beautiful church music ever written.

The Anglican Church had three different types of services: the Short service, the Great service, and the Verse service. A Short service used simple chordal, homophonic, full anthems; a Great service admitted music with modified polyphony and could use a variety of instruments; and a Verse service style used verse-style anthems. The style of music used for each fitted the type of service for which it was written. The queen, however, could have whatever type of service she wished with the style of music she liked most.

QUEEN ELIZABETH'S PRIVATE WORSHIP

When Queen Elizabeth ascended the throne in 1558, her religious tolerance extended to her own style of worship. Elizabeth enjoyed ritual, and she ran her own chapel as she wished. The queen's private chapel used a service so close to that of Catholicism that when a Spanish ambassador went to one, he fully expected England to return to Catholicism.[9] Not only were her services full of ritual, but she loved polyphonic music and made liberal use of instruments in her services as well. As one eyewitness put it:

> The altar was furnished with rich plate, with two gilt candlesticks, with lighted candles, and a massy [massive] crucifix in the midst, and that the service was sung not only with organs, but with artificial music of cornets, sacbuts [a type of early trombone] &c. on solemn festivals. That the ceremonies observed by the knights of the garter in their adoration towards the altar, which have been abolished by Edward VI and revived by Queen Mary, were retained. That, in short, the service performed in the queen's chapel, and in sundry cathedrals, was so splendid and showy, that foreigners could not distinguish it from the Roman, except that it was performed in the English tongue.[10]

In her new Act of Uniformity from 1559, the queen ordered endowments allowed for choirs. An endowment is money given permanently to an organization for a specific purpose. If a church had an endowment for a choir already in place, the queen ordered that this arrangement was inviolable and the money could not be taken for any other purpose. An endowment, in her opinion, was the "means whereof the laudable science of music has been had in estimation, and preserved in knowledge."[11]

PROTESTANTS, PURITANS, AND CHURCH MUSIC

After the Church of England had established itself as the country's Protestant religion, some citizens felt that it had not moved far enough away from Roman Catholicism and its practices. The new group called themselves Puritans because they wanted to purify the Church of England. They were horrified to hear that their sovereign used a crucifix on her altar, allowed Latin to be sung by her choir, and used complicated music. They felt that except for psalm singing by the congregation, music in church was an unnecessary distraction and that paying musicians to sing or play subtracted money needed for more godly causes. In 1572, two London clergymen wrote an *Admonition to Parliament: A view of Popish Abuses*. Of musicians, it said:

> The chief cantor, singing men . . . squeaking choristers, organ players, Gospellers, Epistolers, Pensioners, Readers, Vergers, etc. live in great idleness and have their abiding. If you would know whence all these came we can easily answer you that they came from the Pope, as out of the Trojan horse's belly, to the destruction of God's kingdom. The church of God never knew them, neither doth any reformed church in the world know them.[12]

To Puritans, polyphony was practically a Catholic plot designed to obscure sacred words. If anything were worse, it would be antiphonal choirs—that is, two choirs that sang facing one another, which made a kind of Elizabethan stereophonic effect. The same pair of clergymen complained that antiphonal choirs "tosse the Psalmes in most places like tennice-balls."[13]

Puritans felt that music should be restricted to congregational psalm singing. They did not like instrumental accompaniment, feeling that the human voice was the only music God wanted to hear and all else was vanity. In a book entitled *Jewel of Joy*, Thomas Becom wrote:

> A Christian man's melody, after St. Paul's mind, consisteth in heart, while we recite psalms, hymns, and spiritual songs, and sing to the Lord in our hearts. . . . All other outward melody is vain and transitory, and passeth away and cometh to nought. Vain and transitory it is indeed; notwithstanding, music may be used, so it be not abused. If it be soberly exercised and

reputed as an handmaid unto virtue, it is tolerable; otherwise it is execrable and to be abhorred of all good men. So ye perceive that music is not so excellent a thing, that a Christian ought earnestly to rejoice in it.[14]

Instrumental music in church came in for some harsh words. In 1563, a book of homilies entitled *Tome of Homelyes* was published. This work was meant to be used in every parish church, and it decreed that the piping, singing, chanting, and organ playing were "things which displeased God so sore, and filthily defiled his holy house and place of prayer."[15]

The effect of Puritan diatribes against choirs, organists, and any music in church that wasn't a congregational psalm had a chilling effect on many churches. Some abandoned the idea of having a choir altogether. Others found funding for music greatly reduced and had to cut the size of their choirs down. Some churches began "renting" town musicians—paying singers for one rehearsal and a Sunday service, rather than supporting them on a daily basis. Musical training, too, was largely left in the cold. The result was fewer singers of less skill singing less well for people all too ready to criticize them. Church musicians were described in the crudest terms. The following is from a Royal Injunction against St. George's Chapel, Windsor:

Also, whereas heretofore, when descant [additional melody added above the original melody line], prick-song [music written out, i.e., "pricked" with a quill pen], and organs were too much used . . . great search was made for cunning men in that faculty, among whom there were many that had joined with such cunning evil conditions, as pride, contention, railing, drunkenness, contempt of their superiors, or such-like vice.

St. George's was urged to find musicians who might not have the same skill level, but who were more acceptable morally:

We now . . . do enjoin that from henceforth when the room of any of the clerks shall be void, the Dean and prebendaries [clergyman receiving a stipend from the church] of this church shall make search for quiet and honest men . . . which have competent voices and can sing, apt to study and willing to increase in learning: so that they may be first deacons . . . having always more regard to their virtue and learning than to excellency in music.[16]

Some members of congregations who listened to their preachers and read reforming tracts condemning music in the church actually chose to go outside during the singing. A later treatise outlining the decline of church music explained:

> Then divers preachers being set a work by the humours of these aforesaid reformers were bold to set out books, and also in their sermons did persuade the people from the reverent use of service in song, affirming it to be nothing but an unneccessary piping and minstrelsy. . . . So as few or none of the people would vouchsafe to come into the choir during the singing service, but would stand without, dancing and sporting themselves, until the sermons and lectures did begin, scorning and deriding both the service and those which were employed therein.[17]

This must have been terrifically demoralizing to the musicians attempting to make music while much of the congregation walked out! As church music outside London took more and more abuse, training of musicians came under criticism:

> So as hereby the practice and use of skilful music, and those which exercised the same, began to be odious, and the professors to be accounted but as rogues, drunkards and idle persons . . . all endeavour for teaching of music or the forming of voices by good teachers was altogether neglected, as well in men as children, which . . . continueth to this day.[18]

Some musicians left music altogether. Others worked as town musicians, or supplemented their wages working for private patrons. Large families maintained their own small chapels, and patrons such as the Kytsons and Petries hired singers (both boys and adults) to perform at weddings, funerals, and other private functions. These families commissioned works from composers for their own chapels, where they used their own singers to perform it. A few, such as John Wilbye, ended up as a private musician permanently. He worked for the Kytson family his entire life.

THE CHAPEL ROYAL

The Chapel Royal was the private chapel for the reigning monarch of England and had been in existence since about 1135. During Queen Elizabeth's time, this was the place for the best and brightest names in English music. Gentlemen of the Chapel Royal included Tallis, Byrd, Tye, and Morley. This was the place where musicians were in the closest proximity to the queen herself. A musician who captured her notice might do better than he ever imagined. It is not an accident that music printing monopolies were all granted to members of the Chapel Royal—Tallis, Byrd, and Morley.

Chapel Royal musicians auditioned for the honor. Religion did not matter—Tallis and Byrd were both lifelong Catholics. Nor did nationality matter. Although many Chapel Royal members were English, the Bassanos and Ferraboscos were Italian and the Laniers were French. Several members of each of those families served the queen as musicians. Candidates sang for the subdean first, as a semifinalist trial. If they were recommended, the candidate next sang for the dean in whose hands rested the final decision. If admitted, a new member started as an "Epistoler," a junior member with lower pay. When deemed ready, the member would be promoted to "Gospeller" and a better paying job. Finally, he might reach the top of the heap as a "Gentleman in ordinary." For many years, wealthy people could pay a fee and become "probationary members." This allowed them a one or two-year grace period to determine whether they were worthy of staying. Unfortunately, this practice admitted some members who were less talented. In 1592, the practice was halted. Benefactors who gave large sums to the Chapel Royal were honorary members but were not asked to perform.[19]

Being a member of the Chapel Royal provided a good job. Pay for a gentleman was about twice as high as that for the usual church musician. Travel and board expenses were added in, and additional fees were given for singing at weddings, funerals, christenings, and other functions. As long as the activity did not interfere with their main duties, they could earn extra money singing freelance in the cities. They also were granted a vote on what happened in the Chapel, whereas most cathedral musicians had absolutely no say in their business.[20] Chapel Royal members didn't sing services in London between the end of June and the end of September. They also had off the weeks after Epiphany, Candlemas, Easter, St. George's Day, and the week before Christmas. They didn't sing services when the court was on Progresses unless they were at one of the queen's own castles. And for weekday services, half the choir was used. All these days off amounted to about 100 days a year.[21]

Choirboys

Choirboys for the Chapel Royal took the highest voice parts—the soprano parts. Women were not permitted to sing in the same choir as men, and the English were not about to begin the Italian practice of using *castrati*—adult men who had been castrated as boys and whose voices had remained unnaturally high—in their own choirs. Choirboys went to choir school and learned not only reading, writing, and other such subjects, but also music subjects.

The Reformation had dried up funds for music in many ordinary schools. In 1587, for example, Christ's Hospital School had been a place where children would "learne to singe, to play uppon all sorts of instruments, as to sounde the trumpett, the cornet, the recorder or flute, to play uppon the shagbolts, shalmes, & all other instruments that are to be plaid upon, either with winde or finger." But in 1589 the governors of the school decreed that "Henceforth none of the children in this Hospital shall be apprenticed to any musyssionar [musicianer] other than such as be blinde, lame, and not able to be put to other service."[22]

The boys of the Chapel Royal went to their own special school. Unless recruited from another choir, students at the Chapel Royal started their studies at about the age of seven. The religious upheaval before Queen Elizabeth's reign didn't have an enormous effect on the actual training of the choristers. In Henry's reign and even during Edward VI's reign, choristers mainly had to learn different words, and not necessarily different music.

They began with reading, writing, and "song." These were plainsongs, that is, old-style church chants with Latin words. This taught the boys both the chants and was an introduction to Latin grammar. They also learned *solmization*—what we call the "do-re-mi" of singing. And they were trained to sing intervals at the correct pitches by learning from an older boy or by singing along with an instrument such as a virginal (a keyboard instrument).

Next, students learned to read written music, known as "pricksong" since it was "pricked out"—written—on paper. They learned note values and time signatures, and they learned how to apply certain rhythms to a chant line and then how to improvise on that chant. One style of learning to improvise was *faburden*. Although some choristers sang a chant at its proper pitches, others sang the same chant a certain amount of pitches above the chant line and still others sang the same chant a certain amount of pitches below the chant line. The result was something that sounds like chords to modern ears.[23] After faburden, boys in training learned a more sophisticated improvisational technique called *descant*. They had to know which notes would produce a "pleasing melody" when sung along with a chant line. In other words, they had to learn how to make up a harmony line on the spot.[24] Later, choristers learned "square note." That is, they learned to harmonize with melodies other than chant music. And finally, they learned how to play an instrument.

Most choristers before 1565 learned to play on an organ. Mainly they learned how to play chant lines along with the choir, and then they learned to harmonize that line in the same way they did vocally.[25] A number of chant-based keyboard works can be found in an Elizabethan collection of keyboard works entitled the *Mulliner Book*. Scholars believe that some of the works in this book illustrate how beginners learned to play. "Those [works] towards the beginning of the manuscript are in two or three voices . . . towards the middle, most are in three voices, some are based on the faburden, and many have breaking or ornamenting of the chant; towards the end of the manuscript, most are in four voices and are highly contrapuntal."[26] By the middle of the sixteenth century, some boys were also learning to play the viols.

Older boys learned English grammar, advanced Latin grammar, and morals. Morals lessons came in the form of singing secular songs and then learning a lesson from the text. Many of the lyrics to these songs were known as *sententiae*—wise sayings. One example is a portion of text from "By Painted Words," with a text taken from Thomas Elyot's *Bankett of Sapience* (Banquet of Wisdom): "The greattest token and offyce of sapyence [wisdom], is that the dedes [deeds] do agree with the wordes."[27] Another example from the same source included the Latin refrain "Servire Deo regnare est," which means "to serve God is to reign."[28]

Advanced Latin grammar meant that older boys were only allowed to speak to one another in Latin. Some of the sentences they learned bring their lives into vivid relief, such as "Guttur meum est raucum," Latin for "My throat is hoarse."[29]

After 1565, the Church of England's liturgy was set, and it became more important for choristers to learn to read written music at sight than to learn plainchant. The study of Latin was increasingly less important as a music subject, and the boys were sent to the regular grammar schools two hours a day to learn Latin grammar. Improvisation skills were also less needed, since liturgical music was no longer based on plainchant. Choristers still learned solmization, but they even began learning their intervals more from the frets on viols than from learning solmization syllables. In other words, the boys were learning music more as a specialized subject than as their entire education. After 1565, the boys learned much more about instrumental playing than they had before. As the production of Choirboy Plays increased, the boys had more reason to learn instruments—particularly viols.

A boy's use to the Chapel was over when his voice broke. At that point, the choirmaster informed the master of requests of the occurrence, and the boy would either be put into a good trade or profession or be placed in a good school such as Oxford or Cambridge.[30] The boy might also opt to stay in music as a singer with a deeper voice, or as an instrumentalist, joining the town waits or teaching privately.

MASTER OF THE CHILDREN

During times of religious upheaval, and even into Elizabeth's reign, the master of the children—even those of the Chapel Royal—had a hard time maintaining their charges. These masters were in charge of their own households and also had to provide room and board for the children and teach them as well. As William Hunnis wrote Queen Elizabeth, "some of them died in so poor a case, and so deeply indebted that they have not left scarcely wherewith to bury them."[31]

William Hunnis was master of the children of the Chapel Royal during much of Queen Elizabeth's reign. This honor was no walk in the park. He oversaw the boys' training, fed, clothed, and housed them out of his own allowance. And he scouted out new talent, scouring other cathedrals and chapels looking for new boys of talent. Thanks to rising prices and a fixed salary, Hunnis found himself in the uncomfortable position of petitioning the queen for more funding in 1583. He was faced with feeding a dozen children every day at what amounted to sixpence a day per child. He had no allowance for help to keep these dozen children clean. When he and the children traveled, there was no allowance to board himself, the children, and any servants, nor did he have an allowance for his travels as a talent scout. And there was no extra money available for boys whose voices had changed and were thus unusable in the choir, but for whom a suitable profession had not yet been found. All these items were coming out of his budget, which was becoming stretched beyond belief.

Choirboy Plays

One method of earning extra money to stretch that budget was to hire the boys out for choirboy plays. These plays began as an entertainment at court. Instead of using professional adult actors, plays were presented using boys of the Chapel Royal or St. Paul's Chapel. They played character parts, sang as part of the entertainment, and accompanied one another on instruments. The popularity and growth of choirboy plays is one reason instrumental music and learning secular songs became increasingly important at the choir schools. A visiting duke saw a choirboy play in 1602 and wrote:

> The Queen keeps a number of young boys, who are taught to sing and play on all sorts of musical instruments—they are also expected to continue their school studies at the same time. These boys have special instructors in the various arts, and especially in music. As part of their education in courtly manners they are required to put on a play once a week, and for this purpose the queen has provided them with a theatre and with a great deal of rich apparel. Those who wish to see one of the performances must pay as much as eight shillings of our Pomeranian money [that is in English terms the equivalent of a shilling—about four times the price of a normal theater seat]. Yet there are always a good many people present, including ladies of the highest repute, since the plots are always well developed, and of a suitably elevated character. All the performances are by candlelight and the effect is indeed spectacular. For a whole hour before the play begins there is a concert of music for organs, lutes, pandoras, citterns, viols, and recorders. When we were there a boy "cum voce tremula" sang so charmingly to the accompaniment of a bass viol that with the possible exception of the Nuns at Milan, we heard nothing to equal him anywhere.[32]

Puritans were appalled at this use of church singers and wholeheartedly condemned the practice:

> Plays will never be suppressed, while her Majesty's unfledged minions flaunt it in silks and satins. They had as well be at their popish service, in the Devil's garments. Even in her Majesty's Chapel do these pretty, upstart youths profane the Lord's Day by the lascivious writhing of their tender limbs, and gorgeous decking of their apparel, in feigning bawdy fables gathered from the idolatrous heathen poets.[33]

Despite Puritanical objections, choirboy plays became popular spectacles. It was possible to buy a ticket not only to a performance, but also for a rehearsal as it took place in their rented rehearsal rooms. London society took full advantage of this opportunity, and the high-paying tenants in the area were not amused by all the extra traffic. Puritans added to their discomfort when they began handing out pamphlets condemning the plays.

During the performances, boys sang laments for solo voice and viol accompaniment, consort songs, madrigals, and popular songs of the day.

They provided the instrumental accompaniments and also played instrumental music before the play, between the acts, and at the finale. The boys became so adept at their instrumental playing that they were hired out for noncourt functions from time to time. St. Paul's boys sang for the Grocers' Guild's annual feast. The London Guild of Parish clerks hired the boys of Westminster to sing at their annual meeting. Presumably, funds made at these functions helped to defray the costs facing the master of the children.

To be fair, as time went on the plays became less moralistic and more for the entertainment of the audience. Choirboy plays became increasingly secular, until the boys of St. Paul's and the Chapel Royal were actually in competition with men's companies. To that end, the boys were putting on plays involving racy comedy and vicious political satire. It was at this point that the Puritans' objections seemed to have some validity.[34]

MUSIC IN CHURCHES OUTSIDE LONDON

Parish churches were much more under the sway of Puritanism than the city churches. There was a great deal less music in their services, and they relied on psalm singing from *psalters*. Psalters contained words to the Book of Psalms from the Bible's Old Testament, translated into English and rhymed. Early psalters contained only words and the name of the tune to which the words were to be sung. Later psalters included music as well. Throughout Elizabeth's reign, the public grew used to the Anglican liturgy. Although it is an oversimplification, it is helpful to compare the English and Catholic styles of worship. Whereas Catholics celebrated Mass with Latin ritual leading up to Holy Communion, Anglicans held services with a sermon and English-language rituals leading up to Holy Communion. Anglicans had an English-language Book of Common Prayer to follow instead of the Latin Vulgate. Anglicans sang psalms instead of hymns and anthems instead of Catholic motets.

Texts to sung psalms were set in both prose and verse form. Prose texts were reprinted from Coverdale's Great Bible of 1539–1540; the most popular texts were rhymed, metrical verses of paraphrased psalms. Several of these texts were attempted. Archbishop Matthew Parker's Psalter contained nine tunes by Tallis, which fitted paraphrased psalms worked out by the archbishop. Done in 1557, it was never sold but was finally printed in 1567–1568. Attempts were made to get people to sing psalms not only for church, but also as recreation instead of singing secular ballads. Some examples were *Day's Psalter* of 1563, *Daman's Psalter* of 1579, and *Cosyn's*

Psalter of 1585. As Cosyn printed in the dedication of his psalter, "I was encouraged by some to publish them for the private use and comfort of the godlie, in place of many other songs neither tending to the praise of God, nor conteining any thing fit for Christian eares."[35]

But the most popular psalter was the Sternhold and Hopkins Psalter. At first only the words were printed, with the titles of appropriate tunes given. Later, the tunes were printed along with the words, and finally four-part harmonies were printed along with the words. The best tunes came from France, adapted from a French Huguenot psalter. Other tunes included adaptations of court songs and dance tunes such as galliards and measures.[36] This psalter made congregational singing a requirement, and as the bishop of Salisbury wrote in 1560:

> Religion is now somewhat more established than it was. The people are everywhere exceedingly inclined to the better part. The practice of joining in church music [i.e., the psalms] has very much helped this. For as soon as they had once begun singing in public, in only one little church in London, immediately not only the churches in the neighbourhood, but even the towns far distant began to vie with each other in the same practice. You may now sometimes see at St. Paul's Cross, after the service, six thousand persons, old and young, of both sexes, all singing together and praising God. This sadly annoys the Mass priests and the devil. For they perceive that by these means the sacred discourses sink more deeply into the minds of men, and that their kingdom is weakened and shakened at almost every note. . . . [37]

CAROLS

It would be a mistake to say that the English never sang religious songs in English before the Reformation because they had been singing carols in the vernacular for hundreds of years (see Chapter 3). The term *carol* comes from the old French word *carole*, which was a joyous song usually danced to. By the 1400s in England, the carol was a song on whatever subject one pleased, but it had stanzas and a burden. The burden was a short phrase repeated between each stanza, usually in Latin. Today, when one thinks of a carol one thinks of Christmas. This was not always the case, however. Religious carols ran the gamut of subjects such as carols to the Virgin, carols to the Trinity, carols of Repentance or of Mortality, or the Epiphany, and so on. There were even many carols that were not remotely religious. The following is one stanza and the (English) burden from a satirical carol:

STANZA:

>Envy is Thick and love thin
>And specially among our kin
>For love is without the door and envy within
>And so kyndness away will flee

BURDEN:

>God, that sittith in Trinite
>Amend this world, if thye will it be.[38]

Another sample of a satirical carol tells of bribery, justice for sale, and fair weather friends:

(1) Penny is a hardy knight;
     Penny is right full of might;
     Penny, of wrongs he maketh right
     In every country where he goes.

(2) Though I have a man enslaved
     And forfeited the king's law,
     I shall find a man of law
     Who will take my penny and let me go.

(3) And if I have pence good and fine,
     Men will bid me to the wine;
     "All that I have shall be thine,"
     Such they will say so.

BURDEN:

>Go bet, Penny, go bet, go,
>For thou must make both friend and foe.[39]

There were also carols of marriage, of childhood, of ale, and of hunting. Here is a stanza from the 1500s and its (English) burden from a carol about Women:

>Some be merry and some be sad
>And some be busy and some be bad
>Some be wild, by Saint Chad
>   Yet all be not so,
>For some be lewd
>And some be shrewd
>   Go, shrew wheresoever ye go

BURDEN:
> Women, women, love of women
> Maketh bare purses with some men.[40]

One famous old carol concerned the Hundred Years' War between England and France. It is in celebration of a stunning victory of the English over the French on the field of Agincourt. Here is one verse and its Latin burden:

> Our King went forth to Normandy
> With grace and might of chivalry
> There God for him wrought marvelously
> Wherefore England may call and cry (pronounced "cree")
> "Deo Gracias"

BURDEN:
> Deo gracias Anglia
> Redde pro victoria.[41]

CHURCH MUSIC INSTRUMENTATION

The organ was the most commonly used instrument in Elizabethan churches. During the Reformation many organs were abandoned before they were finished. Others—about 100 by one contemporary account—were torn down by overzealous reformers. Later, however, many were rebuilt, and larger churches in particular began playing the organ along with the choir. Scholars believe that keyboard reductions of church works were meant for rehearsal purposes. During services, the organ might play directly with the choir or might improvise their tune at a different pitch, much as boys did when they sang faburden. Organs of the day had a considerable range of tone colors that would have lent some variety to the music.

In some churches, particularly on special days such as holy days, other instruments found a use in the church. Written references of the time mention cornetts and sackbuts as the most commonly used. The cornett was a wooden instrument with a mouthpiece something like a brass instrument. It was thought to be closest in timbre to a human voice. It could play as softly as a recorder, and according to one source a good player could play up to 80 measures in one breath.[42] The sackbut was something like a modern trombone, but smaller and with thinner tubing.

The sackbut had a soft, clear sound. Both instruments could be played in a processional, the cornett supporting the upper voices and the sackbut(s) supporting the lower ones. Other wind instruments may have also been used, but they are almost never named. Most sources mention the cornett and sackbut and then say, "and other excellent instruments of music" but don't name them.[43] Viols may have been used, but they may have presented more problems than wind instruments. Viol players would need extra room and seats to sit in, and they would not be able to join a procession.[44]

CONCLUSION

The Reformation in England and the establishment of the Church of England during Henry VIII's reign wreaked havoc with church music and musicians. Many valuable manuscripts were lost during the Dissolution of the Abbeys. Church musicians were suddenly out of work and choir schools closed. Under the new church, there was a sudden and desperate need for church music. The religious alterations during the reigns of Edward VI, Mary I, and Elizabeth I caused many English musicians to leave the country.

Elizabeth's reign restored some religious stability to England, and many of her finest musicians were Catholic. Music became an important part of Church of England services. Rather than using women in church choirs, singing parts usually given to sopranos were sung instead by boys whose voices had not yet changed. Choir schools provided training and special schools were provided for the most talented singers who would sing for Elizabeth's Chapel Royal. These boys might also be used as actor-singers in a genre of theater known as Choirboy plays.

While the Church of England used richly textured music, the ultra-Protestant sect known as Puritans developed a plainer style of melody and harmony and an aversion to allowing instruments in church. In rural areas people continued singing English carols, many of which had nothing to do with Christmas, as carols do today. No matter what religion the citizens of Shakespeare's England followed, music was used as a means to bring the human spirit closer to divinity.

NOTES

1. P. Le Huray, *Music and the Reformation in England 1549–1660* (New York: St. Martin's Press, 1964), p. 2.

2. Ibid., p. 4.

3. H. Raynor, *Music in England* (Plymouth: Clarke, Doble & Brendon, 1980), pp. 45–46.

4. D. Stevens, *Tudor Church Music* (New York: W.W. Norton, 1966), p. 19.

5. J. Buxton, *Elizabethan Taste* (New York: St. Martin's Press, 1964), p. 179.

6. E. Doughtie, *English Renaissance Song* (Boston: G.K. Hall & Co., 1986), p. 30.

7. Stevens, p. 20.

8. Le Huray, pp. 217–218.

9. Ibid., p. 33.

10. M.C. Boyd, *Elizabethan Music and Musical Criticism* (Philadelphia: University of Pennsylvania Press, 1962), p. 10.

11. Buxton, p. 180.

12. Le Huray, pp. 38–39.

13. Stevens, p. 55.

14. Le Huray, p. 12.

15. Stevens, p. 64.

16. Le Huray, p. 24.

17. Ibid., pp. 36–37.

18. Ibid.

19. Le Huray, p. 70.

20. Ibid., p. 72.

21. Ibid.

22. Boyd, p. 15.

23. J. Morehen (ed.), *English Choral Practice 1400–1650* (Cambridge: Cambridge University Press, 1995), p. 183.

24. Ibid., p. 186.

25. Ibid., p. 189.

26. Ibid.

27. Ibid., p. 191.

28. Ibid.

29. Ibid., p. 190.

30. Le Huray, p. 63.

31. Stevens, p. 59.

32. Le Huray, p. 220.

33. Ibid.

34. Morehen, p. 197.

35. Boyd, p. 53.

36. Doughtie, p. 30.

37. Le Huray, p. 375.

38. R.L. Greene (ed.), *The Early English Carols* (Oxford: Clarendon Press, 1935), p. 257.

39. Ibid., p. 261.

40. Ibid., p. 267.
41. Ibid., p. 289.
42. Le Huray, p. 127.
43. Ibid.
44. Ibid., p. 129.

REFERENCES

Boyd, M.C. *Elizabethan Music and Musical Criticism.* Phildelphia: University of Pennsylvania Press, 1962.
Buxton, J. *Elizabethan Taste.* New York: St. Martin's Press, 1964.
Doughtie, E. *English Renaissance Song.* Boston: G.K. Hall & Co., 1986.
Greene, R.L. (ed.). *The Early English Carols.* Oxford: Clarendon Press, 1935.
Le Huray, P. *Music and the Reformation in England 1549–1660.* New York: Oxford University Press, 1967.
Morehen J. (ed.). *English Choral Practice 1400–1650.* Cambridge: Cambridge University Press, 1995.
Raynor, H. *Music in England.* Plymouth: Clarke, Doble & Brendon, 1980.
Stevens, D. *Tudor Church Music.* New York: W.W. Norton, 1966.

Chapter 6

Elizabethan Musical Instruments

For centuries, instrumental music in Western Europe was so unimportant that it was rarely represented in musical scores. It was during the Renaissance that instruments became important elements of music. During Henry VIII's reign, England's instrumental music gained some of the respect formerly held by vocal music. This tendency continued throughout Queen Elizabeth's reign until vocal and instrumental music was equally regarded.

The Elizabethan era was a time of transition. Older instruments of medieval times, used in the queen's early reign, were phased out. It is fascinating to read court accounts and records of instrument purchases in some of England's great houses which show new instruments appearing over Queen Elizabeth's 40-year reign. Some of these instruments would not survive; others would continue into the Baroque Era; and still others continue to be used today.

There are several major sources of information about Elizabethan-era instruments. One major source is a series of woodcuts made for Maximilian I, the Holy Roman Emperor in 1519. This unique—and ultimately unfinished—record shows a procession of instruments. Some are grouped in families of "like" instruments, such as various-sized flutes; others are in mixed groups of the time, such as a flute, a lute, and a violin. All the various instrument groups are shown being played in carts drawn by a menagerie of various animals. Although 1519 predates Elizabeth, many of the instruments shown were still used in her time. Sebastian Virdung (1511) and Martin Agricola (1528) also published works that show woodcuts of contemporary instruments. However, Michael Praetorius's book *Syntagma Musicum* (1618) is the next best source of information after Maximilian's woodcuts. Praetorius's illustrations are much more detailed than Virdung's or Agricola's, and he writes about their sounds, tuning, and performance details.

Elizabethans classified these instruments into families, or "consorts." A consort is a group of instruments from the same family, meant to be played together. A consort of flutes, for instance, would contain an ensemble of different-sized flutes—from soprano to bass. Ensembles using instruments from different families were known as "mixed" or "broken" consorts. That is, a flute playing along with a keyboard instrument such as a virginal and a reed instrument such as a shawm would be a broken consort. A consort of either type was usually made up of any three to five instruments.

Elizabethans would have further classified instruments into loud ("haut") instruments and soft ("bas") instruments. Haut and bass mean high and low in Germanic, respectively, and is a classification held over from medieval times. Thinking of instruments as high and low can be confusing, but if one adds the word "volume" after each of those terms, their meaning becomes clear—high volume and low volume. High-volume instruments would be played outdoors. Low-volume instruments would be played indoors, more for private functions than public ones. Mixing haut and bas instruments within the same consort would cause obvious problems, so mixed consorts had to be careful that one or two instruments wouldn't drown out any others.

Although Elizabethan citizens revered vocal music most of all, they loved to play instruments or hear others do so. Formal venues for instrumental music could be found in court circles, at weddings, in church, or during civic occasions. Informal occasions might be amateur music-making after dinner with either family members or guests, listening to a pipe and tabor player or a fiddler at a country fair, singing a love song while strumming a lute, or playing a gittern while waiting to get a trim at the barbershop. Instrumental music also accompanied dancers at both formal and informal events. And anyone able to play a keyboard instrument had some of the finest music of the age to practice on or play at social gatherings.

Elizabethan instruments sounded different from today's instruments. They had a more restricted dynamic range and generally did not have the deep sonorous quality of present-day instruments. To modern ears, Elizabethan wind instruments have a reedy, nasal quality. Strings may sound thin and have a brighter timbre than modern stringed instruments. Brass may sound slightly out of tune, brighter, and less mellow than to-day's brass instruments. All this sounds rather unpleasant, but after a moment or two Elizabethan instruments prove that they have a charm all their own, which is especially evident when they play together. Listening to Elizabethan music played on a consort of viols in a live performance is like looking through a window of time.

PLUCKED STRINGED INSTRUMENTS

An important class of Elizabethan instruments was fretted, plucked stringed instruments. These were classified by having bowed-out or flat backs, by their various tunings, and by their use of gut or metal strings and frets.

Bandore

Also known as the Bandora, Pandore, or Pandora, this bass instrument had 15 frets and six or sometimes seven "courses." A contemporary writer observed in 1561, "In the fourth year of Queen Elizabeth, John Rose, dwelling in Bridewell, devised and made an instrument with wire strings, commonly called the Bandora, and left a son, far excelling himself in making Bandores, Voyall de Gamboes, and other instruments."[1]

Although there was a consort of Bandores—the smallest size was tiny enough to fit inside a musician's cloak—the Bandore is usually referred to as a bass instrument.

The bandore was used mostly in consorts, where it was often paired with the cittern and the lute. Its bass tones complemented the bright sound of the cittern. Queen Elizabeth once planned a Music Academy; although it never got off the ground, one of the plans was to have a teacher of music "to play the lute, the bandora, and the cittern" (1572).[2] The bandore is also named as one of the instruments that played between the acts of "dumb shows."[3] Thomas Morley wrote some works that were meant to be played on the bandore in 1599. And Queen Elizabeth gave one as a gift to a noble whose estate she had visited.[4] It was also used to accompany vocal works. Anthony Munday's 1588 work, A Banquet of Daintie Conceits, says that the works printed were meant to be sung "either to the lute, bandora, virginalles, or anie other instrument."[5]

Cittarone

The citaronne (or chittarone), also known as the "archlute," was huge—over six feet high. It had an enormously long neck and is the largest member of the lute family. The neck was so long that it doubled back in a "swan's neck" formation.[6] This instrument had normal strings that were fretted and plucked, but it also had two additional bass strings running along the neck of the instrument lengthwise. The two bass strings were not used to play different pitches but instead were plucked at whatever pitch they were tuned to. Occasional confusion arises among scholars about this instrument's name because the Italian word for guitar was "chitarra."

Cittern

The cittern was a hybrid between a gittern and a lute. It was pear-shaped like a lute but had a flat back like a gittern—not a round back like a lute (or a mandolin). The cittern has always been difficult to identify because of the various ways its name was spelled. Among its variant spellings are sytholle, sitole, cythol, cytol, citole, or cittern.[7]

The cittern was a popular plucked, fretted instrument. It had its own instruction book—Anthony Holborne's book, *The Cittharn School*, published in 1597. The cittern was known as the "poor man's lute."[8] It was tuned in a particular way to make the playing of certain chords easier, and it held its tuning better because it used wire strings. It was easier to handle because its frets were also metal, which meant they didn't slip like gut ones.[9] Having a flat back instead of a round one made this a sturdier instrument—and cheaper, since it didn't require the subtle work of rounded "ribs" to hold the wood's shape.[10]

The cittern did not have a standard amount of strings, and although one tuning was more popular, the instrument could be tuned in several ways. It had its own body of literature, ranging from simple dance tunes to advanced polyphonic works. The cittern was popular with less wealthy amateurs, but wealthy patrons bought them too. There are some beautifully carved citterns made for the very rich. This instrument was characteristically carved so that the top of the neck ended in a grotesquely carved head. A joke based on this then-common knowledge shows up in Shakespeare's play *Love's Labour's Lost*, Act V, scene 2:

Schoolmaster Holofernes: I will not be put out of countenance.

First Lord: Because thou has no face!

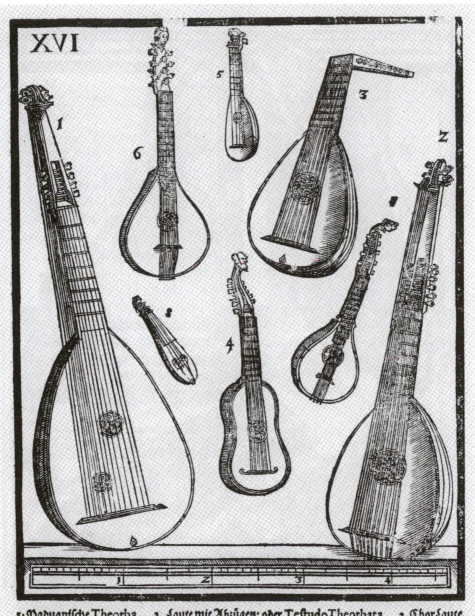

XVI

Figure 4. Plucked stringed instruments: (1) Paduan theorba, (3) lute, (5) mandora, (6) cittern.

Holofernes: What is *this*? (points to his face)
Second Lord: A cittern head! [i.e., wooden and ugly][11]

Gittern

The Gittern (sometimes spelled Gittron) most closely resembles a guitar, an instrument that did not come into England until after the Elizabethan era. Like a guitar, the gittern was a fretted instrument, with curved-in sides and a flat back. It was plucked with a "plectrum"—usually a quill. There was a sound hole in the middle of the body, or sometimes curved slits on either side of the bridge (like a violin). There the resemblance to a guitar ends. The neck of the gittern was not attached separately, but rather was carved from the same piece of wood as the body. The gittern had four gut strings, attached to a tail piece that was itself attached to an ornately carved knob. Although it was not a problem for a player to reach the frets around the thick neck, a thumb hole was carved at some point. Apparently, the performer sometimes used the thumb of his fret hand to pluck the top string of the gittern.[12]

Before lutes took over, the gittern was the instrument of choice for accompanying singers. Henry VIII had four of them, which he called "Spanish Vialls."[13] Queen Elizabeth gave one of her favorite courtiers a gittern as a gift. This instrument was preserved in Warwick Castle. So little was known about it that for many years it was thought to be a variety of violin!

Lute

The lute was by far the most popular stringed instrument of the Elizabethan era. It was known as the "queen of instruments."[14] The lute family came in a "mean" (normal), descant, and octave lute (that is, small, medium, and large sizes). Some even larger sizes had names other than "lute," which is confusing to the present-day scholar. The lute itself owes its name to its Arabic ancestry; the Arabs called it "el oud"—the oud being an Arabic stringed instrument still played today.[15]

In appearance the lute was a gut- and metal-stringed instrument with gut frets. Its body was shaped like the bottom of a pear that had been cut in half, flat on the part holding the strings and round on the back. It had a "rose" opening in the face, under the strings, and it was played with the fingers, not a plectrum (i.e., a pick).

The most striking characteristic of the lute's appearance, however, is not its body but its neck. The lute's neck is bent back at a 45-degree angle. This odd distinction may have come about to give the gut strings a firmer bearing on the bar they must stretch over before reaching the fingerboard. Or perhaps the lute neck is simply so long that it was awkward to hold in an "unbent" form.[16]

The lute had its own system of notation called "tablature"—a series of lines that look like ordinary staves of music but actually represented the strings on the lute. A letter written on the string to be fingered was the "fret letter," the fret to put one's finger on. Dots immediately below this letter indicated which finger was supposed to pluck the string, and a note above indicated its length. If there were several notes without any timing indicated, that meant that the last indication would hold until it was changed. In other words, if a note had an eighth note indication and then several notes following with no time, they were assumed to be eighth notes also.

Actually, there were several ways of writing tablature. Different composers might use slightly different systems, which could prove confusing for any performer. For instance, sometimes the top line on a tablature staff meant to play the top string of the instrument, and at other times the top line of tablature meant the opposite—the performer was supposed to play the string on the bottom of the instrument! Still, lute tablature was as well known to lutenists as our music notation system is to us today.

Early lutes started with four pairs of strings, but that number grew to a mind-boggling 26 to 30 strings. An Elizabethan would call this 13 to 15 "courses." A course was a double string, which meant that a six-course instrument actually had twelve strings. Using finger technique instead of a plectrum brought about "a new delicacy and expressiveness in playing, a breadth of technique, and a range of nuances never possible before."[17] The lute's frets were made of sheep gut and tended to stretch and slip out of place, or tighten and break. It was the responsibility of each player to keep frets in the right place, and to put on as many or as few as needed. As a result, their number and placement varied greatly from one instrument to the next. The frets also didn't necessarily go all the way up to the highest notes possible, since advanced lute-playing technique included learning notes "beyond the frets."[18] Because of its tuning problems and the sheer number of strings lutenists had to tune, there was a common saying that if a lutenist lived to the age of 80, it was certain that he had spent 60 of those years tuning the instrument.[19]

Despite all its drawbacks—or perhaps because of its challenge—the lute was second only to the human voice in musical "musts" for the Elizabethan citizen to learn. Queen Elizabeth herself played this instrument, as had her sister Mary and her father. Lute players were some of the highest-paid musicians in Elizabeth's court. It was in Elizabeth's time that lute music reached its high point. Paintings of the era show many men and women posing for their portraits either playing a lute, holding a lute, or with a lute in the background to let everyone know that they could play it. The lute is played by angels in paintings, it shows up in poetry, and it has its place in the literature of the time.

As with other Elizabethan instruments, there was a consort of lutes, from small to large. Smaller lutes were fragile and did not travel well. Possibly because they were prone to being broken, lutes were commonly given as presents. Even Queen Elizabeth accepted lutes as gifts. Nobles collected lutes. Sir Thomas Kytson, in his 1603 account, speaks of "one great base lute and a mean lute . . . one trebble lute and a meane lute."[20]

The lute was used as an accompaniment to the solo voice, as well as a solo instrument, much as the guitar is today. Performers had many tricks of the trade, which were not necessarily written into their music. Just as musicians today might add a trill or a glissando, Elizabethan lutenists might put in a "back-fall," "elevation," "single or double relish," "slide," a "springer," a "sting," a "rake," "shake," or "futt."[21] Later lutes were made with permanent, metal frets and some acquired soft-tempered steel or brass strings.

Eventually, the lute dropped out of favor, and many lutes were refashioned into guitars. By the first decade of the twentieth century, lutes were so little known that many people actually spoke of them being "blown like a flute."[22] Thanks to the revival of period instruments and thanks to people willing to learn to play them, curious listeners are again able to hear why the lute was the "courtly instrument par excellence."[23]

Mandora

The mandora was a smaller, simpler, lute-like instrument. Mandoras had a bowed-out back like the lute but did not have the bent neck. It was played with a plectrum and is the ancestor of the mandolin. This instrument was most popular in France. It became very popular in Scotland during the reign of Mary Queen of Scots, who had been raised in France. An instrument case surviving from Elizabethan times indicates that mandoras and lutes were meant to be played together as a kind of soprano (mandora) and alto (lute) combination. In this particular instrument case, the lute was on top. But where the lute neck bent, there was a smaller compartment which, when opened, contained a mandora.[24]

Orpharion

The orpharion, named for the mythological musician Orpheus, was "the wire-strung equivalent of the lute."[25] It could therefore use the same tablature and the same literature as the lute. It had seven courses. The string holder was slanted, which shortened the length of the upper strings. The frets were arranged to accommodate this unusual arrangement.[26] Its body shape was also rather unusual. Instead of having one "waist" in the middle, like a guitar, it was more of an oval with several "wavy" indentations, ending up as a "scalloped" shape.

The orpharion was often mentioned along with the bandora. William Barley's 1596 work, *New Booke of Tabliture*, states that the orpharion and bandora finger-work must be done differently than that of the lute. Fingers must be "easily drawn over the strings, and not suddenly gripped or sharply stroken as the lute is: for if ye should do so, then the wire strings would clash or jarre together the one against the other. . . . Therefore it is meet that you observe the difference of the stroke."[27] The orpharion was also paired with the lute in lute duet literature. Having these two instruments playing together instead of two lutes gave extra contrast to the sound and allowed the listener to more clearly appreciate the intricacies of the imitative lines.

WIND INSTRUMENTS

Wind instruments exploded into an unheard of variety during the Renaissance period. Elizabethan England was quick to utilize their individual qualities.

Fife

The fife was a transverse flute used mainly in military fife and drum ensembles. The main difference from the civilian transverse flute is its length (very short) and its bore (very narrow). A 1588 treatise explains, "What we call the fife is a little transverse flute with six holes, which the Germans and the Swiss use, and as its bore is very narrow—only the width of a pistol bullet—it gets a shrill sound."[28]

Recorders

The recorder, also known as the Flute Douce or Doucet, was the flute of choice for mixed consort playing in Elizabethan England, but the Elizabethan recorder is not the same as the instrument that we know today. Today's recorders have a head shaped something like a whistle at the top. The walls of the instrument, though wood, are fairly thin, and they come apart in sections. Elizabethan recorders were shaped like a round block of wood at the top. In fact, for that reason they were known as a "block-flute."[29] The wood of Elizabethan recorders was much thicker, and they were generally made in a single piece.

The Elizabethan recorder, like that of today, was a "fipple" flute. That means the player blew into a hole and the air was automatically directed over a fipple, or whistle-like opening. Recorders did not require much force to play. They were "bas" instruments, meant for indoor use. They came in consorts of treble, mean, and bass but could also have a Tenor, or Counter tenor. Generally, they had a range of about two octaves. Although recorders were used in mixed consorts, the recorder consort was itself quite popular. A recorder consort was typically made up of three or four instruments—soprano, alto, and tenor—with an additional tenor added for the fourth instrument. Praetorius gives eight recorder sizes from sopranino to great bass, but he also says that the number of recorders was split into various types of consorts. In other words, there would never be an eight-voiced recorder consort. Praetorius had a real preference for the lower-voiced instruments and writes in Volume III of *Syntagma Musicum*:

> When a canzona, motet, or concert per choros [i.e., consort] is to be played on recorders alone, without other instruments, it is very good and fitting to use the whole range of recorders, especially the five largest kinds, for the small ones are much too loud and piercing. This gives a very soft, sweet, and pleasant harmony, especially in rooms and chambers.[30]

Elizabethan recorders had six tone holes and a thumb hole in the back. When partially uncovered, the thumb hole acted as an octave key. Tone holes of Elizabethan recorders were not set for correct pitch but for the player's comfort.[31] That made it essential for players to collect their own consorts of instruments, to make sure that they were tuned to one another.

Recorders could be played with either the right hand on top or the left;

with no keys to push, it didn't really matter. Sometimes there were two holes for the bottom note—one for the left-hand little finger and one for the right-hand little finger. The player decided which hand to use on the bottom key and stopped up the "extra" hole with wax. Larger recorders acquired a key to reach their bottom note, but even then it was lyre-shaped where the finger would hit it, so that either the right-hand or left-hand little finger could be used. One of the oldest British drawings of a recorder is a painting in a twelfth-century psalter in Glasgow. The player clearly looks puzzled and is obviously trying to figure out which fingers to put onto which holes.[32] Shakespeare has Hamlet teaching Rosencrantz and Guildenstern how to play the recorder:

> Govern these ventages with your fingers and thumb, give it breath with your mouth, and it will discourse most eloquent music. Look, you, these are the stops.[33]

Tabor Pipe

This Elizabethan fipple flute was a holdover from medieval times. The three-holed, one-handed flute was played by one person, who simultaneously beat out a catchy rhythm on a small drum known as a "tabor." A pipe and tabor player would typically play in rural country fairs, where they often accompanied Morris-dancers. When the court entertainment included Morris-dancers, a pipe and tabor player would also be hired.

One famous tabor piper born early in Henry VIII's reign was still piping in 1609, at 96 years of age. A contemporary who heard him wrote that Mr. Hall of Herefordshire was "giving the men light hearts by thy pipe and the women light heels by thy tabor. O wonderful piper! O admirable tabor man!"[34]

Transverse Flute

In Elizabethan times, the word "flute" is often used for both the transverse flute and the recorder, which causes a lot of confusion for scholars. The transverse flute was not held up-and-down when played, like the recorder; rather it was held to the side, cross-wise at a right angle to the body. The performer did not blow into a fipple but had to aim the air across a mouthhole so that the air split over and under the hole to create a sound. The player-directed airstream is the method used by modern flutists. However, this flute was made of a single piece of wood (or ivory),

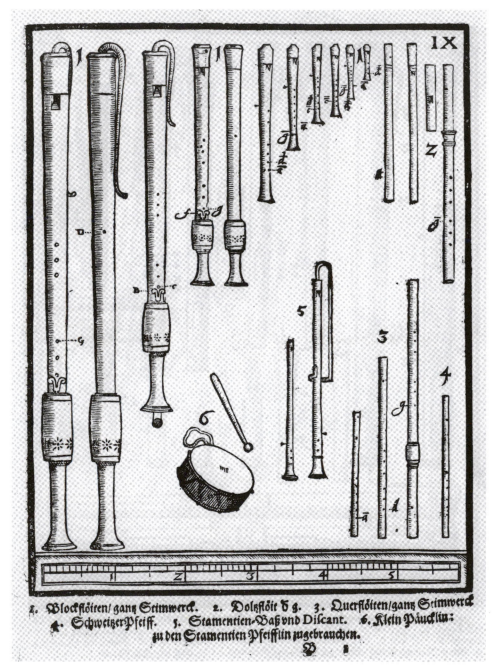

IX

1. Blockflöiten/ ganz Stimwerck.   2. Dolzflöit b g.   3. Querflöiten/ganz Stimwerck
4. SchweizerPfeiff.   5. Stamentien-Baß vnd Discant.   6. Klein Päucklin:
zu den Stamentien Pfeifflin zugebrauchen.

Figure 5. Woodwinds (flutes): (1) the recorder family, (3) transverse flutes, (5, 6) tabor pipe and tabor drum.

had six finger holes without keys of any sort, and lacked a thumb hole. Moreover, as the mouth hole was rather small and round, the Elizabethan flute player had a hard time getting a sound out of this temperamental instrument. One musician wrote, "It is a great deal more difficult to make this flute speak than the other which are blown at the end [i.e., recorders] since everyone can use the latter but few know how to sound the former because of the difficulty found in placing the lips as required on the first [mouth] hole."[35]

Transverse flutes generally formed a consort of three instruments—an alto, a tenor, and a bass. Each flute had a two-octave range—the fundamental fingerings plus one overblown octave. A wise collector would keep a complete consort, since tuning on the transverse flute was difficult at best. In fact, Baroque flutes later began to change and acquire keys because Renaissance transverse flutes were so very much out of tune.

DOUBLE-REED WIND INSTRUMENTS

The sound of a double-reed instrument is produced by vibrating the thinnest edges of two flat pieces of cane together, by means of the player's breath, making a distinctive (and somewhat duck-like) sound. Larger double-reed instruments require larger sized reeds, and they sound proportionately lower in pitch than smaller instruments.[36]

Bagpipes

Bagpipes were still used in Elizabethan days. This instrument had been brought to England from Eastern lands, probably Syria, by Roman soldiers during the Roman occupation of Britain.[37] Bagpipers were favorite performers in early English courts. Edward III sent his court bagpiper to the Continent to learn the most current techniques. Henry VIII kept a bagpiper and had four bagpipes with "pipes of ivorie" in his personal instrument collection.[38]

Bagpipes were favorites with English religious pilgrims because they traveled well. The Miller in Chaucer's *Canterbury Tales* played one. Bagpipers were welcome on pilgrimages as a kind of morale booster. As one person wrote:

> I say to thee that it is right well done that Pylgremys have with them both singers and also [bag]pipers, that when one of them that goeth barefoote, striketh his too [toe] upon a stone, and hurteth hym sore and maketh hym

to blede, it is well done that he and his fellow begyn then a Songe, or else take out of his bosome a Baggepipe for to drive away with soche myrthe the hurte of his felow.[39]

Opinions of bagpipe playing eroded over Queen Elizabeth's 40-year reign. Apparently, musical tastes changed, and bagpipe playing fell out of favor. What had once been considered a pleasant, happy sound was later seen as a nuisance. For instance, in 1561 a story gives a positive spin to a parish priest who not only married his parishioners to one another, but brought them to the church playing merry tunes on his bagpipe.[40] In 1592, however, one Humphrey Sydenham was called before the law and charged for "causing the bells to be rung, and dyvers baggepipes to be blown" during divine services "to the grete dishonour of Almighty God."[41]

Crumhorn

The crumhorn was a Renaissance double-reed "haut" instrument with a cap. The player blew into the cap, which completely covered the reed; the actual reed never touched the player's lips. For that reason, crumhorns had a certain lack of control and were not known for their subtlety. They came in consorts of descant, alto, tenor, and bass. Each instrument had a range of about a ninth (and octave, plus one or two more notes). Its bore was cylindrical (not conical), and the instrument curved up at the bottom. The largest crumhorns had a slider that could act as a sort of "key" to control low notes whose finger holes would have been out of the range of the human hand. Henry VIII had 25 crumhorns in his instrument collection, but there is no indication where or when they may have been used. Elizabethan music shows no music written specifically for crumhorn, and they probably would have been used in the early years of Elizabeth's reign since they are a holdover instrument from the medieval era.

Curtall

This "haut" double-reed instrument is the ancestor of the bassoon. Its name came from the term already used for a type of English short-barreled cannon.[42] Curtalls came into use in Elizabethan mixed consorts because bass and great bass shawms were hard to hold, and they could only play a certain number of notes in the bottom of its range before its tone began to sound "disappointingly weak and wheezy" before failing altogether.[43] Curtalls found a place in waits bands after about 1580 for the same reason—it was a lot easier to lug around than a bass shawm, and it was also quite loud.[44] As one writer put it in 1582, "The common bleting [bleating] musicke is the drone, hobuis, and curtoll." [i.e., the bagpipe, shawm, and curtall].[45]

The main body of the curtall was a single piece of wood with two bores drilled inside. These two bores were connected at the bottom by carving a linking U-shaped horizontal bore carved from another piece of wood, which was plugged at the bottom with a metal cap, as the bassoon is. This gave the curtall twice the depth for its height and weight. Like the bassoon, the curtalls also used a crook to hold its reed. Curtalls had seven tone holes—three on top and four on the bottom. Some curtalls had a key to cover the bottom hole. There was a consort of curtalls, but all were lower-range instruments. Curtalls were normally used to carry a bass line in court instrumental music as well as to play along with the basses in church choir music. This latter job earned the curtall the name "Chorist-Fagott" (the term *fagott* is another word for bassoon).[46]

Rackett

The rackett was another "haut" double-reed wooden instrument. The difference between the rackett and curtall is the amazing amount of connecting bores in the rackett. Racketts may look small, but inside are up to nine thin, parallel bores connected with multiple U-bends at the top and bottom. Its reed is capped. The tone holes seem to be in strange places, but that is because they have to be connected to all the different bores inside the wood. Rackett holes were tricky to drill because they had to be drilled at various angles to connect with the proper section of the proper bore.[47] Despite its inner complications, all the viewer saw was a cylindrical piece of wood that to a modern person looks something like a small wooden car muffler—the smaller reed cap attached to the larger body. Because of its shape, this instrument was also known as the "sausage bassoon."[48]

There was a consort of racketts, and the family group did play together. But its real forte was playing the bass lines in mixed consort music. Like the curtall, the rackett was played in place of the more awkward bass shawm. Unlike the curtall, the rackett was not a particularly raucous instrument. As Praetorius put it:

In sound racketts are quite soft, almost as if one were blowing through a comb. They have no particular grace when a whole set of them is used

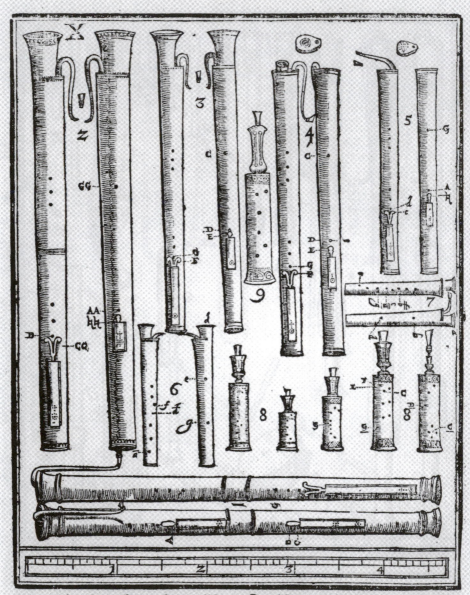

Figure 6. Double reeds: (2–7) curtalls, (8, 9) racketts.

together; but when viols da gamba are used with them, or when a single rackett is used together with other wind or stringed instruments and a harpsichord or the like, and is played by a good musician, it is indeed a lovely instrument. It is particularly pleasing and fine to hear on bass parts.[49]

Shawm

The shawm was a double-reed instrument that has been described as a "more pungent relative of the oboe."[50] The shawm family had its own consort of descant, treble, nocolo, tenor, bass, and great bass.[51] Shawms were "haut", or loud, outdoor instruments and were a main item in the waits bands. Shawms were played by waits musicians all through the night, to make a "bon gayte" [good noise] at every shop door, office, and home as a deterrent to "pickers and pillers [pillagers]."[52] This use of shawms led to their nickname—"wayte pipe."[53]

Because shawms were built to be rugged, their weakest point—the reed—needed to be protected. The smaller shawms had a reed holder called a "pirouette." The pirouette covered just enough of the reed to allow the player to control the actual reed by lip pressure. To any observer, however, it looked as though the player had a trumpet mouthpiece up to his lips. Larger shawms were equipped with a "crook"—a metal holder that bent down to enable the player to reach the reed. The larger the shawm, the longer the crook and the farther down it had to reach. The great bass shawm actually ended up as a modified "s" shape winding down to the player's mouth.

The shawm had a conical bore, which meant that the bottom end was larger than the top end (cylindrical bores are the same size at both ends). Shawms had seven tone holes—three for the top hand and four for the bottom hand. Some of the larger instruments had a key to allow players to reach the bottom hole, and also a protective key cover called a "fontinelle." Actually, the great bass finger holes were so spread out that it had keys for both the lower tone hole and the top tone hole.[54] One characteristic of shawms is that they had unfingered vent holes in the lowest part of the instrument. That section was "often quite extensive, occupying more than half the overall length on some instruments." The vent holes and extra length contributed to the shawms' loud, piercing tone and its considerable carrying power.[55]

Henry VIII had a number of "shawlms" in his enormous collection of instruments. In Queen Elizabeth's time, shawms were sometimes referred to as "howeboies." Also spelled hoboy, hoeboy, howboy, and hautboy, these words were all corruptions of the French term for "high wood"—haut-bois. When used in theater productions, shawms denoted violent emotions. A play in 1561 used the "Musicke of Howeboies" to represent mythological Furies and murder.[56]

The tenor shawm developed into a tenor oboe, also known as Cor Anglois—which is French for English Horn.

BRASS INSTRUMENTS

Not all Elizabethan "brass" instruments were actually made of brass. They could be made of more precious metals, such as silver or gold, and some were made of hard wood, ivory, or animal horn. The two basic types of Elizabethan brass instruments were trumpet-like instruments with a mostly cylindrical tube flaring out only near the end of the instrument, and horn types that gradually grew bigger until they culminated at the bell.[57]

Hunting Horns

Elizabeth inherited a wide variety of hunting horns from her father. These horns were made of a variety of metals but were also often made of wood, "covered with leather or satin."[58] As their name implies, the primary use of these horns was to give calls during hunts, when hunters might be out of earshot from one another. At first, hunting horns were straight, but when their length became unwieldy, they needed to be turned into ever-increasing semicircles. Metal became the more practical material for circular horns. Besides giving hunting calls, horns also gave battle calls loud enough for soldiers to hear. During Elizabethan times horns stopped citizens in their tracks when a public announcement was about to be made.[59]

Cornett

This horn was a hybrid instrument that hovered between being a brass instrument and a woodwind instrument. It was short, could be curved or straight, and like a brass instrument, players made it sound by buzzing the lips into a cup-like mouthpiece. On the other hand, like a woodwind instrument, it was made of wood and had six (or sometimes seven) finger holes drilled into it. Scholars believe that cornetts were originally made from an animal's horn and retained its curved, conical shape. Cornetts came in a consort of sizes—High treble, Ordinary, and Great.

Henry VIII owned many cornetts. Some were made of ivory, others of animal horn, and still others of wood covered in black leather.[60] Curved cornetts had a separate, cup-shaped mouthpiece. Straight cornetts had a conical mouthpiece carved as one piece with the body of the instrument. The straight cornett was known as a "mute" cornett because it was quieter.[61] The curved cornett was preferred because it could be played at either dynamic—loud or soft. In Elizabethan times, the cornett "was the great virtuoso instrument of the Renaissance."[62]

The cornett was equally at home as a solo instrument, in a consort of cornetts, or in a mixed consort. One of its most popular pairings was with sackbuts (an early type of trombone). Apparently, the top-voiced sackbut was not satisfactory even in a sackbut consort, since an essentially low-range instrument sounded strained when played exclusively in its highest range. The cornett, however, made a perfect top voice. It was smaller, which made its higher tones more natural sounding. Today when musicians play a reproduction instrument, they use a trumpet-style mouthpiece and play in the middle of their lips as though playing a trumpet. Elizabethan cornettists used a smaller, acorn-shaped mouthpiece and played on one side of their lips, where the lips are thinner.[63]

Sackbut

The sackbut may have started as a long trumpet. This instrument, too, was folded into a "paperclip" shape, but it also acquired something completely different from its trumpet ancestors—a slide.

Because the slide went up and down with a pumping action, the sackbut got its name from the Spanish words *sacar* (to draw) and *bucha* (a tube). As was true of other instruments, its name was corrupted many times, and it was known as a shakbusshe, saykebud, sakbud, sacbut, shakebutte, sagbut, shagbushe, shagbolt, and finally sackbut.[64] Sackbuts came in a consort of High, Alto, Tenor, and Bass, but was ordinarily used in a mixed consort with the cornett as the treble instrument.

The sackbut had a lot going for it. It had a greater dynamic range than most Elizabethan instruments, so it could fit into both haut and bas mixed consorts in both indoor and outdoor situations. Sackbuts were played in church to support plainsong melodies, and they were also popular instruments in waits bands, as well as theater and pageant music groups. Best of all, the sackbut's slide mechanism allowed it to play absolutely in tune.

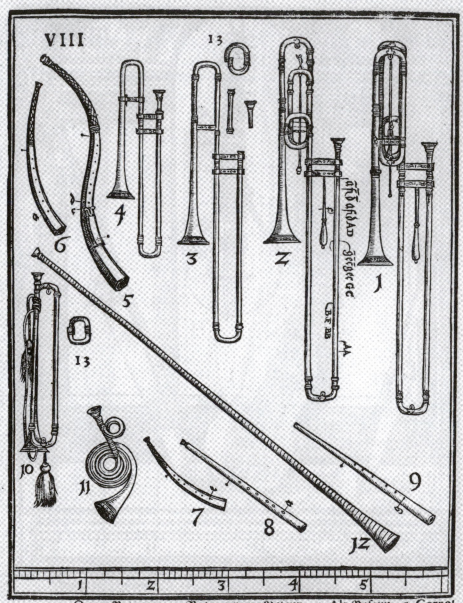

Figure 7. Brass blown instruments: (1–4) sackbuts (with slides), (6, 7) cornetts.

This was a real plus in Elizabethan times, when tuning systems varied from country to country, city to city, and instrument to instrument. Eventually, the sackbut evolved into the modern trombone.

Serpent

The serpent was a sort of bass cornett. Instead of having one curve, it had several, which caused it to look like an enormous snake. In Elizabethan times, when the serpent was used at all, it was played in church to augment lower voiced choir parts.[65]

Trumpet

Trumpeters were the elite of Elizabethan musicians. Even in medieval times they were a special corps with their own guild (an early type of union). The three basic jobs of trumpeters were playing the field trumpet for military operations, playing the tower trumpet for the town waits, and playing clareta trumpet in professional music.[66]

Trumpeters and drummers were often paired together for ceremonial occasions and served as the heralds for their respective lords. These musicians led their lord's retinue wherever it traveled, playing "brilliant tuckets and fanfares" whenever the group passed through a town. They played to announce dinners and stood behind the lord's chair during dinner. A foreign visitor to Elizabethan England wrote that when the guard brought in their dinner, a dozen trumpeters and two kettledrums played for half an hour.[67]

Because trumpets were restricted to notes in the harmonic series, the instruments became increasingly longer so that the trumpeters could get into the top of the harmonic series in order to play diatonic melodies. Tuning was not good in the top of the trumpet range, and players learned to "lip" notes up or down in order to stay relatively in tune. Eventually, trumpet tubes became too long to handle easily and were bent back into their now-familiar "paperclip" shape. The trumpet bell still faced away from the player as it does today, not toward the player's back as the French horn eventually did. Early bent trumpets were referred to as "clarions" to distinguish them from straight trumpets.[68]

BOWED STRINGED INSTRUMENTS

Unlike the stringed instruments already discussed, these instruments were played with a bow instead of being plucked with a plectrum or with finger-work.

Rebec

The rebec was a holdover from medieval times and was on the way out during the Elizabethan period, but it was still used occasionally. Its body resembled the lute in that it was pear-shaped and bowed out in the back. But this instrument had no frets and was played by drawing a bow over its strings. In contemporary writings, the rebec was also occasionally referred to as a lyra.[69]

Viols

The ancestor of the viol family is most likely the medieval fiddle. Viols seem to have appeared quite suddenly, in the generation before Elizabeth. An Englishman named John Cooper went to live on the Continent, returned from Italy as Giovanni Coperario, and practically singlehandedly founded the English school of chamber music.[70] In Elizabethan times, much of the chamber music came from consorts of viols, which was the Renaissance equivalent of the string quartet.[71]

Outwardly, viols resemble the violin family. Made of wood, they have a flat back and sloping shoulders, and, like violins, are narrower at the instrument body. Unlike violins, however, the viol neck has frets. Viols were played with a bow. Viol bows actually look rather like bow-and-arrow bows and were held "underhand" rather than over the top of the bow, as violin bows are. Like modern bows, viol bows were rubbed with resin to make sure they scraped across the sounding strings correctly.[72] Viols were capable of much dynamic variation and emotive power.

The viol family came in consorts from soprano to bass. A "sett" or "chest" of viols would contain two trebles, two tenors, and two basses. They were also known as viol "da gambas," *gamba* being Italian for "leg," because rather than being held under the performer's chin like a violin, viols were supported either on or between the knees. Viols of any size usually had six strings, although some viols also had five or even seven strings. Viol bodies were deeper than those of violins of similar size. The belly and back of viols were fitted to the ribs and did not overhang on the sides. They had sound holes on the front of the instrument. Most Elizabethan viols had no sound post and no bass bar. The sound depended on string vibrations resonating the instrument's facing wood, with the sides and back acting as a reflector of the sound waves.[73] Viol strings were made of thin gut, with a fairly low tension. Viol consorts were capable of great emotional intensity and dynamic variety, even though their sound has a "wiry intensity" unlike the "plummier sound of Baroque viols."[74]

Besides professional viol players, many cultured amateurs took up viol playing. Actually, some aristocrats took their viol playing so seriously that it became a byword for making fun of a person who was either socially out of his depth or who was an affected ass. In Ben Jonson's play, *Every Man Out of His Humour*, the character Sir Fastidious Brisk courts a woman while simultaneously scraping away at a viol and puffing tobacco. In a play entitled *A Trick to Catch the Old One*, by Thomas Middleton, a proud uncle describes his niece's accomplishments in a riot of double-entendres: "The voice between her lips, and the viol between her legs, she'll be fit for a consort very speedily."[75]

With all its positive aspects, as well as the body of literature accorded it, why did the viol consort die out? Actually, the tenor viol continued as a solo instrument for another hundred years. And there was nothing wrong with any of the viols: It was simply its misfortune to be a victim of taste and to be eclipsed by the violin family.

Violin

The violin has been described as having "the most incredible success story of any instrument in the whole history of music."[76] The violin may have evolved out of the rebec. Originally, like a rebec, it had three strings but it developed a bigger body and thus more volume. Who invented it and exactly why? The only person who wrote about the violin's early history within living memory—Praetorius, in his *Syntagma Musicum*—maddeningly stated that "since everyone knows about the violin family, it is unnecessary to indicate or write anything further about it."[77]

The violin family was apparently born all together as a consort of three—treble, alto, and bass—which would become the violin, viola, and violincello. The violin had a sound post and bass bar from the start. It had no frets and it possessed a stronger belly and back to support more string tension, as well as a new longer neck canted back to increase the string tension and a different tuning system from the viol family. Its bow also was less arched, and it was held differently so that performers were able to use a more forceful bowing technique.

Because of its sturdier construction and louder sound, early violins were used to accompany dances and were also played in waits bands. It seems to have always been a professional instrument, played for profit. A musician wrote in 1556, "it is commonly used for dancing, and with good

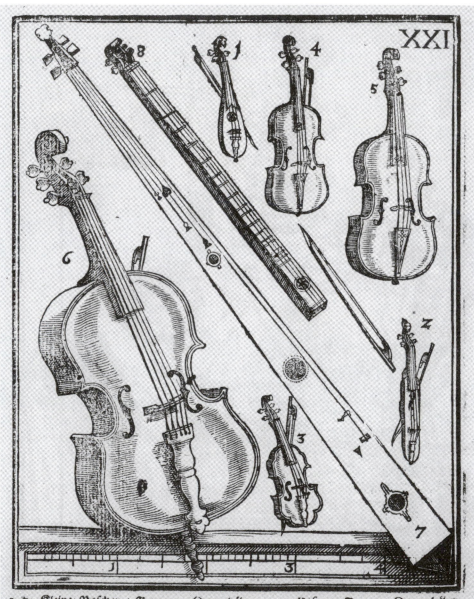

XXI

Figure 8. Bowed stringed instruments: (3–6) the violin family and (7) marine trumpet.

reason, for it is much easier to tune. . . . It is also easier to carry, a very necessary thing while leading wedding processions or mummeries."[78] As a for-profit instrument, violin playing was sometimes denigrated. There was some reason for this attitude, for some Elizabethan violinists apparently did not play very well. A French ambassador visiting Mary Queen of Scots in Edinburgh, wrote in 1561:

> In the evening as she [the queen] wished to sleep, five or six hundred scoundrels of the town serenaded her with wretched violins and small rebecs, of which there is no lack in this country; and they began to sing psalms that which nothing more badly sung or out of tune could be imagined. Alas, what music and what repose for her night![79]

With such an early reputation, it is astounding that the violin family not only outlived its early days but became the dominant string family and the foundation of the modern orchestra.

KEYBOARD INSTRUMENTS

Two basic types of instruments utilized a keyboard: organs and variants on the harpsichord. Organ keyboards allowed forced air to enter flute-like fipple pipes to create their sounds. The harpsichord-like instruments used the keyboard as a mechanism to strike tuned strings in some fashion.

Clavichord

The clavichord was a small keyboard instrument, with a maximum range of about four octaves. It was in one way more akin to today's piano than to any harpsichord—its strings were hit with a hammer, not plucked with a quill. However, the clavichord's dynamic range went from soft to softer, and it was not meant to be played in large rooms, in public performances, or in a mixed consort. Clavichords came early to England; one is mentioned as far back as Henry VII.[80] They were set in rectangular boxes, with the strings running at a right angle to the keys. Some early clavichords had strings that were all the same length but were stopped in different places to get different pitches. They were small enough to be portable, and players could set their instrument on any available table. It had no foot pedals. The clavichord was prized for its intimacy and expressive possibilities, well beyond the Elizabethan age, but it never achieved the wide popularity or varied repertoire of the virginal/spinet.

Organs

Organ building was not the advanced art in England that it was in Germany. As one writer put it:

> There could scarcely be a greater contrast between the English organs of the 16th century, with only one manual, no pedals, and a few flute stops, and those of the North German School with three manuals, a pedalboard, and a host of colourful mixtures, flutes, and reeds to choose from.[81]

To the modern reader accustomed to the organ as a church instrument, it might come as a surprise that small organs were a source of personal amusement among Elizabethans. The "portative" organ was, as its name implies, portable and could be played by one person. The player picked out a melody on the the two-octave keyboard with one hand, while the other hand worked a small bellows. The bellows had no air reservoir, so the air had to be drawn in by phrase, just as one breathes in when singing. According to paintings of the time, portative organs could be held on the player's knee or held up by a strap over the player's shoulder. Sometimes one hand can be seen on the keyboard and the other hand seems to be hidden. Scholars believe that the bellows on some instruments was on the side facing away from the viewer, or sometimes on the bottom of the instrument.[82]

Elizabethans also had a larger type of organ called a "positive." Its name came from the Latin word "to put"—*posit* (think: deposit, or position). This was a two-person organ and had to be placed on a table or some other support in order to be played. One person worked a double-bellows system, while the other played the manual.[83]

Regal

The regal is a variety of organ that did not have pipes. Unlike most organs, this one operated with a bellows that forced air through a set of metal reeds, each "responsible for its own pitch."[84] Its name is possibly a corruption of the Latin word *regula*, which means "order," because in medieval times this instrument played along with church plainsong singers to keep the singers on pitch.[85]

There are many references to regals in the literature during Henry VIII's time, for buying, moving, and mending them. Henry had 22 regals listed in his instrument inventory. At least one had a "nightingale-pipe,"

Figure 9. Organs: (1) positive organ, (2) regal.

which contained water and gave a bird-like twittering sound when activated.[86] Later, Queen Elizabeth played the regal. Expenses for regals are listed separately from other organ expenses, so they must have been considered to be different from the organ. A 1582 list records payment for "crimson vellat [velvet] for covering, lining, and ornamenting divers of Queen Elizabeth's Regals and Virginals."[87]

Regals were quite popular with Elizabethans. Although they are listed as positive organs, some were small enough to be portable. One type was the ultimate in portability. The bellows folded over the keyboard and reeds, and then that folded in half as well. Known as the "Bible Regal" it folded to about the size of a large book, such as a Bible.[88]

Regals did pose some problems, however. Apparently, they went out of tune with amazing rapidity; it was said that a regal could go out of tune from one hour to the next.[89] Praetorius wrote:

> I know only too well how much difficulty is caused the organist or director of an ensemble when several regals are to be played together in churches or at court dinners—and especially when in winter a regal must be brought out of the coldness of the church into a warm dining room. It is indeed true that metal pipes [reeds] are forced down in pitch to such an extent by the cold of winter that they sink by half a semitone, if not more.[90]

Elizabethans referred to a "pair" of organs or a "pair" of regals. It does not mean that everyone had two of these instruments, but it is like saying that a person has a "pair" of scissors.

Virginal

The virginal, or spinet, was the Elizabethan equivalent of the harpsichord. This instrument had strings and a keyboard, something like a piano, but the strings were not hit with a hammer. Instead, the keyboard caused a mechanism equipped with a quill to pluck the strings. Many people assume that the virginal got it name because Queen Elizabeth—known as the "Virgin Queen"—played the instrument quite well. But virginals were already so-named before Queen Elizabeth ever earned her nickname.[91]

Another name for a virginal was the "spinet" because the quill point looked something like a small fishbone ("spine-ette").[92]

The virginal keyboard had about four octaves of notes, more or less. Some were in rectangular cases, and others were in pentagonal cases, which actually looked like rectangles with an extra little piece. Its strings looked extremely harp-like, even though they lay flat in the case. Unlike many harpsichords, the virginal did not have a double keyboard (as the modern organ does) but only one (as the modern piano does). However, because of the way the key jacks had to be placed in relation to where the strings were, the virginal keyboard was not in the middle of the instrument. Sometimes it was on the right side and sometimes on the left side—and there were people who would swear that this made a difference in the instrument's sounds. That said, the cover of a famous book of virginal music, *Parthenia*, shows a drawing of a young lady on its cover playing a virginal with the keyboard squarely in the middle.[93]

Learning to play the virginal was as much a part of a young gentlewoman's education as learning to play the lute was for young gentlemen. The virginal's popularity was no doubt boosted by the fact that Queen Elizabeth herself was a fine virginal player. Quite a few Elizabethan upper-class and middle-class families owned at least one virginal, and some owned a "small chamber organ" as well.[94]

PERCUSSION INSTRUMENTS

The Elizabethan age sported a wide variety of percussion instruments, with and without fixed pitches. Drummers in Queen Elizabeth's day were called "timpanists," but that referred to any kind of drum—not necessarily what we call a tympani today.[95]

Elizabethan march cadences were dignified and rather slow. Once a visiting French nobleman commented to a British officer about the sluggish pace of English drum cadences. The officer answered, "It may be true, but slow as it is, it has traversed *your* master's country [i.e., France] from one end to the other."[96]

Bells

In England as on the Continent, large bells called churchgoers to services. Small bells were not only used to brighten dance music and singing, but were also applied to practically anything that moved in Elizabethan England. Tuned or untuned, small bells were applied to clothing, shoes, and horses' harnesses, to name just a few places they were used. The old nursery rhyme about Mary Queen of Scots alludes to her habit of adorning herself with bells:

Mistress Mary, Quite Contrary,
How does your garden grow?
With cockle shells and silver bells
And little maids, all in a row.

Sometimes tuned bells were suspended on a frame, which was either put on a stand in front of the performer or suspended over his head. The player hit the proper bell with either one hammer or sometimes two. These bells were known as "chyme-bells."[97]

Cymbals

Cymbals were used as war instruments in Greece and related countries. Elizabethan cymbals could be flat or cupped and came in various sizes. The smallest—finger cymbals—were very popular to accompany singing and dancing.[98]

Drum and Fife

The military drum in Elizabethan times was about 2 feet in diameter and 2 feet deep. It was not an easy instrument to march with, and it was no doubt quite heavy. The drummer slung the drum diagonally by a strap over his shoulder and hit it with two sticks as drummers do today, while the drum hung by the player's side. Fifes piped out a melody while the drummers played a cadence. The drum and fife corps so beloved in America today is its descendant.

Nakkers

Nakkers were various sizes of kettledrums. These tuned drums originated in Arab lands, as did the name—*noqqaryeh*—and they probably came to England during the Crusades. In medieval times, the largest nakkers were war drums. They hung on either side of a horse and were used to give battle cadences. Other large-sized nakkers had to be carried by one person and played by another in processions. There were also smaller sizes that could be carried and played by one performer.[99]

Tabor

This small, unpitched tom-tom was played along with the tabor pipe by a single performer who piped with one hand and drummed with the

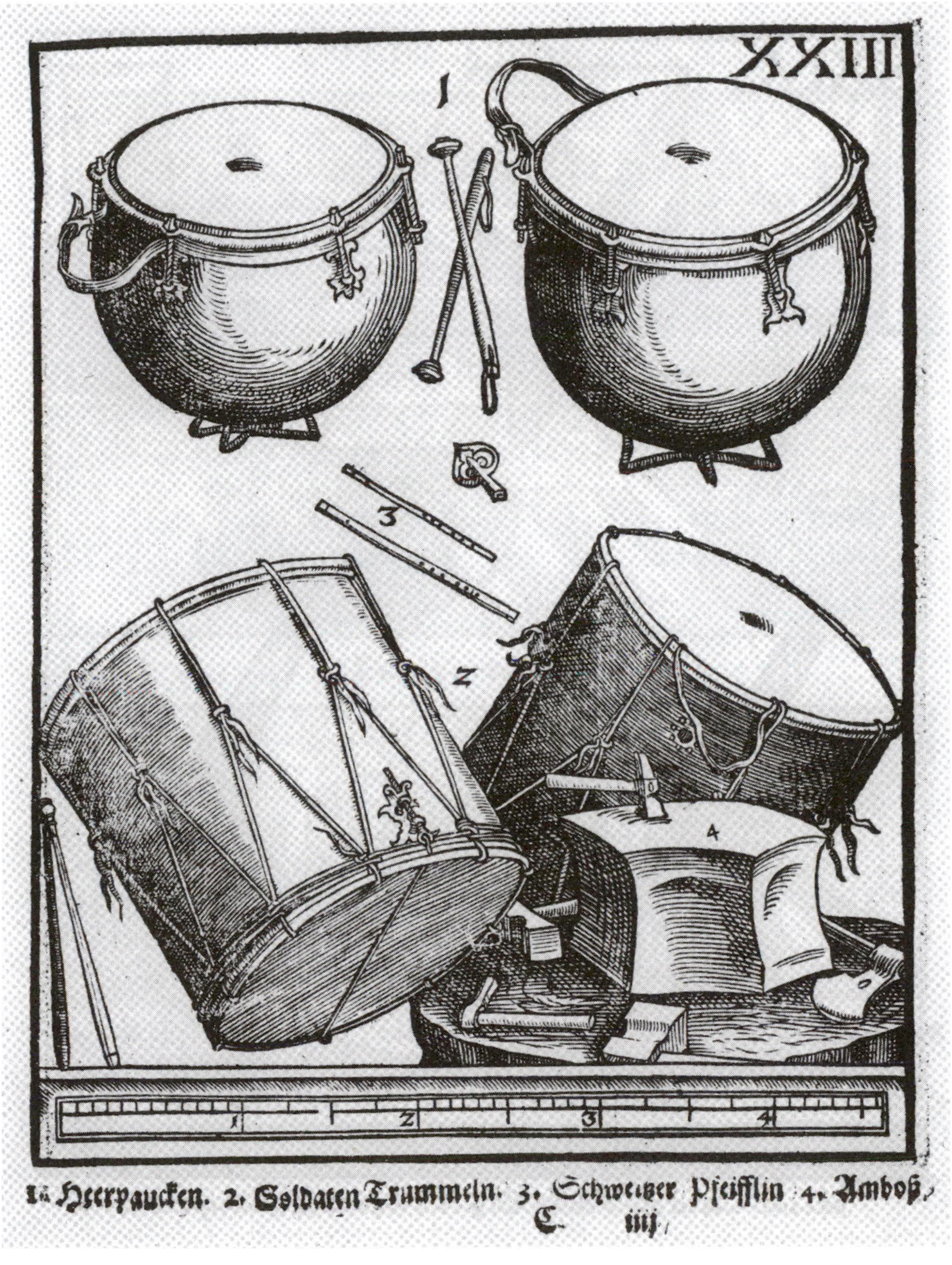
XXIII
1
3
2
4
1. Heerpaucken. 2. Soldaten Trummeln. 3. Schweitzer Pfeifflin 4. Amboß.
C. iiij

Figure 10. Drums: (1) kettledrums, (2) snare drums, (3) Swiss fifes (played with drums).

other. The player wore the tabor slung over his body by a leather strap and beat it with either a drumstick or a bone. Although the tabor was a holdover from medieval times, it was a popular part of the equipment that accompanied Morris-dancers in country entertainments right up to the nineteenth century.

Tambourine

Also known as a timbrel, the tambourine was not just a gypsy instrument. In Elizabethan times, various sizes of tambourines accompanied both singers and dancers.[100]

Xylophone

The Elizabethan xylophone was a set of tuned wooden bars laid on "hanks of straw tied to wooden struts."[101] Even in Elizabethan times a connection was made between this instrument and the clatter of dry bones, a connection that persists to the present day.

ELIZABETHAN CONSORTS

Today, many countries enjoy a pitch standard. That is, the note A in France or Spain is going to be the same pitch (or very close to it) as the note A in Germany or the United States. There was no such pitch standard in Elizabethan times. The note that a Londoner played as an A might sound like an F# to a player in Lincolnshire, or a Bb to a player in Dover. For that reason, buying a ready-made consort was the only way to make absolutely sure that a family of instruments would play in tune together.[102] Instrument collecting grew into somewhat of a mania among upper- and middle-class Elizabethans. The Kytson collection of music and instruments from an inventory of 1602–1603 listed the following:

> six viols, six violins (probably in both cases, two trebles, two means and two basses), seven recorders, four cornetts and a mute cornett, four lutes (one treble, two means and one great bass), a bandore, a cittern, two sackbuts, three hautbois, a curtall (bassoon), a lysarden (probably a serpent), two flutes, a pair of little virginals, a pair of double virginals, "a wind instrument like a virginall" [probably a regal] and a pair of great organs. The music included two "lewting books," many song books, five books with pavines, galliards, measures and country dances, five books of levaulties

and corantoes, and five books with pavines and galliards "for the consort."[103]

During Elizabeth's reign, improvements were made in the construction of instruments—particularly wind instruments, but because of pitch and balance problems, the whole consort was the more normal one. A family of three to five like instruments, from treble to bass, would play together. A 1561 play production that included musical interludes specifies that the groups of instruments were kept apart. There were five sections: consorts of violins, cornetts, flutes, hautboys, and drums/fifes, "each section playing separately."[104] Broken consorts did exist, however. A famous painting from 1596 shows scenes in the life of Sir Henry Upton. One scene includes a masque accompanied by a broken consort. The players are treble violin, bass viol, lute, cittern, transverse flute, and something that looks like a pandore (although only the neck of the instrument is visible).[105]

CONCLUSION

Elizabethan England's interest in playing music as an amateur occupation, in hiring professional musicians for various functions, and in playing instrumental music from English music publishers, all contributed to the manufacture, development, and use of a wide variety of instruments. It also contributed to the growing respect for instrumental music in the face of vocal music, which had always been dominant. Dissatisfaction with instrumental tuning, dynamic capabilities, and range led to improvements among instruments, which ultimately became the instruments we know today.

NOTES

1. D. Munrow, *Instruments of the Middle Ages and Renaissance* (London: Oxford University Press Music Department, 1976), p. 82.
2. Ibid.
3. F.W. Galpin, *Old English Instruments of Music: Their History and Character* (London: Methuen & Co., 1932), p. 31.
4. Ibid.
5. Munrow, p. 82.
6. Ibid., p. 79.
7. Galpin, p. 29.

8. R. Donington, "Music and Musical Instruments," in R. Edwards and L.G.G. Ramsey (eds.), *The Connoisseur Period Guides to the Houses, Decoration, Furnishing, and Chattels of the Classic Periods. Vol. I: The Tudor Period, 1500– 1603* (London: Rainbird, McLean, 1956), p. 163.

9. Munrow, p. 80.

10. J. Montague, *The World of Medieval & Renaissance Musical Instruments* (London: David & Charles, 1976), p. 119.

11. Galpin, p. 29.

12. Ibid., p. 22.

13. Ibid., p. 25.

14. Montague, p. 118.

15. Galpin, p. 40.

16. Ibid., p. 41.

17. Munrow, p. 75.

18. Ibid., p. 72.

19. Galpin, pp. 37–38.

20. Ibid., p. 44.

21. Ibid., p. 45.

22. Ibid., p. 44.

23. Munrow, p. 75.

24. Galpin, p. 40.

25. Munrow, p. 83.

26. Galpin, p. 31.

27. Munrow, p. 83.

28. Ibid., p. 55.

29. Ibid., p. 53.

30. Ibid., p. 56.

31. Montague, p. 99.

32. Galpin, p. 140.

33. Munrow, p. 56.

34. Galpin, p. 150.

35. Munrow, p. 54.

36. Galpin, p. 162.

37. Ibid., pp. 173–174.

38. Ibid., p. 175.

39. Ibid., p. 176.

40. Ibid., pp. 176–177.

41. Ibid.

42. Munrow, p. 43.

43. Ibid.

44. Ibid.

45. Ibid.

46. Ibid.

47. Ibid., p. 47.
48. Galpin, p. 167.
49. Munrow, p. 46.
50. Donington, p. 163.
51. Montague, p. 99.
52. Galpin, p. 160.
53. Ibid., p. 162.
54. Montague, p. 100.
55. Munrow, p. 40.
56. Galpin, p. 164.
57. Ibid., p. 182.
58. Ibid., p. 184.
59. Ibid.
60. Ibid., p. 191.
61. Montague, p. 104.
62. Ibid., p. 106.
63. Munrow, p. 69.
64. Galpin, p. 208.
65. Montague, p. 106.
66. Galpin, p. 199.
67. Ibid., pp. 199–200.
68. Ibid., p. 201.
69. Ibid., p. 80.
70. Donington, p. 165.
71. Ibid., p. 164.
72. Galpin, p. 89.
73. Montague, p. 112.
74. Ibid.
75. Munrow, p. 87.
76. Ibid., p. 91.
77. Ibid., p. 90.
78. Ibid., p. 91.
79. Ibid.
80. Galpin, p. 118.
81. Munrow, p. 59.
82. Galpin, p. 229.
83. Ibid.
84. Montague, p. 126.
85. Galpin, p. 230.
86. Ibid., p. 231.
87. Ibid., p. 232.
88. Ibid., p. 230.
89. Munrow, p. 61.

90. Ibid.
91. Galpin, p. 123.
92. Ibid., p. 120.
93. Munrow, p. 64.
94. Donington, p. 163.
95. Galpin, p. 252.
96. Ibid., pp. 246–247.
97. Ibid., p. 261.
98. Ibid., pp. 255–256.
99. Ibid., p. 249.
100. Ibid., p. 239.
101. Montague, p. 109.
102. Munrow, p. 38.
103. Galpin, p. 280.
104. Ibid., p. 276.
105. Ibid., p. 279.

REFERENCES

Brown, H.M., and Stein, L.K. *Music in the Renaissance* (2nd ed.). Upper Saddle River, NJ: Prentice Hall, 1999.

Donington, R. "Music and Musical Instruments." In R. Edwards and L.G.G. Ramsey (eds.), *The Connoisseur Period Guides to the Houses, Decoration, Furnishing, and Chattels of the Classic Periods. Vol. 1: The Tudor Period, 1500–1603.* London: Rainbird, McLean, 1956, pp. 159–165.

Galpin, F.W. *Old English Instruments of Music: Their History and Character.* London: Methuen & Co., 1932.

Montague, J. *The World of Medieval & Renaissance Musical Instruments.* London: David & Charles, 1976.

Munrow, D. *Instruments of the Middle Ages and Renaissance.* London: Oxford University Press Music Department, 1976.

Chapter 7

Instrumental Music and Dance Music

Instrumental music is written specifically to be played on instruments, as opposed to music written to be sung. This distinction may sound obvious, but the concept was a rather new one in Elizabethan times. Vocal music had been all-important up to this time. Instruments either played along with voices, played vocal parts, or played improvised music that was not put down in writing. Writing down music meant only for instruments was a new wrinkle.

Instrumental music gained respect from composers and patrons during the Elizabethan era and began to catch up to vocal music in popularity by the end of Queen Elizabeth's reign. But it was an evolving, not a fully developed, art form. The rise of printed music helped, but published instrumental music didn't catch on as fast in England as it had in Italy. England's first printed instrumental music was for keyboard playing, the *Mulliner Book*, first published in 1530.[1] By contrast, the earliest printed book for purely instrumental ensemble music was published in Rome in 1521, and German composer Arnold Schlick's printed instruction manual for organ playing was published in 1511.[2] Although Elizabethans played instrumental music throughout the 1500s, putting it into print really got started near the end of that century.

INSTRUMENTAL MUSIC FORMS

Instrumental music took several forms, most of which were direct offshoots of vocal and dance forms. The following quotation from the Elizabethan era points out that there was hardly any tune sung or danced to that every fiddler did not know:

> Neither is there anie tune or stroke which may be sung or plaide on instruments which hath not some poetical ditties framed according to the numbers thereof, some to Rogero, some to Trenchmore, to down right Squire, to Galliardes, to Pauines, to Iygges, to Brawles, to all manner of tunes which euerie Fidler knows better then my selfe.[3]

Intabulations

One of the most common instrumental forms was the "intabulation," parts originally written for voices played by instruments instead. Even in medieval times, when monks sang chant melodies with no harmony, an instrument played the tune along with the singers to keep them on pitch and in time. The instrument was usually a portative organ (see page 118) but could also be a wind or brass instrument. As harmony lines began to be added to church music, instruments continued to play along with the voices. Since the individual range of instruments was not great, several instruments of varying sizes belonging to the same family were developed (see "Elizabethan Consorts," p. 124) to follow what evolved into the soprano, alto, tenor, and bass vocal lines. When the tenor line began using extremely long notes during the late medieval and early Renaissance eras, those notes were usually completely taken over by instruments such as a sackbut, an early type of trombone. Scholars base this on the fact that while other voices have text, these lines have only notes with no words. Further evidence is provided in visual arts of the times. By the Renaissance era, church instruments sometimes took over all the sung parts and played one or more strains of a vocal work instead of having an entire work sung.

Similar developments occurred in secular music. If there weren't enough people who could sing, an instrument might take over a vocal line. Eventually, as consorts of instruments became common, vocal works were entirely played on instruments. In Elizabethan England, any sort of vocal music could become an intabulation. Secular works such as ballads, vocal chansons (French secular polyphonic songs), madrigals, lieder (German secular songs), and "catches" (what we know today as a "round") were commonly played on instruments. More surprisingly, sacred works were also played on instruments—not only motets, but actual Mass movements as well.

Cantus Firmus Instrumental Works

In vocal music, the *cantus firmus* was a compositional device used since medieval times. The *cantus firmus* line was a preexisting melody (usually part of a Gregorian chant) put into very long notes and sung as the bottom line of a three- or four-voiced work. The composers wrote new lines of music over this older, slower line. The result was a new work built over an older one. Later, composers spread the idea of a *cantus firmus* to include popular tunes, slowed down, put in the bottom voice, and with new lines of music written over the slowed-down popular tune.

In a form related to intabulation, instrumental composers sometimes arranged a new harmony to preexisting melodies, either plainchants or popular secular tunes. Or they might add a second melody to fit with the original melody and its original harmony. This practice was known as adding a "counter melody." Thus, even though the work was based on a vocal model, composers used the older vocal part as the basis for a newer instrumental work.

One such work was a very popular Elizabethan form known as an "In Nomine." To understand In Nomines, one must return to the early days of the English Catholic Church. Although Continental Europe used Gregorian chants, the island of England developed its own variety known as "Sarum" chants, which developed from the Catholic rite as it was practiced in medieval Salisbury, England. In the Benediction section of one Mass, part of a Sarum plainsong became a very popular tune on which to build musical works. It was the part where the Latin words for "In the name of the Father, Son, and Holy Ghost" were sung. ("In Nomine" is Latin for "In the name of. . . .")

Henry VIII's favorite composer, John Taverner, started a fad when he used this melody in a Mass, as a six-part vocal work. This In Nomine setting broke away from its original Mass setting and began to circulate as an instrumental, textless work.[4] Soon other composers were trying their hand at building instrumental works over the In Nomine melody, and for about 100 years a variety of composers set this melody in over 150 different instrumental works. Most of the settings were for viol consorts, but some were keyboard works.

Variation Sets

Variation sets became very popular in Elizabethan England, particularly on keyboard instruments, but also with consorts (groups of instruments

played together). In this type of music, a particular line or chord pro-
gression repeated again and again, while contrasting music occurred
around it. Since the repeated line was "ground out" in the bass part—
cranked out, as coffee is ground out in a coffeemill or as meat is ground
out to become hamburger—it became known as a "ground bass" or (because it repeated, as in a round) a "ground round." Elizabethans liked the
ground bass form so much because it was directly descended from the
familiar *cantus firmus* techniques of sacred music. Taking this sacred music
technique and placing it firmly into the secular world showed that secular
music was gaining respect. Playing this music as a purely instrumental
genre was a great leap forward toward a new respect for instrumental music
and a new self-confidence within its composers.

One popular instrumental composition technique was "divisions upon
a ground." The divisions referred to the notes *not* part of the ground, but
proportionate to it. For instance, the division might be twice as fast—
two notes for every one of the ground (a ratio of 2 to 1). Or the division
might be more complicated, such as three notes for every two notes of
the ground (that is, a ratio of 2 to 3).

In other eras, when instrumentalists played a theme and variations,
they generally inserted a slight pause after the theme, as well as after each
variation to clearly set them apart from one another. In Elizabethan times
many variation sets, particularly those based on a ground bass, were played
without any pause between variations. Sometimes the melody of an especially popular ground bass acquired a name, such as the Romanesca and
Ruggiero. Variation sets of this type were also known as "Dumps." The
tunes to Dumps were generally rather sad and mournful, from which
comes the expression to be "down in the dumps."[5]

Other Elizabethan variation sets based themselves not on a repeating
bass line but on a popular tune. These paused between each variation. A
famous variation of this type is William Byrd's treatment of "The Carman's Whistle." (The popular tune originally imitated the whistling of
an Elizabethan cab driver to his horse.) Other variation sets used dance
forms as inspiration. In these, variations came at the point in which a
dance pattern would have been repeated. Instead of a musical repeat, the
instrumental version had a variation.

Some methods for making variations on popular tunes were to take a
melody originally in duple meter and rework it into triple meter. A composer might also keep the melody line intact and change the harmonies
or counter-melodies around it. Another common treatment was to add
more (and more complicated) ornaments to the original melody. A less

common but very interesting technique was the following: After several treatments in which a melody line was firmly cemented in the listeners' heads, the composer left the melody out altogether and kept only its form and harmony.

All types of variation sets were very popular as works for instrumental consorts; they were also particularly good as keyboard pieces. Variation sets by composers such as William Byrd and John Bull may be found in books such as the *Fitzwilliam Virginal Book*. The variation set is one of the types of music that England may not have invented, but English composers took to its "highest peak of perfection."[6]

Fantasias and Ricercars

In the last half of the sixteenth century, Fantasias (also known as Fantasies, or Fancies) dominated instrumental music forms. For most of the English Renaissance, Ricercars and Fantasias were interchangeable terms. The Ricercar was an Italian import, and originally meant "seek-find," a reference to its imitative counterpoint. The Fantasia arrived in England from Italy when Elizabeth was still a baby. Both John Taverner and Christopher Tye wrote Fantasies, taking the Italian form and adapting it to English tastes. Music of this form is *not* based on anything preexisting—a preexisting melody or dance scheme, for instance. For composers, this was an amazingly free moment. As Thomas Morley wrote in 1597:

> The most principal and chiefest kind of musicke which is made without a dittie [without words] is the fantasie, that is, when a musician taketh a point at his pleasure and wresteth and turneth it as he list, making either much or little of it according as shell seeme best in his own conceit. In this may more art be showne then in any other musicke, because the composer is tide [tied] to nothing but that he may adde, diminish, and alter at his pleasure. . . . Other thinges you may use at your pleasure, as bindings with discordes, quicke motions, slow motions, proportions, and what you list. Likewise, this kind of musick is with them who practice instruments of parts in greatest use, but for voices it is but sildone [seldom] used.[7]

The opening and closing sections of Fantasies tended to have a lot of imitative counterpoint, meaning that small bits of music appeared and reappeared throughout various melodic lines, like musical hide-and-seek. The central section(s) were more homophonic, meaning that they were more chordal. Fantasies and Ricercar sections were very clear and separated from one another, with a cadence and sometimes a double bar (a double perpendicular mark on a music staff that marks the end of a section, or of a work).[8]

The title *Fantasie* or *Fancy* was rather freely used for many abstract instrumental works in collections such as the *Fitzwilliam Virginal Book*, even though some of these works look more like variations than Fantasies. Fantasies for keyboard tend to have a lot of notes because the Elizabethan keyboard instruments had no sustain pedals. To take the place of what might have been a sustained note or passage in a violin or vocal work, composers used elaborate filigrees of fast notes instead.

Canzonas

Instrumental canzonas were a direct descendant of French vocal works called "chansons." The giveaway is a particular rhythm with which certain types of chansons, and also English canzonas, began. The characteristic rhythm is a single long note taking up two beats, followed by two notes taking up one beat each. Canzonas are built in contrasting sections. The sections might be contrasted by style, as in an imitative style followed by a very chordal style. Or they might be contrasted by rhythms, such as a duple section followed by one in triple time. Sometimes canzonas were built on simple repetition forms, such as ABA, ABB, or AABC.

Preludes, Preambles, and Toccatas

This type of instrumental form worked best on keyboards, but it was also used for lute, or even harp, music. It was meant to sound improvised, as if the performer were making it up on the spot. As the least restrictive form imaginable, Elizabethan composers must have had a sense of freedom akin to taking a roller coaster ride. That sense of freedom is still evident today in these forms' abrupt textural changes, brilliant scale passages, and quirky tempo changes.

This instrumental form, like the Fantasia, is not based on any other related form, such as vocal models or dance rhythms. As such, it is one of the first types of instrumental writing to lean toward "idiomatic" writing. That is, the music written for these forms suited a particular instrument, and it would be difficult or impossible to either sing it or to play the music on another instrument.

INSTRUMENTAL COLLECTIONS

The First Booke of Consort Lessons

Thomas Morley's *The First Booke of Consort Lessons* was first published in 1599. The good news is that its 25 pieces are a prime source of Elizabethan music for broken consorts. The bad news is that this collection, one of the earliest published with particular instrumentation in mind, came in separate part books and that no complete set of part books remains. Six part books existed, one each for treble lute, pandora, cittern, basse-viol, treble-viol, and flute. Fortunately for today's musicians, scholars have pieced together parts from existing part books and manuscript copies of other books and reconstructed the works in score form.

Fitzwilliam Virginal Book

The *Fitzwilliam Virginal Book*, consisting of 297 keyboard works originally written within a 50-year period, was collected and put together by Francis Tregian around 1609. Even though it appeared after Queen Elizabeth's death, it contains music from the Elizabethan era. Oddly, we owe its existence to London's Fleet Prison. After being implicated in a plot against the crown, Tregian was jailed in 1577 for "recusancy"—leaving the Church of England and reverting to Catholicism. To pass the time of the 24 years he spent in jail, Tregian copied out all the keyboard works he could get his hands on. Unfortunately, he was unable to proofread his publication or check his sources. So the book's first printing has many errors and was not a reliable source for knowing who wrote which works. Still, reprints of this book continue to be used today, and it is a major source of Elizabethan keyboard music. Tregian was finally released in 1602, moved to Spain, and died in Lisbon, Portugal, in 1608.

Mulliner Book

The *Mulliner Book* is an early collection of English keyboard works that actually predates Elizabeth's reign. Compiled by organist Thomas Mulliner, the book contains a variety of keyboard works (probably for small organs or regals) by famous composers such as John Taverner and Thomas Tallis, and by others not as well known, such as John Shepherd and Richard Allwood. The *Mulliner Book* is a valuable guide to keyboard music that the young Elizabeth might have known as a musically inclined princess.

My Ladye Nevells Booke

My Ladye Nevells Booke is a collection of William Byrd's secular keyboard works dated 1591. It is unknown whether the Lady Nevell was a pupil or a patron of Byrd's. The book contains a virtual anthology of 42 of Byrd's secular keyboard compositions, and it is possible for scholars to trace Byrd's maturation from early works to later ones. The book begins with "My Ladye Nevells Grownde" and also contains character pieces, Pavans and Galliards, variations on popular tunes, and Fancies. It is a major source of Byrd's secular compositions and of Elizabethan keyboard music—and a major source of delight for musicians.

Parthenia

Parthenia or *The Maydenhead of the First Musicke that Ever was Printed for the Virginalls* is a collection of mostly Pavans and Galliards written by William Byrd, John Bull, and Orlando Gibbons. Although at first glance the music looks reasonably familiar to the modern eye, at second glance most musicians do a double-take because the music has six staves instead of five. Musical staves are the setup of lines and spaces on which notes are placed to show musicians what pitches to play. An extra line is very confusing to a person used to seeing the top line of a treble clef stave as an F. With a sixth stave, that note might be an A instead. Although the book was printed in 1611 or 1612, years after Elizabeth's death, it is still an important source of contemporary instrumental forms.

DANCE MUSIC

In Elizabethan times, as today, people danced to both instrumental music and to music sung with lyrics. This is why dance music is considered both instrumental and vocal. Queen Elizabeth loved to dance. It was said that, even in her old age, Elizabeth exercised each morning by dancing six or seven Galliards. In fact, a Spanish ambassador expressed some outrage at seeing the queen dance three or four strenuous Galliards "in her old age" at a Twelfth Night revel in 1599. A letter from 1602 reads in part: "We frolic here in Court; much dancing in the Privy Chamber of Country Dances before the Queen's Majesty, who is exceedingly pleased therewith."[9] Sometimes the queen made important post appointments on the basis of one's dancing skill. One Sir Christopher Hatton received his post "as a result of his dancing abilities."[10]

Dancing was a very important social institution in the Elizabethan era. For one thing, it was a socially acceptable way for young people to meet one another. Dances and balls were a venue for serious matchmaking where "joyous flirtation and the exhibition through dance of delightful feminine charms and lusty male prowess were vital to social intercourse."[11] Dancing masters were hired to teach the newest steps, and instruction books (mostly from the Continent) were also available. Not only the invention of music printing, but also the birth of dance script helped preserve at least some Elizabethan era dances.

Even though Queen Elizabeth loved dancing, some religious leaders gave dance and dancing music a mixed review, or condemned it outright. One of the more virulent churchmen wrote:

> Dancing is for the most part attended with many amorous smiles, wanton compliments, unchaste kisses, scurrilous songs & sonnets, effeminate music, lust-provoking attire, ridiculous love-pranks, all which savour only of sensuality, of raging fleshly lusts. Therefore, it is wholly to be abandoned of all good Christians. Dancing serves no necessary use, no profitable, laudable or pious end at all. It issues only from the inbred pravity, vanity, wantonness, incontinency, pride, profaneness or madness of men's depraved natures. Therefore, it must needs be unlawful unto Christians. The way to Heaven is too steep, too narrow for men to dance and keep revel rout. No way is large or smooth enough for capering roysters, for jumping, skipping, dancing dames but that broad, beaten, pleasant road that leads to hell. The gate of Heaven is too narrow for . . . whole troops of dancers to march in together.[12]

Instruction Books

Of the several dancing books available, some of the most popular were Fabritio Caroso's *Nobilta di Dame* (1600), Thoinot Arbeau's *Orchesography* (1589), and the part of Thomas Morley's *A Plaine and Easie Introduction to Practicall Musicke* (1597) which dealt with dance forms. Both Caroso and Arbeau were old men when they wrote their books, and both felt they had to defend dance against those who thought it a frivolous or even a wicked way to spend one's time.

Caroso claimed that dancing balanced out the hardships of life as one of the "pleasant and merry" activities available to humankind "for in human converse and society it rouses the spirit to joy, and when we find ourselves oppressed by our troubles it relieves and refreshes us, keeping away annoying or unpleasant thoughts."[13] He taught that besides being good physical exercise, attending dances taught manners and bearing.

Arbeau's book is something like a play, with two characters—Capriol and Arbeau—talking about dancing. Capriol is a lawyer and has come to learn dancing because he's having trouble meeting women. His instructor Arbeau agrees that social dancing is a great place to show himself off in front of women, "because ladies do not like to be present at fencing or tennis, lest a splintered sword or a blow from a tennis ball should cause them injury."[14]

Capriol admits that he's a little embarrassed to be wasting his time on a "shameless and effeminate pastime." He has been told that Cicero and Moses disapproved of dancing. Arbeau says that Cicero was jealous because he had varicose veins and couldn't dance himself, and Moses wasn't angry at the dancing itself but the fact that his people were dancing around an idol. Then Arbeau cements his argument by bringing up King David dancing before the Ark of the Covenant.[15]

Warming to his subject, Arbeau says that dancing is "both a pleasant and a profitable art which confers and preserves health; proper to youth, agreeable to the old and suitable to all."[16] He suggests that dancing is a "peaceful counterpart to the art of war."[17] For young women especially, he says that dancing will "contribute greatly to health, even to that of young girls, who, leading sedentary lives, intent upon their knitting, embroidery and needlework, are subject to a variety of ill-humours which have need to be dispelled by some temperate exercise."[18]

Comforted, Capriol embarked on his learning campaign, and, by extension, so did French and English readers.

TYPES OF ELIZABETHAN DANCE

Elizabethans had a wide variety of dances from which to choose. There were group dances for unlimited amounts of dancers, which could either be danced in circles or "longways." There were also dances for fixed amounts of participants, such as trios, two or three couples, or an odd number of dancers. There were mimed dances that acted out stories, usually of the "battle of the sexes" type. And there were flirting dances with chances to embrace, kiss, or engage in pretend chases.

Three distinct styles of dance existed in Elizabethan England, at court and otherwise. One style was the ancient ritual dance, such as Morris dances; another was the Country dance which came to court from rural areas; and the third were the Court dances, generally danced by the nobility.

Country Dances

This kind of dancing may have begun in medieval times in France, and spread to England when refugees from a French religious sect fled from southern France to England "where the dance tradition they started was permitted to develop almost in isolation from the rest of the world."[19] In 1591, Queen Elizabeth was visiting Lord and Lady Montague at their manor in Sussex, and watched as both hosts and tenants danced Country dances together. After that, Country dancing came to court. A report from 1600 said that the Maids of Honour were dancing both "the old and the new country dances," and young noblemen were learning Country dances along with court dances at the Inns of Court. A line from a 1600 play describes the popularity of Country dancing and its effect on wood floors:

> the mad lads and country lasses, every mother's child, with nosegays and bride-laces in their hats, dance all their country measures, rounds and jigs, what shall we do? Hark! . . . they toil like mill-horses. . . . you shall see tomorrow the hall floor peck'd and dinted like a mill-stone, made by their high shoes: though their skill be small, yet they tread heavy where their hob-nails fall.[20]

Country dances were not standardized. Such things as the number of dancers and which foot to start on changed from region to region. Country dances were interactive. Partners not only danced with one another, but also had steps with other peoples' partners. Steps were simple, there weren't too many of them, and they were usually on the music's beats. Each complete move tended to correspond to a musical phrase—including adding an extra step if the music called for it. Many country dances had steps that described a tight circle or square formation. This started because rural dancers didn't have much space in which to dance. By the time Country dancing came to court, the formations had become set.

The one "rule" of Country dancing was that they began and ended with "Honours": a bow for men and a courtesy (curtsy) for women. Most Elizabethan dance music had an introductory phrase intended for the

Honours at the beginning of each dance. There were specific instructions for bowing and curtsying:

> The man places his right foot back about a foot behind his left and pointing at right angles to it. He then bends his right knee but keeps his left leg straight and his waist almost straight, and gazes at his partner. The woman keeps both feet together at a 45-degree angle, or she may place her left foot ever so slightly behind the right, and, bending her knees outwards but not her waist, gracefully sinks and rises again, her glance slightly downcast.[21]

Court Dances

Court dances were imported from the hotbed of Renaissance culture, Italy, through both traveling courtiers and visiting ambassadors. Even French dances had an Italian origin, imported into France by Catherine de Medici who brought her court to France after her marriage. It was therefore no accident that many dancing books were Italian and French.

Court dances came in pairs, and the custom was to start with a slower, more stately dance and then progress to a quicker one. Slower dances were called "basse" because they were "low" dances; that is, the dancers' feet did not leave the floor. In contrast, more lively "haute" (high) dances involved skipping, hopping, or jumping.

The following are some of the most common Elizabethan Court dances. The instructional sources used are the Caroso, Arbeau, and Morley books.

The Alman, or Allemagne

The Alman was a basse dance apparently of German origin—Allemagne being an old name for Germany. Arbeau calls it a "plain dance of a certain gravity . . . with little variety of movement."[22] Morley wrote that "The Alman is a more heavie daunce then this (fitlie representing the nature of the people, whose name it carieth) so that no extraordinarie motions are used in daucing of it."[23]

Music for the Alman was in duple time and written in "cut" time. However, it was not a fast dance. Its characteristic rhythm was quarter note/two eighth notes/quarter note/two eighth notes. Musically, the Alman closely resembled the Pavane. Arbeau described it as a "simple, rather sedate dance."[24] It became known as the most sentimental Court dance because its partners held one another's hands the entire time.[25] Its beauty lay not in whirling steps, but in its grace and tenderness.

The Alman musical form survived its dance. Later, the word became a verb. To "allemande" became a term for interlacing partners' arms during a turn.[26] As a musical form, it became one of the required movements of an instrumental dance suite. In the dance suite, just as in the actual dances, the Alman comes before the more lively Coranto.

The Branle

Elizabethans danced the Branle (Bransle, Brawle, or Brawl) during the entire Elizabethan era. Although most Branle music was in three groups of two notes each, it was sometimes written in two groups of three notes each instead. The characteristic rhythm of a Branle was three notes of one beat each, one note two beats long, and another note of one beat's worth. Branles could be danced as a line dance or in a ring. This, and the fact that Branles might be accompanied by singing, points to its old-fashioned, Country dancing roots.

Apparently, there were four basic types of Branles, suitable for people of various years and energies. Older partners danced a "double" and "single" Branle in a rather slow manner. Young married people danced the "gay branle." And young unmarried people danced the liveliest of all Branles—the "branles of Burgundy."[27]

Dancers could choose from an amazing number of Branle versions, such as the Scottish Branle, Brittany Branle, Maltese Branle, the Washerwomen's Branle (the outstanding gesture in this one comes when the women put their hands on their hips and the men shake their fingers at them, and then the gesture is reversed), the Pease Branle, the Hermits' Branle (dancers greet one another with crossed arms and a nod of the head, as religious hermits greet one another), the Candlestick Branle (or Torch Branle) (the man chooses his partner and they dance with a candle, when he takes her back to her place he hands her the candle, and then it's her turn to choose, etc.), the Clog Branle, the Horses Branle (dancers tap their feet), the Montarde Branle, and the Hay Branle (the dancers interweave at the end).[28]

The Canary

The Canary was a very lively Elizabethan dance in triple time, usually either 3/8 or 6/8. The first eighth note of each group of three notes is dotted, which gives it a lilting rhythm. It contains stamps, heel-and-toe steps, and something called a "swishing slide."[29] The Canary is mentioned in at least two Shakespeare plays. In *Love's Labour's Lost* (1588), a character urges someone "To Jigge off a tune at the tongues end, Canarie it with the feet." In *All's Well That Ends Well* (1601), a character describes "A medicine that's able to breathe life into a stone and make you dance Canari."[30]

It is not clear whether the dance actually came from the Canary Isles or whether it developed from a masque in which players dressed as savages and danced wearing costumes made mainly of feathers. Arbeau mentions that the music to this dance has passages that are lively but "nevertheless strange and fantastic with a strong barbaric flavour."[31]

Although it never became part of the dance suite form, the Canary shows up in French Baroque ballets. In that capacity, Jean-Baptiste Lully, Jean-Philippe Rameau, François Couperin, and the Baroque English composer Henry Purcell all wrote Canaries.[32]

The Coranto

The Coranto (or Courante) was a haute dance, lively, and in triple time. Coranto music had two sections of either 16 or 32 bars each, both of which were repeated. It was a favorite Court dance for 200 years, from the 1550s to the 1750s. The only other dance to survive that length of time as an actual dance was the Minuet. The name of this dance was taken from the Latin word *curro* meaning to run.[33] Although it may be compared to the Galliard (or, more likely the Volte), Morley wrote that the Coranto was more of a "travising and running" dance than the Volte's rising and leaping.[34] An introduction to an edition of Arbeau's book states that the Courante "is danced with short passages of coming and going, and has a very pliant movement of the knees, which recalls that of a fish when it plunges lightly through the water and returns suddenly to the surface."[35]

Courante music also outlived its dance steps. The Courante became a favorite musical form for lute composers. As one German composer said almost 200 years later, "The masterpiece of the lutenists, especially in France, is generally the Courante, upon which one can employ his efforts and skill to good purpose."[36] The Courante became the fourth required dance form for the instrumental dance suite, along with the Allemande, Sarabande, and Gigue. As such, many composers of dance suites including J.S. Bach, wrote delightful Courantes played by instrumentalists to this day. Scholars also believe that the Courante was the seminal form for the Scherzo—a later lively, graceful musical form.[37]

The Galliard

Pavanes were almost always followed by a "haute" dance called the Galliard, which got its name from the old French word *galach* which meant a dashing, vibrant person.[38] This lively, nimble dance was in triple time, generally made up of a five-step set and a leap (called a "caper") on the sixth beat. Its music had no pickup note (one or more notes preceding the first downbeat of a work), and Galliard music was generally in two groups of three notes, making six beats per note group. The Galliard's most striking rhythm was three notes of one beat each (three dance steps), followed by a note lasting two beats (one dance step), and a final note of one beat (the final "caper" step). This early five-step form, known as the "cinquepace," was quickly added to. One older dancer wrote in complaint:

> Our Galliardes are so curious, that they are not for my daunsing, for thei are so full of trickes and tournes, that he which hath no more but the plaine Sinquepace is no better accumpted of that a verie bongler.[39]

Arbeau advised that even when a Galliard was "performed reasonably slowly, the movements are light-hearted."[40] Morley observed that, however many strains of fours the preceding Pavane had in duple time, the Galliard that follows should have an equal number in triple time. Some later Galliard moves bordered on the gymnastic. Multiple turns on the ground, turns in midair, and taking turning jumps while kicking a tassel raised high above the floor were some of the gyrations attempted by Galliard-dancing gentlemen.

Arbeau called Galliard leaps "postures." He warned dancers not to clump down on both feet after a posture, "for when they both come down together it looks as if a sack of grain had been dumped on the ground."[41] He also warned against showing off:

> There are some persons so nimble in the air that they have invented numerous leaps, sometimes doubling or tripling them . . . and upon completing these leaps they have finished so neatly on the cadence as to gain the reputation of being very fine dancers. But it has often come to pass that in performing these feats of agility they have fallen down, when laughter and jeers have ensued. Wherefore the prudent have always advised against such leaps, unless they are performed so easily that no ill consequence could befall the dancer.[42]

Galliards were also popular as music alone, without actual dancing. They were particularly written as keyboard pieces for virginals. Elizabethan composers William Byrd and John Dowland wrote excellent instrumental Galliards.

The Gavotte

Originally a Country dance, the Gavotte evolved from the Branle. Arbeau wrote, "Gavottes are a miscellany of double branles, selected by musicians and arranged in a sequence. . . . They have named this suite the gavotte."[43] In the country, Gavottes had been a rough-and-ready dance with plenty of capering and kissing. At court, the dance acquired some class and became more stately. Instead of kisses, court girls received flower bouquets.

> Gavotte music is in duple time, either 2/2 or 2/4. Its characteristic rhythm is an upbeat of two quarter notes (in 2/2). In dance suites, it is usually situated between the Sarabande and the Gigue.[44]

The Gigue

The Gigue was a haut dance, and some varieties were known as the fastest of all the Elizabethan dance forms. The Gigue's name came from Italy, either from the word *giga* which was the name of an ancient instrument, or for an old Italian word for leg.[45] This dance came to England early and quickly became Anglicized. Commonly known as a "jig," Elizabethans also recognized its spelling as Iyg, Iigge, Ieig, Iig, Ijyge, Gigge, Gig, Gygge, or Jegg. They also changed its meter from triple to duple—usually a lively 2/4.

Although the Gigue was known in Queen Elizabeth's day, it was most popular as an actual dance in Ireland, where it became known as the Irish Jig. In 1559, one of Queen Elizabeth's courtiers wrote to her that he had seen Anglo-Irish ladies dancing the Irish Jig in Galway County. He wrote that they were "very beautiful, magnificently dressed, and first-class dancers."[46]

In England it was the custom to end theater plays with a jig—singing silly or bawdy lyrics and dancing to the accompaniment of a fiddle. Possibly because of its use in this way, the jig became known as a low-class dance and does not seem to have been actually danced at the Elizabethan court. Instead, known as the Gigue, this was known at court more as an instrumental form included in instrumental dance suites and keyboard collections. As such, it had two sections that were a bit longer than most dance forms, and they often contained more imitative counterpoint than most dance forms.

The Lavolta

The Lavolta (or "Volte") was more violent than the trickiest Galliard. This was not a polite dance and for its time bordered on the obscene.

Arbeau claimed that the Lavolta came from the south of France. It was full of leaps that were a matter of some discussion and shock for more conservative dancers. Skirts flew, ladies' knees were exposed, and people sweated. Ladies who intended to dance a Lavolta decorated their garters with gold and silver ornaments because those garters *would* be seen during the dance. In France, Lavolta dancers perspired so much that the ladies at court had to change their linen after dancing it.[47]

The Lavolta shocked some people because of the body parts dancers of the opposite sex were permitted to touch during the infamous leaping turns. While the woman prepared to leap, the man helped her by putting his right hand on her back, his left underneath her bosom, and pushing her with all his might under her rump with his right thigh. Scholars believe that it was this form of the Galliard that Praetorius railed against when he called it "an invention of the devil, full of shameful and obscene gestures and immodest movements."[48]

Arbeau described the aftermath of such a strenuous workout:

> After having spun round for as many cadences as you wish, return the damsel to her place, when, however brave a face she shows, she will feel her brain reeling and her head full of dizzy whirlings; and you yourself will perhaps be no better off. I leave it to you to judge whether it is a becoming thing for a young girl to take long strides and separations of the legs, and whether in this lavolta both honour and health are not involved and at stake.[49]

In Arbeau's book, even Capriol had some reservations about the Lavolta, saying "The dizziness and whirling head would annoy me." Arbeau seems to snap at his pupil when he answers, "Then dance some other kind of dance."[50]

The Pavane

The Pavane was a stately basse dance originally from Spain that got its name from the Latin word for peacock, *pavo*.[51] Dancers moved to music in duple time in a grand procession that was often the dance that started the ball. Pavanes were set up for display. As Arbeau wrote:

> On solemn feast days the pavan is employed by kings, princes and great noblemen to display themselves in their fine mantles and ceremonial robes. They are accompanied by queens, princesses and great ladies, the long trains of their dresses loosened and sweeping behind them, sometimes borne by damsels. And it is the said pavans, played by hautboys and sack-

buts, that announce the grant ball and are arranged to last until the dancers have circled the hall two or three times.[52]

Pavane steps were simple—basically "advancing" and "retreating" with the gentlemen slightly behind their ladies but leading them by the hand. There were bows and curtseys, and some sliding steps. "Next, one of the gentlemen advanced alone, and, describing a slight curve in the middle of the ballroom, went en se pavanant (strutting like a peacock) to salute the lady opposite him. Finally, taking some backward steps, he regained his place, bowing to his own lady."[53] The music was generally made of three repeated strains of mostly slow notes. The only rule was that the music should end with a number of beats divisible by four, so that the dance would come out right. As Morley put it:

> you must cast your musicke by foure, so that if you keepe that rule it is no matter how many foures you put in your straine, for it will fall out well enough in the end, the arte of dauncing being come to that perfection . . . so that it is no great matter of what number you make your strayne.[54]

Elizabethans also danced a Passamezzo, variously known as a "Passing Measures Pavan" which was like a Pavane but not as slow.[55] There are two Passamezzo Pavanas in the *Fitzwilliam Virginal Book*, one by William Byrd.[56] Another of these dances is the "Earl of Essex Measure" from about 1570. The earl of Essex, whose name was Robert Devereaux, was a favorite of Queen Elizabeth who ultimately fell out of favor and was executed for high treason in 1601.

The Sarabande

The Elizabethan Sarabande was something like a Pavane but was in triple time instead of duple time. The name seems to be Arabic or Moorish, deriving either from the word *serbend* for song, *sarband-a* which was a lady's headdress, or *zarabanda* which meant noise.[57] Whatever its origin, Sarabande music was proud, grave, and solemn. The Sarabande was generally followed by a Gavotte.

The Tordion

The Tordion was a less violent version of a Galliard. Its steps were glided instead of kicked, hopped, and jumped. The music, however, was identical. As Arbeau wrote:

The tune of a tordion and that of a galliard are the same, and there is no difference between them save that the tordion is danced close to the ground to a light, lively beat and the galliard is danced higher off the ground to a slower, stronger beat.[58]

DANCE AND ELIZABETHAN DRESS

When reading about Elizabethan dance, it is important to remember that their clothing influenced their style of dance. Dances of peasants wearing looser clothing more conducive to their work, and dancing outside where high steps were necessary, are described as very active. Dances of the nobility who moved across polished floors, with women wearing heavy skirts, are described as more graceful and gliding.[59] Clothing of the upper classes was bulky. Women's upper bodies were encased in stiff corsets, and men's in tightly laced doublets. In addition, neck ruffs kept the heads of both sexes relatively restricted.[60] Although some dances used fancy footwork, the majority of steps were small.

On first glance it might seem that women would trip over their long skirts, but stiff petticoats held them far enough out that women were not actually in danger of falling. Their lack of more active movement came from the weight of their clothing.[61] Men were able to move about more freely. Their breeches came only to their knees or mid-thigh, and men were quite proud of the fine shape of their legs. So men's footwork was more vigorous, calling for strength in kicking, endurance, and elevation.

Dance books included rules for handling accessories such as gloves, fans, and men's swords. Dancers used their hands for leading, holding, clapping, or holding objects such as a hat, sword, or flower. However, they generally held their bodies and arms relatively still and did not usually raise their hands above the head. Gentlemen wearing long capes generally had to use one arm to keep their dress from flying up. A woman danced on the right side of her partner so that his sword would not hit her as they danced.

GENERAL DANCE COMPORTMENT

Dancing at balls was not only a test of one's dancing ability but a school of etiquette. Thus dancing masters taught manners as well as dance steps. The following are a few Elizabethan etiquette tips.

The only parts of a dancer that should touch the floor are the feet and the lady's dress. Dancers should charm their partner, not flirt with other dancers. After a dance, the man should escort his lady back to the place where he took her from and thank her for the dance. Dancers should not look at their feet when dancing. They should at least appear self-confident, even if they didn't feel that way. Dancers should be clean, neatly dressed, and dressed properly for the occasion. Men should make sure that their hose are straight and well-secured so that they wouldn't sag during dancing.[62]

When speaking to one's partner, dancers should speak "affably in a low, modest voice, your hands at your sides, neither hanging limp nor moving nervously." If the occasion arose, the dancer should "spit and blow your nose sparingly, or if needs must, turn your head away and use a fair white handkerchief."[63]

THE EFFECT OF DANCE FORMS ON MUSICAL FORMS

Renaissance dance music was some of the first music written for instruments alone. Dancing does not happen in a vacuum; music of some sort is needed. In the case of dance, the number of steps, where the leaps or hops occur, and the tempo and mood of each dance all had an enormous effect on its music. Because there were no vocal parts, music for dancing did not have to conform to a certain amount of poetry lines or rhythms derived from speech. Setting music to dance steps established patterns of strong and weak beats that helped develop present-day time signatures and phrases of regular lengths. Dance music contrasted sections where rhythms expressed in twos were interspersed with other sections expressed in threes. Over time these sections would become more formally separated and in some cases would become separate movements. Phrases, cadences, and repeated areas followed various dance patterns, thereby helping to shape dance music into recognizable, set forms that remained popular even after the dances themselves ceased to be used.

Dance music is generally short. In vocal music, poems may go on for many stanzas. But people only want to dance for a short while before taking a break or changing moods for the next dance. This set up a pattern of slow-fast–slow-fast dances that helped instrumental music develop the movements of sonatas, concertos, and symphonies in later years. Last, but certainly not least, Renaissance dance music evolved into the Baroque dance suite—a set of dances enjoyed for their music alone and never meant to be danced to.

NOTES

1. H.M. Brown and L.K. Stein, *Music in the Renaissance* (2nd ed.) (Englewood Cliffs, NJ: Prentice Hall, 1999), p. 254.

2. Ibid., p. 253.

3. B. Pattison, *Music and Poetry of the English Renaissance* (London: Methuen & Co., 1948), p. 181.

4. A.W. Atlas, *Renaissance Music* (New York: W.W. Norton, 1998), p. 692.

5. F. Keel, *Music in the Time of Queen Elizabeth* (February 24, 1914), p. 53.

6. Brown, p. 262.

7. T. Morley, *A Plaine and Easie Introduction to Practicall Musicke* (New York: Da Capo Press, 1969 [originally published in 1597]), p. 181.

8. H. Raynor, *Music in England* (Plymouth: Clarke, Doble & Brendon, 1980), p. 69.

9. J.F. Millar, *Elizabethan Country Dances* (Williamsburg, VA: Thirteen Colonies Press, 1985), pp. 12–13.

10. Ibid., p. 2.

11. F. Caroso, *Nobilta di Dame* (Julia Sutton, trans.) (Oxford: Oxford University Press, 1986 [originally published in 1600]), p. 21.

12. Millar, pp. 12–13.

13. Caroso, p. 87.

14. T. Arbeau, *Orchesography* (Mary Stewart Evans, trans.) (New York: Dover Publications, 1967 [originally published in 1589]), p. 12.

15. Ibid., pp. 12–13.

16. Ibid., pp. 15–16.

17. Ibid., p. 17.

18. Ibid., p. 18.

19. Millar, p. 2.

20. Ibid., pp. 12–13.

21. Ibid.

22. L. Horst, *Pre-Classic Dance Forms* (Princeton, NJ: Princeton Book Company, 1968), p. 25.

23. Morley, p. 181.

24. Arbeau, p. 125.

25. Horst, p. 28.

26. Ibid.

27. Arbeau, p. 129.

28. Ibid., pp. 128–153.

29. Horst, p. 109.

30. Ibid.

31. Arbeau, pp. 179–180.

32. Horst, p. 109.

33. Ibid., p. 34.

34. Ibid., p. 35.

35. Ibid.

36. Horst, p. 39.

37. Ibid., p. 43.

38. Ibid., p. 18.

39. Keel, p. 53.

40. Arbeau, p. 78.

41. Ibid., p. 89.

42. Ibid., p. 119.

43. Ibid., p. 175.

44. Horst, p. 74.

45. Ibid., p. 54.

46. Ibid., p. 55.

47. Pattison, p. 187.

48. Horst, p. 22.

49. Arbeau, p. 121.

50. Ibid., pp. 121–122.

51. Ibid.

52. Arbeau, p. 59.

53. Horst, p. 12.

54. Morley, p. 181.

55. Horst, p. 110.

56. Ibid., p. 111.

57. Ibid., p. 45.

58. Arbeau, p. 93.

59. Janelyn of Fenmere, *Letter of Dance*, Vol. 3, "Stepping on our Toes: Garb," http://www.pbm.ocm/~lindahl/lod/vol3/garb.html, p. 1 of 2.

60. Andrew Draskoy, *Western Social Dance*, "Renaissance Dance," http://www.rendance.org/site/history.html, last modified June 2, 2001, p. 1 of 4.

61. Janelyn, p. 1 of 2.

62. Ibid., pp. 118–119.

63. Ibid.

REFERENCES

Arbeau, T. *Orchesography* (Mary Stewart Evans, trans.). New York: Dover Publications, 1967 [originally published in 1589].

Atlas, A.W. *Renaissance Music*. New York: W.W. Norton, 1998.

Brown, H.M., and Stein, L.K. *Music in the Renaissance* (2nd ed.). Englewood Cliffs, NJ: Prentice Hall, 1994.

Caroso, Fabritio. *Nobilta di Dame* (Julia Sutton, trans.). Oxford: Oxford University Press, 1986, [originally published in 1600].

Draskoy, Andrew, "Renaissance Dance." *Western Social Dance*, http://www.rendance.org/site/history.html, last modified June 2, 2001.

Horst, L. *Pre-Classic Dance Forms*. Princeton, NJ: Princeton Book Company, 1968.

Janelyn of Fenmere. "Stepping on our Toes: Garb." *Letter of Dance*, Vol. 3, http://www.pbm.com/~lindahl/lod/vol3/garb.html.

Keel, F. *Music in the Time of Queen Elizabeth*. A paper read before ye sette of odd volumes February 24th, 1914. Presented to the sette by Brother John Lane bibliographer: at the 341st meeting, Tuesday, May 26th, 1914.

Millar, J. F. *Elizabethan Country Dances*. Williamsburg, VA: Thirteen Colonies Press, 1985.

Morley, T. *A Plaine and Easie Introduction to Practicall Musicke*. New York: Da Capo Press, 1969 [originally published in 1597].

Pattison, B. *Music and Poetry of the English Renaissance*. London: Methuen & Co., 1948.

Raynor, H. *Music in England*. Plymouth: Clarke, Doble & Brendon, 1980.

Chapter 8

Secular Vocal Music

QUEEN ELIZABETH AND VOCAL MUSIC

Queen Elizabeth inherited her love of singing. Her father, Henry VIII, sang, and her mother, Anne Boleyn, also sang while accompanying herself on the lute. Although the queen is usually praised for her instrument playing, there is evidence that she did sing herself, as well as encouraging others to do so. A poem from 1575 said in part:

> The Queen, the glory of our age and isle
> With royal favor bids this science smile;
> Nor hears she only others' labor'd lays,
> But, artist-like herself both sings and plays.[1]

A biography written after Elizabeth's death also attested that she had sung in the days of her youth. "Neither did she neglect Musicke, so farre forth as might beseeme a Princess, being able to sing and play on the Lute prettily and sweetly."[2] One of the glories of the Elizabethan age was its secular music for voices. Before her time, and even during her early reign, the most important vocal music was religious. The rise of secular vocal music to a fine art was largely due to her royal support.

Advice from a book of the time, *Introduction to the Skill of Music* gives Elizabethans some rules for singing that hold good in any age:

> Observe that in tuning your Voice you strive to have it clear. Also in the expressing your Voice, or tuning of Notes, let the sound come clear from

your throat, and not through your teeth, by sucking in your breath, for that is a great obstruction to the clear utterance of the Voice. . . . Lastly, observe that in tuning your first note of your Plain Song, you equal it so to the Pitch of your Voice, that when you come to your highest note, you may reach it without squeaking; and your lowest note without grumbling.[3]

ELIZABETHAN SECULAR VOCAL WORKS

Elizabethans sang or heard part-songs, consort songs, lute and voice songs, and madrigals (although many times part-songs were loosely grouped under the "madrigal" umbrella). As one scholar put it, "there was no lack of music wherever you went; in fact, it was difficult to get away from it."[4] Enormous numbers of songs attempted to satisfy the Elizabethan craving for something new to sing. Enormous amounts of poetry were written or pressed into service, supplying tunes with lyrics ranging from crude to sublime.

Text is an integral part of vocal music. Before the 1530s, most English verse had been called a "metrical swamp."[5] Although English poets had long felt that lines should have a certain number of syllables, when it came to stresses many poets tried to squash the English language into a Latin or Ancient Greek poetic scheme and found it a difficult fit.[6] Somewhere around the time of Elizabeth's birth, poets influenced from the Continent began to put their words into regular patterns of strong and weak syllables and to solidify rhyming patterns. Thus, music and poetry developed together throughout Queen Elizabeth's reign.

A problem of this era's secular vocal works is that one type of song might be described by several different names. Any work with a "dittie" (text) was a song. Part-songs had more than one vocal part but could also be called canzonets, ballades, sonets, balletts, or madrigals. Lute songs could also be known as "airs" or "ayres." Elizabethans were as loose with their nomenclature as they were with their spelling.

One thing the majority of Elizabethans agreed on was that people should learn to sing. In 1588 William Byrd listed eight reasons for singing in the preface to his *Psalmes, Sonets, and Songs*:

1. It is a knowledge easily taught and quickly learned where there is a good master and an apt scholar.
2. The exercise of singing is delightful to nature, and good to preserve the health of man.
3. It doth strengthen all parts of the breast, and doth open the pipes.

4. It is a singular good remedy for a stutting and stammering in the speech.

5. It is the best means to procure a perfect pronunciation, and to make a good orator.

6. It is the only way to know where Nature hath bestowed a good voice, and in many that excellent gift is lost because they want Art to express Nature.

7. There is not any music of instruments whatsoever comparable to that which is made of the voices of men; where the voices are good, and the same well sorted and ordered.

8. The better the voice is, the meeter it is to honour and serve God therewith; and the voice of man is chiefly to be employed to that end.

Byrd ends with the delightful couplet, "Since singing is so good a thing, I wish all men would learn to sing."[7]

Part-Songs

The heart of Elizabethan secular vocal music is the part-song. Part-song singing was one of the main recreations of choice for upper-class and middle-class Elizabethans, and in some forms it filtered down to the lower class. People in cities and in the most remote country areas all indulged in some kind of part-singing. In fact, the madrigal may also be categorized as a type of part-song.

Even the least tutored Elizabethan could indulge in "catches"—a type of song that is known today as a "round." They also sang an astounding variety of songs known as "ballads." Some ballads—particularly the lowest type of "broadside" ballads, sold on the street for a penny a page—had the tune only, with no harmony voices. Others, however, might be sung with as many as five parts. One collection of these songs, also called "sonets" and "histories" was very popular. Clement Robinson published his collection, *A Handefull of Pleasant Delites*, in 1566. Its hack-written poetry was fitted to tunes written by London composers. One contemporary wrote sarcastically that without these songs, "cuntry striplings" would lack "ditties to sing at the maydes windowes" and "cart-horses will grow discontented for want of them."[8]

Lower- and middle-class ballads were often a mix-and-match situation. The poetry book, *The Paradise of Daynty Devises* for instance, advises its buyers that the poems in this book are "aptly made to be set to any song in 5 partes, or song to instrument."[9] In other words, you might buy the book for the text but it was up to you to find tunes for the poems. Many lyrics that have become associated with certain tunes were not actually written for them. An easy example for the modern reader to understand would be how the words of "What Child is This," have become indelibly associated with the tune of "Greensleeves."

During the Elizabethan age, people of good birth or gentle rearing were expected to know how to sing part-songs at sight. Thomas Morley's *A Plaine and Easie Introduction to Practicall Musicke* opens with an embarrassing incident in which a guest must confess that he cannot join his hosts in an after-dinner sing-along entertainment because he does not know how to sing a part at first sight. His hosts, embarrassed for him, wonder how he was raised.

Persons of a serious nature might sing Elizabethan religious tunes or madrigals for after-dinner fun, but most Elizabethans were more likely to sing works of a less serious nature. Morley's book describes several types of light vocal part-songs, as follows.

The Ballette

Note that the word "ballet" appears within the word "ballette," which brings to mind a certain type of dance. Originally ballettes were sung while people danced. Now we know the ballett (or ballette) as a type of song containing the nonsense syllables "fa la la." Morley wrote one of the most famous balletts ever written—"Now is the Month of Maying." And every December, Christians sing "Deck the Halls with Boughs of Holly" (fa la la . . .).

> There is also another kind more light then this, [i.e., the villanella] which they tearme Ballete or daunces, and are songs, which being song to a dittie may likewise be daunced: these and all other kinds of light musicke saving the Madrigal are by a generall name called ayres. There be also an other kind of Ballets, commonlie called fa las . . . but a slight kind of musick it is, & as I take it devised to be daunced to voices.[10]

The lyrics of "Now is the Month of Maying" mentions a game called "barley break." Generations have sung the song wondering how to play barley break. The game consisted of at least three male-female pairs of players who played on a game field divided into three parts. One couple stayed on the right side, one on the left side, and another couple stayed in the middle, which was called Hell. The object was for the couple in Hell to "catch" the other couples to get themselves out of Hell and the

A

HANDEFULL

OF

PLEASANT DELITES:

CONTAINING

𝕾𝖚𝖓𝖉𝖗𝖎𝖊 𝖓𝖊𝖜 𝕾𝖔𝖓𝖊𝖙𝖘 𝖆𝖓𝖉 𝖉𝖊𝖑𝖊𝖈𝖙𝖆𝖇𝖑𝖊 𝕳𝖎𝖘𝖙𝖔𝖗𝖎𝖊𝖘

IN DIVERS KINDES OF MEETER.

NEWLY DEVISED TO THE NEWEST TUNES, THAT ARE NOW IN USE TO BE SUNG:

EVERIE SONET ORDERLY POINTED TO HIS PROPER TUNE.

WITH

NEW ADDITIONS OF CERTAIN SONGS,

TO VERIE LATE DEVISED NOTES,

NOT COMMONLY KNOWEN, NOR USED HERETOFORE.

BY

CLEMENT ROBINSON:

AND DIVERS OTHERS.

¶ AT LONDON, PRINTED BY RICHARD IHONES:

DWELLING AT THE SIGNE OF THE ROSE AND CROWNE, NEARE HOLBURNE BRIDGE. 1584.

LONDON:

𝕱𝖗𝖔𝖒 𝖙𝖍𝖊 𝕻𝖗𝖎𝖇𝖆𝖙𝖊 𝕻𝖗𝖊𝖘𝖘

OF

LONGMAN, HURST, REES, ORME, AND BROWN.

PRINTED BY T. DAVISON, WHITEFRIARS.

1814.

Figure 11. First page of Clement Robinson's book, A *Handefull of Pleasant Delites* (from an 1814 reprint).

other couple in. The problem was that the couple in Hell could not let go of one another's hands and had to chase the other couples that way. Meanwhile, the other couples could separate when they were hard-pressed. The game was over when the last couple ended up in Hell.[11]

The Canzonet

Canzonet and madrigal styles frequently crossed. Many canzonets are really light madrigals, and some madrigals are actually misnamed canzonets. There is no hard line to separate the two. Even Elizabethans had a hard time putting madrigals and canzonets into separate camps. The only difference Morley came up with was the serious nature of many madrigals contrasted with the less serious nature of the canzonet:

> The seconde degree of gravetie in this light musicke is given to Canzonets that is little shorte songs (wherein little arte can be shewed being made in straines, the beginning of which is some point lightlie touched, and everie straine repeated except the middle) which is in composition of the musick a counterfet of the Madrigal.[12]

The Consort Song

A consort song is a vocal work performed with one voice and a consort of instruments—usually a set of three, four, or five viols. Consort songs are related to the lute song or ayre, which is made up of one voice and one instrument. There is also some crossover with part-songs, which are usually exclusively vocal but which sometimes have one or more part-song vocal parts played on an instrument.

William Byrd wrote many forms of music, but one of his specialties was the consort song. Byrd's genius was not in merely writing consort songs; others had done this before. Byrd tied the vocal and instrumental parts together by using points of imitation. That is, the instruments either anticipated or echoed the vocal melody line. This integrates the parts, making both instruments and vocal lines equal partners in a concerted effort.

William Byrd composed about 100 consort songs. They show up in three publications; the number of consort songs in each work shows this style's decline in popularity. Byrd's 1588 work *Psalmes, Sonets, & songs of sadnes and pietie* contains 10 metrical psalm settings, 16 sonnets and pastorals, seven songs of sadness and pietie, and two funeral songs. Even though all the parts have words, Byrd wrote that the works were originally meant to be consort songs. As he put it, they were "originally made for

Instruments to expresse the harmonie, and one voyce to pronounce the dittie."[13] Scholars believe that Byrd supplied words to all the published parts so that people who were looking for part-songs could be satisfied. It was a sales technique to sell more books. His 1589 book, *Songes of Sundrye Natures, some of gravitie, and others of myrth, fit for all companies and voyces*, has fewer consort songs but more polyphonic part songs for three, four, and six voices, along with some verse anthems. His last work, published in 1611—long after Elizabeth's death in 1603—contained only two consort songs.

Byrd's consort songs generally use a serious text. Since many of the poems he picked are about either morality or mortality, the formal approach he took to fitting the words to music works very well, giving dignity and power to the poetry.

The Lute Song, or Ayre

The "air," "ayre," or "lute song" is related to the consort song in that it is a vocal part plus an instrumental part. In this case, however, the voice is accompanied by only one instrument—the lute. One problem associated with consort songs is that of balance. One voice must sing against anywhere from three to six instruments. With the lute song, one singer and one instrument achieve balance with no problem. Moreover, the possibilities for an intimate and personal performance are raised when the lutenist and singer are the same person. For amateurs, this combination was as popular as singing while strumming a guitar is today. For the less skilled, privacy during practice was highly desirable.

The Elizabethan custom of "crossover" applied to this type of song in a big way. Part-songs, consort songs, instrumental works, and madrigals could all be arranged for one voice and a lute (or gittern) part. Elizabethan lute songs were very popular, but like mushrooms they popped up rather suddenly and were gone within a 25-year period. The difference between Elizabethan lute songs and English lute songs before that time is that actual lute players began composing the lute parts. Having idiomatic lute parts was a different and thrilling experience for a performer.[14] According to scholars and music lovers alike, England's best lute song composer was John Dowland.

John Dowland was not a cheery sort of person, and many of his works have texts so sad that they border on the morbid. The music, however, is so beautifully written that his *First Book of Songes or Ayres*, published in 1597, was reprinted four times during Dowland's lifetime. The parts to this book were printed so that everyone could sit around a table and read their part from the same book at the same time. Like Byrd, Dowland emphasized that the parts to each song could be played exclusively on instruments, sung exclusively with voices, performed with a voice and lute, or performed with voice and either a whole or broken consort of instruments.

By the time Dowland wrote his ayres, English poetry had become easier to set to music. The texts were relatively uncomplicated and came in regular phrases of eight (or sometimes six) syllables, which made them much easier to fit into a musical phrase scheme. A case in point is this typically melancholy poetic text from Dowland's *Second Booke of Songs or Ayres*, published in 1600:

> If fludes of teares could cleanse my follies past,
> And smoakes of sighes might sacrifice for sinne,
> If groning cries might salve my fault at last,
> Or endles mone, for error pardon win,
> Then would I cry, weepe, sigh, and ever mone,
> Mine errors, faults, sins, follies past and gone
>
> I see my hopes must wither in their bud,
> I see my favours are no lasting flowers,
> I see that woords will breede no better good,
> Then losse of time and lightening but at houres,
> Thus when I see then thus I say therefore,
> That favours hopes and words, can blinde no more.[15]

By Dowland's day, some poems were written with the idea that they would be set to music. Some were written with the music in mind. Of the second type of poem, many were set to popular dance tunes. One of Dowland's most famous songs, "Flow my Tears," from 1600, was known as a "contrafact"—text written to fit music that already existed. In this case, the tune already existed as Dowland's *Lachrimae* pavan. The first four verses show the unmistakably melancholy mood of the work:

> Flow my teares, fall from your springs,
> Exilde, for ever let me morne
> Where night's black bird her sad infamy sings,
> There let me live forlorne
>
> Downe, vain lights, shine you no more,
> No nights are dark enough for those

That in dispaire their last fortuns deplore.
Light doth but shame disclose

Never may my woes be relieved,
Since pitie is fled,
And teares, and sighes, and groans my wearie dayes
Of all joyes have deprived.

From the highest spire of contentment
My fortune is throwne,
And feare, and griefe, and paine for my deserts
Are my hopes, since hope is gone.[16]

Four of Dowland's melodies from his first book of ayres began as Galliard dance music, which he also composed. The text "Can shee excuse my wrongs" was put to the music of "The Earl of Essex Galliard."[17] Others supplied with vocal text and arranged for voice and lute were the "Frog Galliard," "Sir John Souch his Galliard," and "Captain Piper's Galliard."[18] Corantos and sarabands also supplied melodies for songs later arranged as lute songs.

The idea of conceiving the music first and later fitting the text to a preexisting melody was a great departure from former eras. In the past, the written word was paramount, and the poem came first. By late Elizabethan times, music was no longer following the text—rather, the text was following the music. In this, the lute song looked to the future when instrumental and vocal music would stand on equal footing.

The Neapolitan

Another secular part-song is so closely related to the Canzonet that even Morley has trouble differentiating them. Mainly, the Neapolitan is more Italian in nature. But, as Morley says, if you know Canzonets, you also know Neapolitans.

Of the nature of these [counterfeits of the madrigal] are the Neapolitans or Canzone a la Napolitana, different from them in nothing saving in name, so that whosoever knoweth the nature of the one must needs know the other also, and if you thinke them worthie of your paines to compose them, you have a patterne of them in Luco Marenzo and John Feretti, who as it should seeme hath imploied most of all his study that way.[19]

The Villenelle

The Villenelle were Country songs that were both fun and funny. As light as air, villenelle lyrics and music were viewed by Elizabethans as "fluff" music. Morley does point out that sometimes a good tune is not judged on its own merits but gets sneered at and ignored simply because it's a villenelle.

> The last degree of gravetie (if they have any at all) is given to the villanelle or countrie songs which are made only for the ditties sake, for so they be aptly set to expresse the nature of the ditty, the composer (though he were never so excellent) will not sticke to take many perfect cordes of one kind together, for in this kind they thinke it no fault (as being a kind of keeping decorum) to make a clownish musicke to a clownish matter, & though many times the dittie be fine enough yet because it carrieth that name villanella they take those disallowances as being good enough for plow and cart.[20]

SECULAR VOCAL SONG IN QUEEN ELIZABETH'S WORLD

Elizabethans sang or heard secular singing outside their homes at festivals, plays, and even during some dances. Elizabethan citizens of all classes enjoyed numerous festivals, from country fairs to highly organized government-sponsored celebrations. These festivals served as a substitute for Catholic feast days of former times and simultaneously bolstered popular support for queen and country.

When Elizabeth's father dissolved the monasteries, all the traditional saint's days and feast days of Catholicism went with them. But people without any holidays are not happy people. The monarchy therefore began to replace church festivities with government holidays, many deliberately set at times of the year normally associated with Catholic festivities. Instead of religious vocal music, government-sponsored celebrations used secular vocal music.[21]

The Elizabethan festival year fell into two large categories. Winter was the time of "Revels," and summer was the time of the "Progresses." The season of Revels began on November 17, known as Accession Day—the day that Elizabeth was crowned queen of England. It was also the traditional day that the queen returned the court to London from her summer Progresses. Revels included the Christmas season, New Year's, Epiphany, Candlemas (February 2), and Shrove Tuesday (also known as "Mardi Gras," the day before Lent begins). The Royal Progresses took place in summer and allowed the people of England to view their sovereign in an era that had no television or photographs. It also allowed Elizabeth to keep a close watch on her kingdom and to keep her nobles closely tied to her so that they would not be tempted to join any rebellious power plays. Elizabeth's visits included her entire court. They might stay for a week, a month, or six weeks at a particular noble's manor. During that time, "mythological and pastoral entertainments, fireworks, water pageants (with barges instead of wagons), banquets, Masques, hunting, and other rural pastimes"[22] ensured that the queen and her courtiers would not become bored. All these activities included secular vocal singing.

An Elizabethan "Progress" Entertainment

In 1591, Queen Elizabeth's last stop on her Summer Progresses was a four-day stay at the estate of Edward Seymour, the earl of Hertford. For various reasons, Edward and his family had been in and out of favor with the queen, so it was important that she have a good time. Edward therefore pulled out all the stops. Getting ready for his extra company, Edward added two new wings to his house. He refurnished an upper gallery for the queen's apartment and added a new fireplace and chimney. Outside, he built a huge artificial lake with a model ship and a castle on a raft. Around the lake he built over 20 temporary structures for nobles, as well as a large hall for knights, ladies, and gentlemen. Hidden among the shrubbery were utility houses, which included a pantry, storage areas for dishes and linen, a wine cellar, a storage area for thousands of candles, a larder, a spicery, a dairy storage area, and a pastry-making facility with five new ovens. He also built a kitchen with four ranges, two "boiling houses" for meat, and another kitchen for extra meals if needed. All the extra cleaning people, cooks, and their helpers had temporary lodgings, as did the queen's footmen, their friends, her armed guard, her steward and his helpers, and her gentlemen-in-waiting.[23]

When the queen arrived on September 20, a poet dressed in green saluted her with a Latin oration of 65 "hexameters" all glowing with praise for the queen. Afterward, six "virgins"—men and boys dressed in costumes—strewed her path with flowers and sweet-smelling herbs and sang "a sweete song of six parts." When the queen and her entourage came to the manor, Edward's family and household greeted the queen who was then taken to her rooms for a short rest. She was awakened by a boom from the artificial ship on the artificial lake. The queen loved it—she liked loud noises. After supper, a consort of six musicians entertained her with music. She liked one of the works—a Pavan—so much that she personally gave it a name.

The next day was stormy, so all the planned entertainments for the day were called off. By lunchtime the weather had cleared. The meal took place in a structure overlooking the artificial lake while listening to a variety of consort music. At about 4 P.M. the queen and the courtiers took seats under a canopy by the edge of the artificial lake. A group of sea-beings swam or waded across, while other sea-beings played trumpets, or Scottish Jigs on cornets from a floating barge.

Suddenly some forest creatures emerged from the bushes, led by "Sylvanus." The forest creatures and sea-beings engaged in a mock battle. Sea-beings pulled forest creatures into the water. Forest creatures fired "darts" from tiny bows, and sea-beings retaliated with "squirts." Finally, peace was restored, and all the actors retreated to the sound of trumpets and cornets. The queen was so amused that she rewarded all the actors handsomely before retiring.

On September 22, the queen rose and opened her casement window to find three waiting musicians who immediately began singing the "Plowman's Song" to her. After lunch, she watched a sporting match—tennis, or perhaps handball—between two teams of Edward's servants. After supper the queen watched a fireworks display while she and her court snacked on "sugar sweet" dishes brought in by 200 gentlemen and lit by 100 torchbearers.

On September 25, the queen woke to three cornet players performing "fantastic dances." Actors dressed as the Fairy Queen and her Maids danced about the garden singing a six-part song accompanied by a mixed consort. The queen liked this so much that she made them repeat it three times, calling her lords and ladies to come and see it. When the queen and her court were ready to leave, all the performers came to bid her goodbye—the sea-beings, forest creatures, Poets, Fairy Queen, and Fairy Maids. As the queen left, she heard a song of farewell sung accompanied by instruments from musicians hidden among the bushes along her route. She was so impressed that she stopped her coach to listen more clearly.

The earl was a hit. Elizabeth told him that she was so pleased "as hereafter hee should finde the rewarde thereof in her especiall favour. . . ."[24] His company of actors was invited to perform at court, which they did in January 1592.

Elizabethan Boys' Companies

Elizabethans heard secular vocal music in plays, where stage directions called for certain songs. Men sang the songs calling for a male voice, but since women were not allowed to be actors, young boys played female parts and also sang songs calling for a female voice. Some boys played in adult companies, such as those performing Shakespeare's plays. But there were also acting companies made up entirely of boys, known as Boys' Companies.

In England, boys trained in choir schools had traditionally sung the top voice in church music. When the Catholic Church was supplanted by the Church of England during the reign of Henry VIII, only the largest choir schools survived the Dissolution of the Abbeys. These boys now sang for the Church of England. Boys entered choir schools at the age of seven or eight, and received a secular education as well as instruction in singing, instrument playing, and acting.[25]

Acting in plays was only a part of the boys' education before Queen Elizabeth's reign, but it grew into an Elizabethan institution. The two main children's companies were the Children of St. Paul's and the Blackfriars, which used boys from both Windsor Chapel and the Children of the Chapel Royal.[26]

During Elizabeth's reign, boys were chosen for their voices and looks. They were not asked about their religion. In fact, one of the choirmasters at St. Paul's was an outspoken Catholic. But because of his excellent training of the boys, he was protected by the Crown from any government harassment.[27]

Early performances were for the upper classes and royalty, and were part of the Christmas Revels. In order for the boys to perform under realistic conditions, a large hall was rented for rehearsals and an audience bought tickets to these "dress rehearsals." Boys' Companies put on plays with singing and instrumental music—all supplied by the boys. The play might be on a stage, but sometimes was on the floor level. In either case there was usually a raised stand for the boys to sit on when they were playing instruments.[28]

At the Revels performance, the audience sat at long banquet tables if the play took place during a meal. Otherwise, audience members might sit in tiered rows like grandstand seats. Usually the audience sat on three sides of the action. However, if the play was put on in the middle of the hall, the actors might be surrounded on all four sides. Of course the upper-class audience had servants, who stood wherever they could find a spot.[29]

Eventually, the plays became public for a paying audience. Each play contained an average of four or five songs. Sometimes words to the songs are included in the plays, but often there is only an indication that a song would be sung at that time. Scholars believe that means that any fashionable song could be inserted, not necessarily something written specifically for the play. Types of songs identified with Boys' Companies include servant songs, pastoral or supernatural songs, choral and religious songs, and complaints.

Servant songs were comical and had anywhere from two to four singers. Many times the words mocked the upper classes, and sometimes involved some sort of practical joke.[30] Pastoral or supernatural songs were usually sung as a chorus. In these songs the boys would appear as fairies, muses, nymphs, or a group of shepherds.[31] Religious songs were also choral, and were natural for the boys who, after all, sang for religious services every week of their lives.[32] Sometimes the song would be a prayer, as part of the play. Other times it would be sung at the end of a play, calling for the Queen's health and for blessings on her nobles and the country.

The Complaint was a very popular type of Boys' Company song. Usually a boy sang solo, masquerading as a female character who is having some reversal of fate. Usually the character has been deserted, or someone has died, or the character is frustrated in love. These songs were accompanied by a viol consort and were set up in a very formal way, with stock texts using alliterations such as "grievously groaning" and "weeping and wailing." At the end, the character pleads for the comfort of death. It is not clear whether adult musicians played the viols, but it is just as likely that the boys played the instruments. Occasionally the singer might be accompanied by a lute or a keyboard instrument instead of a viol consort.[33]

As already noted, Boys' Company children learned to play instruments as well as to sing and act. They played instrumental music before the play began, between the acts, and after the play's conclusion. There may also have been some music accompanying action in the plays, since some plays indicate that music was played offstage.[34]

Through no fault of the boys, their plays became increasingly political. The political satire became so inflammatory that the troupes fell in and out of favor at various times during Queen Elizabeth's reign. After her reign, the Boys' Companies went out of favor and were discontinued.

The Elizabethan Masque

The masque most likely came to England from an Italian tradition. Traveling Italian actors known as Commedia dell'Arte drew upon well-known "stock" characters to make their plays. Characters depicted, such as a blustering Captain, a Miser, a sweet and innocent but slightly bird-brained girlfriend, or an old man hopelessly in love with a young girl were all very familiar to Italian audiences. Indeed, they are familiar today as characters in television sitcoms. Commedia dell'Arte actors wore specific masks for each of these characters.[35] Upper-class Englishmen who had visited the continent undoubtedly saw these plays and brought the idea back to England.

Elizabethan England had wonderful plays, but did not have a thriving opera scene. The masque, which included a plot, singing, costumes, and dancing, was England's answer to opera during Queen Elizabeth's reign. It was an upper-class entertainment, and in Elizabeth's day the masque was used to glorify her reign.

When Queen Elizabeth visited the various areas of her realm during her annual "progresses," her court was wherever she was staying. Masques, either indoor or outdoor spectacles, were often part of the entertainment. Many times masques had an idealized pastoral scene. Other times a masque might have an historical background. But even though the queen herself did not join in the festivities as later monarchs did, she was the star.

In a typical masque, the queen was seen as a pure and unattainable being—the Virgin Queen, or a sort of goddess. Placed firmly on a pedestal, the queen could be part of the festivity, a caring overseer of her people, and at the same time revered and special. The entertainment was a sort of offering to this perfect, remote being. Plots might include idealized versions of country life with the queen as Ceres, goddess of the harvest. Or actors might perform a masque based on Paris having to choose the most beautiful among Venus, Juno, and Athene. In this case, Paris would defer to the queen and choose her instead.[36]

THE MADRIGAL

The Renaissance madrigal was the dominant form of secular polyphonic vocal music in its time. An Italian innovation, madrigals brought the combination of expressive text and expressive music to its highest point. When Elizabethan music is mentioned, often the first thing that springs to mind is the Elizabethan madrigal. Needing no instrumental accompaniment, the Elizabethan madrigal is accessible to elite groups of singers from high school age through adult professionals. Madrigal singing societies the world over perform these delightful works—particularly at Christmas time, for Madrigal Dinners.

Madrigals originated in Italy, where the music fitted itself to the form of the poetry. Most of the poetry had two- or three-line stanzas followed by a refrain of two lines. The music that was fitted to the poetry's stanzas was strophic; that is, the same tune was used for all stanzas (just as hymn verses use different words to the same tune). The refrain had music of its own.[37]

The Word "Madrigal"

Scholars know that the word "madrigal" was used in Italy in the 1100–1200s to mean an unusually complicated composition. Later, still in Italy, the word came to mean a type of poem—a *madriale* or *mandriale*. When Franco-Flemish composers began moving into Italy and working there, they reactivated the word as a musical term. This time the term stayed in the world of music, and in 1533 the word *madrigali* was first used in a printed music title.[38] Some scholars think the word is older than the 1100s and that it comes from the root word *madre* meaning "mother." They speculate that it may have originally applied to musical works praising the Virgin Mary, mother of Jesus, or it may have been a reference to singing in one's native language—their "mother tongue."[39]

The Italian Madrigal and the English Madrigal

The Italian madrigal was an all-vocal work (using no instruments) for four, five, or six voices. Italian madrigals evolved from a long tradition of Italian secular polyphonic vocal music. Their immediate ancestor, the frottola, wrapped music around long poems of unrequited love. To Italian composers, the poetic words were all-powerful. Music took the form of the poetry—words were not composed to fit the tunes. The term for this is *formes fixes*. Although Elizabethan madrigals began moving away from such a one-sided relationship, Italian madrigals always stressed the text.

Italian madrigal texts were serious, many of them contemplating death or exploring feelings of grief over the loss of a beloved figure. Over time, one particular poet's works overshadowed all others, as Italian madrigal writers reached back to the 1300s to set the poetry of Petrarch.

Petrarch's poetry was beautifully constructed and heart-rending. As Franco-Flemish composers began to come into Italy, hired for their musical expertise, they combined their skills in polyphonic voice writing with the expressive poetry they found in their adopted country. The result was madrigals of stunning beauty. Later, as the Franco-Flemish teachers passed their skills on to their willing Italian pupils, madrigals began to express the text through harmonies stretching the tonal scheme to an unheard of extreme. Some of the works of its most extreme composer, Carlo Gesualdo, approach atonality (music without a tonal center).

Besides using different languages and concentrating on different moods, the most striking difference between Italian and English madrigals is that the music instead of the words became the focus of the English form. This was a distinct difference from any Continental treatment, where the words were first and foremost.

The English madrigal reflected its times and its audience as perfectly as music ever has. The first published book of madrigals came to England just after the defeat of the Spanish Armada. Because of the joyous feeling of optimism in England at the time, the tone of Elizabethan madrigals is distinctly lighter than that of their European counterparts. The music is generally lively and as light as a souffle. The words, too, moved away from sadness and death toward springtime and young love.

Far from considering the madrigal a serious work, Thomas Morley, one of England's best madrigal composers, defined it as one of the lighter forms of music. He does not stint to declare that in the writing of madrigals, English composers are on a par with European composers. In his *Plaine and Easie* book, he praises the variety with which the English madrigal shows the human condition:

> As for the musick it is next unto the Motet, the most of artificiall and to men of understanding most delightfull. If therefore you will compose in this kind you must possesse your selfe with an amorus humor . . . so that you must in your musicke be wavering like the wind, sometime wanton, sometime drooping, sometime grave and staide, otherwhile effeminat, you may maintaine points and revert them, use triples and shew the verie uttermost or (of) your varietie, and the more varietie you shew the better shal you please. In this kind our age excelleth, so that if you would imitate any, I would appoint you these for guides: Alfonso Ferrabosco for deepe skill, Luca Marenzo for good ayre and fine invention, Horatio Vecchi, Stephano Venturi, Ruggiero Giovanelli, and John Croce, with divers others who are verie good, but not so generallie good as these.[40]

The English took a foreign form of music and naturalized it to their taste. For the first time since Dunstable in the medieval era, England began turning out better music than that of the rest of Europe. The English wanted less of the extreme chromaticism of the Italian harmonies. They wanted parts that ordinary people could sing rather than professionals. They wanted lyrics in English, fewer of them, and happier ones. But mostly they wanted fuller, more naturally flowing music than they had from Italy.

Italian Madrigals in England

Although madrigals were not commonly known in England before 1588, some had made their way to the upper classes earlier. Queen Elizabeth had Italian musicians in her court, and they knew about madrigals from their homeland. Some were singers or instrumentalists, but at least one—Alfonso Ferrabosco—was a composer living at the Elizabethan court. Alfonso spent at least 16 years in England (1562–1578), and possibly more. His son grew up largely in the English court, and Alfonso had other relatives there as well. Although Alfonso was not a major composer in his native country, he was considered a fine musician in England. Alfonso's own madrigals had been sung at court for some time before 1588. Certainly courtiers, and probably the queen herself, had heard these compositions with their Italian lyrics. Besides his own works, Alphonso had manuscripts of other Italian composers and their madrigals, which would have circulated in manuscript among courtiers.

Extant is a set of part books that have the royal arms of Queen Elizabeth on their covers, dated 1564. These part books contain about 70 Italian works (including madrigals) and 17 French chansons. Although it is unknown whether Queen Elizabeth actually used the part books for recreational singing, she must have been aware of their contents. This set of part books proves that the English court had Italian madrigals for more than 20 years before the "madrigal craze" started.[41]

Besides court circles, Italian madrigals came into England by other means. An indispensable part of any young gentleman's education was the "Grand Tour" of Europe (see Chapter 1). A cornerstone of that tour was Italy. Even though it was a center of Catholicism, Italy was also the center of the Roman Empire, which made it historically, if not politically, correct. In musical matters, the English had a fascination with Italian styles. During their Grand Tour, young English gentlemen studied music from Italian masters, commissioned works, and brought instruments and manuscripts back home. Undoubtedly, some of those manuscripts were madrigals. All of this learning and collecting spread throughout the upper class, priming the pump for later developments.

Madrigals didn't spread faster in England in part because they weren't published there. Ferrabosco's madrigals and other works were published in Italy; only later would his works be fitted with English words and put into print in England. In another instance, Henry Fitzalan, earl of Arundel, ordered madrigals from Innocentio Alberti in 1566. Although they were widely copied, the copies were handwritten and circulated only among his peers. Since the lyrics were Italian, some of his peers copied the notes only, without the words. They played the music on instruments (in direct contrast to Italian taste) and called them "fantasies." The public never saw or heard any of these madrigals.

Lack of suitable text might have also hampered early efforts at setting madrigals in English. Italians had a rich heritage of medieval and Renaissance poetry, including Petrarch, Tasso, Dante, and a number of other widely read poets. Thus, Italians had no lack of suitable poetry to frame their music. In England, poets Sir Philip Sidney and Edmund Spenser called the state of English poetry in their times a "rakehellye route of our ragged rhymers."[42] English poetry had to grow up along with the English madrigal.

Composers (particularly those who performed in the Chapel Royal) would have had access to some of the Italian madrigals circulating in court. But the match that lit the wildfire known as the "madrigal craze" came from Nicholas Yonge.

Musica Transalpina

Nicholas Yonge has been described as a lay-clerk, a London businessman, and a musician who sang at St. Paul's Cathedral. Certainly he was an enthusiast of Italian music. Although he didn't do too much traveling himself, Yonge collected manuscripts of Italian music from merchants who knew they had an easy sale with each new work they brought him. Merchants soon discovered that Yonge was especially keen to collect Italian madrigals. After a while, his house became "madrigal central," and a musical club of like-minded musical enthusiasts had formed itself.

The central item of Yonge's group was singing his imported madrigals. As he explained in the Dedication page of Musica Transalpina:

> since I first began to keepe house in this Citie [London], it hath been no small comfort unto mee, that a great number of Gentlemen and Merchants of good accompt (as well of this realme as of forreine nations) have taken in good part such entertainment of pleasure, as my poor abilitie was able to afford them, both by the exercise of Musicke daily used in my house, and by furnishing them with Bookes of that kinde yeerely sent me out of

Italy and other places, which beeing for the most part Italian Songs, are for sweetness of Aire, verie well liked of all, but most in account with them that understand that language.[43]

Yonge understood that the English were resistant to singing in another language. England had a long and unhappy tradition with foreign languages. Latin had been the language of rule during the Roman occupation of the British Isles. When the Romans left, the Saxons moved in and drove the original English-speaking population west. Then in 1066 the French-speaking Normans conquered the Saxon-speaking English population. Not until Chaucer's *Canterbury Tales* would there be anything like an "English language," which would remain the amalgam it still is today. If for no other reason, Yonge realized that even the most beautiful music would remain unsung if it had words in a foreign language. As he put it, "As for the rest [those who did not understand Italian], they doe either not sing them at all, or at the least with little delight."[44]

Yonge and his friends decided to put the Italian poetry into English as best they could and publish the result, along with the best English songs they could find. He tried to keep both the accents of the original Italian words and as much of the sense of the original poetry as possible. He claimed that those who tried singing the "Englished" words "affirmed the accent of the words to be well mainteined, the descant not hindred, (though some fewe notes altred) and in everie place the due decorum kept."[45] The resulting music collection was published in 1588 as *Musica Transalpina*, which means "music from across the Alps."

Yonge's collection offered the English public madrigals borrowed from Flemish anthologies of Italian madrigals, with their texts translated from Italian to English, as well as several of Alfonso Ferrabosco's works translated into English and two works by William Byrd. *Musica Transalpina* contains madrigals for four voices, for five voices, and for six voices. The list of works is a "Who's Who" of Italian composers including such luminaries as Luca Marenzio, Orlando di Lasso, Fillipe de Monte, and Giaches de Vert. Titles are listed in both Italian and English, but all the lyrics are in English.

In one of history's rare intersections, *Musica Transalpina* couldn't have come along at a luckier time. When Queen Elizabeth ascended the throne in 1558, she knew that there would be trouble from Spain and France. Elizabeth's older sister Mary Tudor had been married to the Spanish monarch Philip II, who now had a claim on Elizabeth's throne—and had actually proposed to Elizabeth at one time. Elizabeth's cousin, Mary Queen of Scots, also had a claim to the English throne, a claim that was supported by France. Both Mary Queen of Scots and Philip were Catholic, so they were likely to get financial and moral support from every Catholic nation in Europe as well as the Vatican. For 30 years Queen Elizabeth managed a balancing act among her country and the countries of France and Spain.

This delicate political dance fell apart when Elizabeth had Mary Queen of Scots executed. Philip had been building a fleet of warships—called an Armada—with which to invade England and take the throne. The invasion started in the spring of 1588, with 130 Spanish ships and 30,000 men headed for English shores. For weeks the English waited in agonized anticipation as weather and politics delayed the coming invasion. Finally, the Armada anchored at Calais, France (just across the English Channel) on August 6, 1588. On August 7, the British slipped in and set fire to as many ships as possible. On August 8, the English and Spanish fleets engaged in battle, and the Spanish Armada was repelled.

Whether the defeat of the Spanish Armada was due to the fighting or whether bad weather actually caused the Spanish Armada to retreat is still debated, but the result was wild elation in England. They had faced a major power and driven it away. The entire country was ready to celebrate. *Musica Transalpina* was published in November by Thomas East, just as the country was ready for something wonderful to sing.

The works are presented in part book form. That means if a person wanted the entire collection, they would have to buy six part books, but each singer would have his own individual part to sing from. Although the first four books had parts to all the madrigals, the fifth book only contained parts for the five- and six-part madrigals, and the sixth book only contained parts for the six-part madrigals. This meant that the books were not necessarily a soprano book, an alto book, and so on. The first book would be the highest part, and the sixth book would contain all basso parts. But book four would contain a mix of voice parts—lowest for the four-part madrigals, higher for the five- and six-part madrigals.

Yonge's collection was available to anyone with the money to purchase it. This was the first chance that the lower gentry and middle class had to enjoy this sort of music making. They liked what they had and wanted more. England was entering a golden age and wanted music of its own to celebrate it.

The Madrigal Craze

The next book of madrigals published was Watson's *Italian Madrigals Englished* (1590), also a collection of Italian madrigals fitted with English

The Table of all the madrigales contayned in these
bookes, with the names of their seuerall authors, and originalls.

Of 4.

These that bee certaine signes. I	Questi ch'inditio.	Noe:Fagnient.
The faire Diana. II	Non piu Diana.	Giouan de Macque.
Ioy so delights my hart. III	Gioia s'abond'all cor.	} Gio:Petraloysio Preneſtino.
False Loue now ſhoot. IIII	Amor ben puoi.	
O griefe, if yet my griefe. V	Dolor, ſe'l mio dolor.	Baldeſſar Donato.
As in the night. VI	Come la notte.	Baldeſſar Donato.
In vayne hee ſeekes for beau-tie. VII	Per diuina bellezza.	Filippo di Monte.
What meaneth Loue to neſt him. VIII	Perche s'annida Amore.	} Gio: Petraloyſio Preneſtino.
Sweet Loue when hope. IX	Amor quando fioriua.	
Lady that hand. X	Donna la bella mano.	Mare' Anconio Pordenone.
Who will aſcend. XI	Chi ſalira.	Giaches de Vuert.
Lady your looke ſo gentle. XII	Donna bella e gentile.	Cornelio Verdonch.

Of 5.

From what part of the Hea-uen. XIII	In qual parte del ciel.	Filippo di Montte.
The ſecond part. XIIII	Per diuina bellezza 2.pars.	
In euery place. XV	Ogni luogo.	
Thirſis to dye deſired. XVI	Tirſi morir volea.	
The ſecond part. XVII	Freno Tirſi il deſio, 2.pars.	} Luca Marenzio.
The third part. XVIII	Coſi moriro. 3.pars.	
Suſanna fayre. XIX	Suſann' vn iour.	Orlando di Laſſo.
Suſanna fayre. XX	Suſann' vn iour.	Alfonſo Feraboſco.
When ſhall I ceaſe. XXI	To the note of Chi per vei non.	Noe: Faignient.
I muſt depart. XXII	Io partiro.	Luca Marenzio.
I ſaw my lady weeping. XXIII	Vidi pianger Madonna.	Alfonſo Feraboſco.
The ſecond part. XXIIII	Come dal ciel.	
So gracious. XXV	Sci tanto gratioſa.	}
Cruell vnkind. XXVI	Donna crudel.	Giouan Ferrettie
What doth my prety dar-ling. XXVII	Che fa.hoggil mio ſole.	Luca Marenzio.
Sleepe mine only Iewell. XXVIII	Sonno ſcendoſti, 1. pars.	} Stefano Felis.
The ſecond part. XXIX	Tu la ritorni, 2.pars.	
Sound out my voyce. XXX	To the note of Veſtiu'icolli.	Gianetto Paleſtina.

Liquid

Figure 12. List of madrigals included in Nicolas Yonge's *Musica Transalpina*.

The Table.

¶ FINIS.

words. This book was mostly a collection of Luca Marenzio's madrigals—
23 of his works and 5 by other composers. Watson was an influential man
in literary circles, and his interest in madrigals stemmed from his interest
in the poetry. Despite his love of Italian poetry, Watson's English translations were not necessarily respectful of text meanings, even though they
followed Italian poetic forms.[46]

The first native madrigal set was published in 1593. By 1597–1598 the
publication of madrigals in English—either using imported tunes or tunes
written by English composers—became a flood. Yonge published a second
collection of "Englished" madrigals entitled *Musica Transalpina II* in 1597.
These madrigals were lighter than the first and fewer in number. Although the original had 57 works, the second book contained only 24.
In that same year, Thomas Morley issued a collection entitled *Selected
Canzonets*. In spite of the title, scholars agree that Morley's canzonets are
really light madrigals. This was followed by another book by Morley entitled *Selected Madrigals*, published in 1598. Weelkes had two books of
madrigals published, and Wilbye, Kirbye, and Farnaby also had one book
each published.

Text and the English Madrigal

One complaint sometimes voiced with regard to madrigals is that the
vocal polyphony obscures the text. The English madrigal sidestepped this
criticism in several ways. Each line of poetry coincides with a line of
musical phrasing, so that the listener can follow the beginning of a line
of music with the beginning of a line of poetry. Rhythmic contrasts among
the voices actually help the listener to get the meaning of a text, even
though it sometimes becomes a game of musical "hide and seek," with
bits of text popping out among the voices. Generally, each voice will
repeat the text once or twice so that the possibilities of hearing the text
are increased without sacrificing musical interest.[47]

As one scholar observed, a madrigal composer could get away with
almost anything he wanted in a madrigal and still have the text understood as long as "each coherent phrase or line of the text must be stated
at least once either in homophony by several voices, or by one voice in
a point of imitation that does not overlap with another voice until the
phrase is complete, or by one voice against other voices singing only one
syllable."[48]

The reality of English madrigal text is that most people are attracted
to the music first and only later to the words. Elizabethans probably

learned the words through repetition, just as one learns the lyrics to some types of rock music today. They probably didn't get the words right the first time, but by the fifth time a person has heard the same work, they probably have a pretty good idea of the lyrics.

Even as the English madrigal flourished and developed musically, their texts were somewhat slighted. In England, poetic texts were often not very good apart from their music. Few major English poets had their works set. Spenser and Thomas Campion were two exceptions. Shakespeare's words were set to vocal music, but it was to other types of part-songs and not to madrigal music. When it came to madrigal texts, the English failed to realize greatness in their midst even when it presented itself. In an age of fine sonnets, surprisingly few were ever set to music. Of all the major Elizabethan madrigalists, only five set sonnets into madrigals.[49] Instead, composers relied on poetic texts chosen by or even written by their amateur friends. Writing poetry was just as much a part of a gentleman's general education as was knowledge of music, but quality suffered. When reading the poetry of English madrigals, readers must not be dismayed at the quality of the poems themselves, because most of them were not meant to stand alone, without music.[50] The music appears all the more fresh and original because the poetry was somewhat conventional and its subjects tended toward stale ideas of lover's pangs.

Atmosphere—contrasting shades of emotion and shifting moods—was important to English madrigal composers. As one scholar noted, "Good music can be made from indifferent poetry."[51]

Of course not all poetry was substandard; somewhere between pathetic laments and light-as-air lyrics stood the narrative madrigal. This interesting and informative madrigal type put slices of Elizabethan life into a musical setting. Thomas Morley was particularly successful at this type of madrigal. His "Arise, get up my dear" describes a wedding celebration with "merry maidens squealing" and "spice-cake, sops in wine."[52]

"Ethical madrigals" contemplated life in well-written verse. John Wilbye set the following lyrics, which sound a great deal like Shakespeare's sentiments about all the world being a stage:

> Happy, o happy he, who not affecting
> The endless toils attending worldly cares,
> With mind reposed, all discontents rejecting,
> In silent peace his way to heaven prepares
> Deeming his life a Scene, the world a Stage
> Whereon man acts his weary Pilgrimage[53]

Another type of madrigal that paid attention to the quality of its text was the "elegy" madrigal, composed upon the death of a teacher or a friend. The following words were set to madrigal music by Orlando Gibbons:

> Ne'er let the Sun with his deceiving light
> Seek to make glad these watery eyes of mine;
> My sorrow suits with melancholy night,
> I joy in dole, in languishment I pine.
> My dearest friend is set, he was my Sun,
> With whom my mirth, my joy and all is done.[54]

When a text seemed suitable for a madrigal setting, a composer might use the same text for a setting of his own composition. For instance, a work originally set by William Byrd in 1588 entitled "Penelope that longed for the sight" was set again by John Mundy to a tune of his own composition in 1594. In another instance, there are two settings of "Hark, did you ever hear" in the same book of madrigals, by two different composers. Though it may be a bit confusing, nobody minded a resetting of text. It was a common Elizabethan practice.

The most successful poems are those that give a composer the chance to use the most variety in the music. This variety could be in the music's texture in which areas of polyphony and homophony alternate. It might show up in flexible rhythms. Or the variety might be in harmonies that outline changing moods of the text or that highlight a particular word.

Madrigalisms

There is one area in which the English madrigal copies the Italian, to great effect, and that is the use of word painting, known in this style as "madrigalisms." Although the music of all madrigals closely follows its text, madrigalisms reflect text in a heightened way. Both English and Italian madrigals used these to great effect. A case in point is Thomas Weelkes's madrigal, "As Vesta was from Latmos Hill Descending." The text is:

> As Vesta was from Latmos hill descending,
> She spied a maiden Queen the same ascending,
> Attended on by all the shepherds' swain,
> To whom Diana's darlings came running down amain,
> First two by two, then three by three together,

Leaving their goddess all alone, hasted thither;
And mingling with the shepherds of her train,
With mirthful tunes her presence entertain.
Then sang the shepherds and nymphs of Diana:
    Long live fair Oriana.[55]

On the word "descending" the music descends; on "ascending" the music goes up. The words "running down amain" are sung to eighth notes descending. "Two by two" is a duet between two voices. "Three by three" is a trio of three voices. On the word "together" the trio sings in homophonic togetherness. And the words "all alone" leave a single voice singing. On the last line, the word "Long" is sung to four whole notes tied together to make one very long note.

English composers loved using madrigalisms. Wilbye put the text "at thy feet I fall" on a descending scale. Morley set the words "Help, I fall!" to descending leaps of a fourth and a fifth. In Morley's book, A *Plaine and Easie Introduction to Practicall Musicke*, he advises novice madrigal composers that:

You must have a care that when your matter signifieth ascending, high heaven, and such like, you make your musicke ascend: and by the contrarie where your dittie speaketh of descending, lowenes, depth, hell, and such others, you must make your musicke descend, for as it will be thought a great absurditie to talke of heaven and point downwarde to the earth: so it will be counted great incongruitie if a musician upon the wordes hee ascended into heaven shoulde cause his musicke deescend, or by the contrarie upon the descension should cause his musicke to ascend.[56]

Rhythmic values also corresponded to certain textual expectations. For instance, Wilbye's "So Heavy is my heart" and Morley's "Grief tormenteth" are going to use longer note values and slower tempos than Wilbye's "Fly love aloft." As Thomas Morley wrote:

If the subject be light, you must cause your musicke to go in motions, which carrie with them a celeritie or quicknesse of time, as minimes, crotchets and quavers: if it be lamentable, the note must goe in slow and heavie motions, as semibreves, breves, and such like, and of all this you shall finde examples everywhere in the workes of the good musicians.[57]

Sometimes the music actually drew a physical picture, known as "eye music." For instance, words about flying birds might be set to a phrase describing a rising and falling arc in the music, resembling a flock of birds in flight. "Aetna's flames" have notes shooting higher and higher. The word "sigh" is preceded by a rest, as though the singer were taking a breath for the sigh just as one does in real life. Notes in two voices moving toward one another in contrary motion and ending on a unison showed lovers coming together into an embrace. Notes in two voices moving apart in contrary motion illustrated a couple breaking up. The Italian madrigalist Luca Marenzio published the most outrageous madrigalism, however, when he set the word "occhi" (eyes) to two whole notes. The result was that the music looked as though it had two open eyes. Another time he set the word "blind" with two black notes set side by side. One of the troubles of English translations of Italian texts was that the madrigalisms used to such great effect in Italian madrigals meant nothing with an English text.

Elizabethan Madrigals and Modern Notation

Madrigal part books had no bar lines. Morley put small dashes into each individual voice to indicate where a periodic beat, or *tactus*, was supposed to happen. He called these "strokes" and they did not conform to any regular accents or rhythmic units.[58]

The lack of bar lines in part books and the flowing, shifting rhythms of intermingling voices pose a problem for musicians trying to put an Elizabethan madrigal into modern notation with bar lines and time signatures. Any sort of rigid system is unlikely to be satisfactory. Frequent changes of time and meter are compounded by complex rhythms among the voices, making any sort of bar lines throughout a score difficult. If one voice turns out pretty well with a modern barring system, another ends up distorted out of all proportion. How may one bar this type of music without feeling like Anastasia trying to stuff her oversized foot into Cinderella's glass slipper?

The latest answer to this problem is to put the voices in score form but to bar each voice separately. This means that every voice has bar lines, but they are not necessarily in the same place. A modern musician might be confused at first glance, seeing one voice in 3/4 and another singing against it in 6/8 or even 4/4. But when actually sung, this method seems to allow the musical flow to fall into place rather naturally.[59]

Dynamic and expressive markings are also absent from the original part books. Modern musicians should not assume that Elizabethans paid no attention to dynamics or balance among the voices. Modern editors must take care when adding these markings, suggesting rather than overguiding the performers.

Triumphs of Oriana (1601)

One of Thomas Morley's most lasting achievements in madrigal history is his collection of madrigals written by England's best composers and published in 1601 as *Triumphs of Oriana*. The *Triumphs of Oriana* dedicated itself to Queen Elizabeth. Because this book was intended for the queen, the works are especially fine. Each madrigal was set to a verse of each composer's choice, but every madrigal in the book ended with the line, "Long Live Oriana." Oriana referred to Queen Elizabeth. The list of composers is a virtual "Who's Who" of Elizabethan madrigal composers. The *Triumphs of Oriana* presents 25 pieces of music from 24 of England's finest Elizabethan composers (Morley wrote two pieces). Although some names may not be as familiar as others, the list of English composers represented is as follows: Michael East, Daniel Norcome, John Mundy, Ellis Gibbons, John Bennet, John Hilton, George Marson, Richard Carlton, John Holmes, Richard Nicolson, Thomas Tomkins, Michael Cavendish, William Cobbold, Thomas Morley, John Farmer, John Wilbye, Thomas Hunt, Thomas Weelkes, John Milton, George Kirbye, Robert Jones, John Lisley, Edward Johnson.[60]

None of the works is overly long. Most are one stanza, and even the longest madrigals have just two or three. The characteristics of the English madrigal may easily be taken from these offerings. The madrigals are all through composed; that is, they are not in verse form with different verses sung to the same tune as hymn tunes are. Using a single stanza from a longer poem was perfectly acceptable. English madrigals could be any "suitable" length, but they were certain to be shorter than their Italian counterparts. The poetry could be in any rhythm, and lines could be rhymed in any way that seemed right. Each poetic line was at the same time a musical phrase. Music texture is one of polyphonic imitation and rhythmic contrast among the voices.

Twilight of the English Madrigal

The "Elizabethan" madrigal outlived its namesake. Some madrigal composers are not listed in this book because they did not mature until James I's reign and are thus not really "Elizabethan." The English Madrigal School continued until the 1620s. After that time, madrigals suffered a benign neglect. They were seen as quaint by later generations, and not until the early twentieth century would this delightful genre of music be revived. Now schools and community groups all over the world have Madrigal Societies, and listeners may have the same joy given to them today that their Elizabethan counterparts experienced over 400 years ago.

CONCLUSION

Always an essential part of England's church life, vocal music was also an integral part of the fabric of everyday Elizabethan life. Whether in the home or as entertainment, all classes of Elizabethan society indulged in a love of song making. The cross-pollination between composers of secular vocal works and a public eager to buy and sing them propelled the Elizabethan into a golden age of secular song.

The madrigal was the dominant secular vocal genre of the Renaissance. From its origins in Italy, the madrigal came late to England. Its rapid popularity was largely due to a book published in 1588 entitled *Musica Transalpina* that put English words to Italian madrigal tunes. This, added to the general euphoria of the English defeat of the Spanish Armada, touched off a madrigal craze. English composers quickly began writing their own madrigals, different from Italian madrigals in their lighter subject matter and extensive use of "madrigalisms" or word painting, in their music. The English madrigal craze culminated in the 1601 publication of Thomas Morley's *Triumphs of Oriana*, a collection of madrigals—all dedicated to Queen Elizabeth—written by England's best madrigal composers. Though the zenith of the English madrigal craze was short and its decline rapid, the English madrigal is still the music most tightly identified with the Shakespearean age.

NOTES

1. M.C. Boyd, *Elizabethan Music and Musical Criticism* (Philadelphia: University of Pennsylvania Press, 1962), p. 7.

2. Ibid.

3. F. Keel, *Music in the Time of Queen Elizabeth* (February 24, 1914), pp. 23–24.

4. Ibid., p. 12.

5. E. Doughtie, *English Renaissance Song* (Boston: G.K. Hall, 1986), p. 12.

6. Ibid., p. 32.

7. Keel, pp. 30–31.

8. B. Pattison, *Music and Poetry of the English Renaissance* (London: Methuen & Co., 1948), p. 163.

9. Ibid., p. 164.

10. Ibid.

11. W. Chappell, *Popular Music of the Olden Time*, Vol. 1 (New York: Dover Publications, 1965), p. 136.

12. Morley, p. 180.

13. Doughtie, p. 68.

14. H. Raynor, *Music in England* (Plymouth: Clarke, Doble & Brendon, 1980), p. 71.

15. Doughtie, pp. 125–126.

16. Pattison, pp. 182–183.

17. Doughtie, p. 129.

18. Pattison, p. 183.

19. Ibid.

20. Ibid.

21. F. Laroque, *Shakespeare's Festive World* (J. Lloyd, trans.) (Cambridge, MA: Cambridge University Press, 1991), pp. 8–9.

22. Ibid., p. 69.

23. J.H. Long, *Music in English Renaissance Drama* (Lexington: University of Kentucky Press, 1968), p. 36.

24. Ibid., p. 55.

25. M. Shapiro, *Children of the Revels* (New York: Columbia University Press, 1977), p. 2.

26. Ibid., pp. 14–15.

27. Ibid., p. 2.

28. Ibid., pp. 32–33.

29. Ibid., p. 34.

30. Ibid., pp. 239–240.

31. Ibid., p. 243.

32. Ibid., p. 244.

33. Ibid., pp. 237–238.

34. Ibid., p. 250.

35. "The Masque," http://www.mtsn.org.uk/acdepts/english/tempest/masque2.htm, p. 1.

36. Ibid.

37. K. Stolba, *The Development of Western Music* (Dubuque, IA: William C. Brown Publishers, 1990).

38. E.H. Fellowes, *The English Madrigal Composers* (London: Oxford University Press, 1950), p. 43.

39. Ibid., p. 48.

40. T. Morley, *A Plaine and Easie Introduction to Practicall Musicke* (New York: Da Capo Press, 1969 [originally published in 1597]), p. 180.

41. Fellowes, p. 38.

42. Pattison, p. 89.

43. N. Yonge, *Musica Transalpina* (New York: Da Capo Press, 1972) [facsimile of original 1588 publication], dedication page.

44. Ibid.

45. Doughtie, p. 88.

46. J. Kerman, *The Elizabethan Madrigal: A Comparative Study* (New York: American Musicological Society, 1962), p. 9.

47. Pattison, pp. 95–96.

48. Doughtie, p. 120.

49. Pattison, p. 15.

50. Doughtie, pp. 101–103.

51. Pattison, p. 100.

52. Doughtie, p. 105.

53. Fellowes, p. 144.

54. Ibid., p. 145.

55. E.H. Fellowes, *The English Madrigal School*, Vol. 32: Madrigals, *The Triumphs of Oriana* (London: Stainer and Bell, 1923, [originally published in 1601]), p. xiii.

56. Pattison, p. 102.

57. Ibid., p. 105.

58. Fellowes (1950), p. 122.

59. Ibid., p. 130.

60. Fellowes (1923), Index page.

REFERENCES

Boyd, M.C. *Elizabethan Music and Musical Criticism.* Philadelphia: University of Pennsylvania Press, 1962.

Chappell, W. *Popular Music of the Olden Time.* New York: Dover Publications, 1965.

Doughtie, E. *English Renaissance Song.* Boston: G.K. Hall & Company, 1986.

Fellowes, E.H. *The English Madrigal School*, Vol. 32: Madrigals, *The Triumphs of Oriana.* London: Stainer and Bell, 1923.

Fellowes, E.H. *The English Madrigal Composers.* London: Oxford University Press, 1950.

Harris, H.W., and Levey, J.S. (eds.). *The New Columbia Encyclopedia.* New York and London: Columbia University Press, 1975.

Keel, F. *Music in the Time of Queen Elizabeth.* A paper read before ye sette of odd volumes February 24th, 1914. Presented to the sette by Brother John Lane bibliographer: at the 341st meeting, Tuesday, May 26th, 1914.

Kerman, J. *The Elizabethan Madrigal: A Comparative Study*. New York: American Musicological Society, 1962.

Laroque, F. *Shakespeare's Festive World* (J. Lloyd, trans.). Cambridge, MA: Cambridge University Press, 1991.

Long, J.H. (ed.). *Music in English Renaissance Drama*. Lexington: University of Kentucky Press, 1968.

"The Masque." http://www.mtsn.org.uk/acdepts/english/tempest/masque2.htm, p. 1.

Morley, T. *A Plaine and Easie Introduction to Practicall Musicke*. New York: Da Capo Press, 1969 [originally published in 1597].

Pattison, B. *Music and Poetry of the English Renaissance*. London: Methuen & Co., 1948.

Raynor, H. *Music in England*. Plymouth: Clarke, Doble & Brendon, 1980.

Shapiro, M. *Children of the Revels*. New York: Columbia University Press, 1977.

Stolba, K. *The Development of Western Music*. Dubuque, IA: William C. Brown Publishers, 1990.

Yonge, N. *The English Experience*, Number 496, *Musica Transalpina*. New York: Da Capo Press, 1972 [originally published in 1588].

Chapter 9

Notable Elizabethan Composers

WILLIAM BYRD (ca. 1543–1623)

Records indicate that William Byrd began composing during his 20s and learned "to play the organ and many other instruments."[1] Byrd was Catholic, but because he began writing after Queen Elizabeth's reign had begun, he did not have to go through the religious and political confusion that some of his predecessors had. In 1563, when he was only 20, Byrd became organist and master of the choristers at the main church in Lincoln, which was one of the largest cities in England at the time. Lincoln Cathedral had once been Catholic but now held Church of England services. "Know ye," the records at Lincoln read, "that we, the dean and chapter, have given to William Byrd the post of master of the chorister boys, with all wages belonging to the said post, namely six pounds thirteen shillings and fourpence of legal English money. We have also granted to the same William Byrd the post of player at the organs."[2] Churches in Elizabethan times did not use women in their choirs. For the high voices, they used boys whose voices had not changed yet. Byrd was not only in charge of playing organ but of training the boys to sing in the choir.

During his time at Lincoln, Byrd spread his wings as a composer and worked on sacred choral music, church organ music, secular virginal (harpsichord) works, and both sacred and secular songs. Even in his early career, Byrd took the styles that influenced him—styles of Thomas Tallis, Christopher Tye, and others—and made them into something uniquely his own. Byrd added sweetness to the contrapuntal skill learned from his teacher, Thomas Tallis, and added a sense of humanity to the severe grandeur of Christopher Tye's musical style. Scholars studying Byrd's works from these years are impressed by his experimentation with different styles of composition and his masterful handling of each.

In 1572, composer Robert Parsons drowned in the Trent River, and Byrd was called in to take his place.[3] Byrd became a Gentleman of the Chapel Royal. For a while it seems that he worked at both Lincoln and the Chapel Royal. From the time Byrd arrived at the Chapel Royal, he and Tallis were fast friends. Byrd learned from the older composer even while they shared the organist's post at the Chapel Royal.

In 1575, Tallis and Byrd received a joint patent from the crown for the printing and marketing of lined music paper and for the printing and marketing of all part-music (music written for several parts) in England. That year Tallis and Byrd together published a work entitled *Cantiones*, a collection of Latin hymns written by the two composers that included a wide range of styles and forms. Although the venture sounds as though it should have made Byrd and Tallis wealthy men, it seems to have been a failure.

In 1577, Tallis and Byrd jointly asked for help. Byrd's petition said that "through great charge of wife and children, [he is] fallen into debt and great necessity."[4] Byrd wrote that because he had been working so much for the queen he could not make his usual income from teaching. Meanwhile, the printing license had "fallen out to their loss and hindrance to the value of 200 marks at least."[5]

Byrd was what one would today call a "wheeler-dealer." He made powerful friends at court and rapidly rose to the "A-list" of courtiers. He wrote music for them and taught their children music, and they helped him out when he needed a favor at court. He ended up with several properties this way. Having some Protestant courtiers on his side helped Byrd's position as a Catholic working in a Protestant environment.

During this time, Byrd's music was changing and taking Elizabethan music into new ground. His sacred works were a mix of the Franco-Flemish polyphonic styles overtaking the rest of Europe (polyphony is the simultaneous combination of two or more equally important melodic lines) and Byrd's highly expressive style. In his secular music, he began writing variations over a continuously repeating bass line (called a "ground") which showed off his unending imagination. He also wrote works for keyboard—particularly pieces based on older dance forms called Pavans and Galliards. These works show up in later keyboard collections and are popular with budding pianists to this day.[6]

Figure 13. A galliard by William Byrd, from *Parthenia*, uses six staff lines.

From 1580 to 1591, Byrd continued writing music that still enthralls churchgoers, singers, and keyboard artists. Unfortunately, Byrd also got into some religious hot water, temporarily allowing his Catholicism to overrule his political sense. Queen Elizabeth expressed her attitude toward Catholic-Protestant differences early in her reign when she said, "some think one thing, some another, and only God can say whose judgement is best."[7] In fact, she had once promised that English Catholics would not be subject to "any molestation by way of inquisition of their secret opinions" and, "let it not be said that *our* Reformation tendeth to cruelty."[8] For some years, Byrd and his family suffered no particular inconveniences because of their faith. Indeed, a number of Chapel Royal musicians were Catholic.

Unfortunately, this situation was about to change. In the early 1590s, Catholic priests of the Jesuit order began arriving in England from the Continent. (These priests were English, but they had been trained for the priesthood overseas.) Instead of quietly practicing their religion, they began attacking the Church of England on the grounds that it was unpatriotic. "[I]n condemning us you condemn all your own ancestors—and the ancient priests and kings—all that was once the glory of England."[9] Some priests were suspected of plotting against Elizabeth and trying to put the Catholic Mary, Queen of Scots on the throne instead. The execution for treason of three Jesuit priests sent a shock wave through England. Being Catholic was about to get tougher.

For some years the restrictions placed on Catholics had been more of an inconvenience than a persecution. Although they could not celebrate Catholic Mass in a public church, they were not prevented from practicing "the older religion" in private chapels or in their homes, although Catholics were fined 12 pence every week for not going to Church of England services. In 1581, the 12 pence fine went up to 5 pounds a week, and anyone guilty of "harboring a priest" was guilty of treason. Byrd's house in Harlington, England, was searched twice. The searchers would "lock the whole family up in a room by themselves and go rifling the house at their will."[10]

A servant of Byrd's rode up while a search was being conducted. Frightened, he turned his horse around and tried to flee. He was stopped, searched, and found to have "an old printed song book . . . and a letter sent from Mr. Byrd of the Queen's Majesty's Chapel." The songbook contained a piece of music based on a banned Catholic chant, and the letter asked help for a Catholic family having a hard financial time because of the latest persecutions. In addition, in 1583 Byrd had stayed for a week at the manor of a Catholic nobleman, who also had Jesuit priests as guests.[11] Although he was never arrested, Byrd lived for a time under suspicion of being a "seducer" for the Catholic cause.

Byrd and his family survived, however, and when Thomas Tallis died in 1587 Byrd found himself the sole surviving member of the printing monopoly. An astute businessman, Byrd could now make business arrangements without having to consult with anyone. Music began to flow out of his printing press, kicking off a golden age of English music printing. If one wanted any music published or music paper in one's shop, one went through Byrd. In 1596, the contract on his patent expired and was granted to another musician—Byrd's student, Thomas Morley.

In 1588, Byrd published one of his most popular works, *Psalmes, Sonets and Songs*. It was only the third book of English songs known to have been published. He wrote in the preface that most of the songs were originally for voice and "consort" but were now rearranged for five voices. His reason was "to perswade every one to learne to singe."[12] It was a potpourri of works, as Byrd writes in his introduction, "If thou be disposed to pray, here are psalms. If to be merry, here are sonnets. If to lament thy sins, here are songs of sadness and piety."[13] The books were published in separate part-books, which meant that if folks wanted to get together and sing these works, they had to have all five books. It was a hit, however, and three editions were printed and sold out before 1593.

In 1591, Byrd published another very popular book—this time of keyboard music for the virginal, entitled *My Ladye Nevells Booke*. This was a collection of some old tunes of Byrd's and some new ones, including variations over a ground, Pavans and Galliards, and Fantasias.

Byrd's wife is believed to have died in 1586, and Byrd remarried. His second wife, Ellen, lived until 1606. After about 1592, Byrd went into in semiretirement. He spent more time at his property in Stondon Massey, where he rented a house on a long lease. He also spent a lot of time in court where his claims to various grants and properties were being challenged. He and his family continued to pay heavy fines for their Catholicism and were constantly being accused of keeping their servants from attending Protestant services.

After Queen Elizabeth's death in 1603, Byrd journeyed to London for the funeral and "walked in procession at the head of the singing-men of the Chapel Royal."[14] The new king, James I, had been raised Catholic (his mother had been Mary, Queen of Scots), even though he had later aligned himself with Queen Elizabeth. But James soon managed to upset both Catholics and Protestants, and there was an infamous attempt to blow him—and Parliament—up in the "Gunpowder Plot." The plotters were Catholic. Because some of them had been friends of Byrd's, he came under suspicion of having had knowledge of the plot. Thanks to his influential noble friends, Byrd once again escaped a very dangerous time.[15]

Surprisingly, in his later years, Byrd's religious works are more frankly Catholic, but after 1590 he also wrote keyboard works and some of his most famous vocal works. For instance, "Go, from my Window" and "John, come kiss me now" are staples of Elizabethan secular vocal music. William Byrd died in Stonden in 1623, and he requested in his will that he be "honourably buried in that parish . . . in the parish of Stondon where my dwellinge is, and . . . be buried near unto the place where my [first] wife lyeth buried."[16] The Royal Chequebook recorded his death and the hiring of his replacement—just as he had replaced Robert Parsons. "1623 . . . Wm Bird died the 4th of July and Joseph Cr[oker] was admitted into his place the 24th of [July] followinge."[17]

Byrd's influence lies not only in his own compositions, but also in the training of his pupils—Thomas Morley, for one. It is thought that Thomas Weelkes and John Bull may also have been his pupils. Byrd's religious music included Catholic motets adapted for use as English anthems, English anthems using expressive techniques taken from secular music, and Anglican music using Latin text. The effect of Byrd's sacred work is highly emotive music that makes a vivid impact. His largest Anglican offering was a Great service (similar to a High Mass) for Elizabeth. Byrd's Anglican Church music still thrives and is sung not only in churches but in concerts; his keyboard music also continues to be reprinted and enjoyed. Byrd did not normally write lighter forms, but on Thomas Wintam's request he did write two madrigals for Watson's book, *First sett of Italian Madrigalls Englished* in 1590. Byrd's madrigals are more serious in nature, following the Italian madrigal tradition.

JOHN DOWLAND (1563–1626)

John Dowland (see also Chapter 8) is identified as an Elizabethan composer, even though he spent a significant amount of time in other countries. He never seemed to have the kind of luck in England that other English musicians of his time did. Nevertheless, he left a legacy of lute and voice music that will live as long as people sing music in which a single voice is accompanied by a plucked stringed instrument, be it lute or guitar or mandolin.

Dowland was born in 1563, supposedly in the city of Westminster,

England, although there have been some claims for Dublin, Ireland. As a teenager, he traveled as a servant with the English ambassador to France. While in Paris, from 1580 to 1584, he converted to Catholicism. In 1588 he received his bachelor of music degree from Oxford.

In 1592, Dowland performed for Queen Elizabeth during an entertainment known as a masque at a castle where she and her traveling court were staying. The entertainment, entitled "Daphne and Apollo," included two musicians, "one who sung and one who plaide." Dowland was the one who "plaide" a lute, and apparently he wrote not only the music but the text as well.[18] That same year, six of his arrangements of psalm tunes were included in a published collection entitled *The Whole Booke of Psalmes*.

Dowland was sure that his star was rising. So when a court lutenist died, Dowland applied for the post. When he was turned down, he left England, this time on his own. As he put it, "I desired to go beyond the seas."[19] He traveled through what is now Germany, spending time at two courts where he was treated very well. In fact, the noblemen of both courts tried to hire Dowland, but he was on a mission to Italy. Dowland wanted to meet a Renaissance composer whose work he admired—Luca Marenzio. Eventually, he made his way to Florence, but besides meeting Marenzio, he also fell into company with a group of exiled English Catholics.[20] Unfortunately, this group was plotting to assassinate Queen Elizabeth. Dowland, terrified at this turn of events, wrote a letter in 1595 exposing the entire plot. "Right honourable this have I written that her Majesty may know the villainy of these most wicked priests and Jesuits, & to beware of them," a portion of the letter reads.[21]

Dowland returned to England in 1597, again applied for a post at Elizabeth's court—and again was turned down rather than being rewarded for exposing a plot against the crown. Dowland bitterly suspected that his Catholicism cost him the post, but his reasoning sounds like "sour grapes." After all, two of Elizabeth's main musicians—Tallis and Byrd—were Catholic. A more likely reason may be that Dowland was not the easiest person in the world to get along with. In the words of one historian, Dowland comes through history as "Immensely self-centred and highly emotional with a just appreciation of his own powers, but with an almost childishly irritable reaction to criticism, subject from time to time to attacks of melancholy."[22]

That same year, Dowland collected 21 of his songs and arranged them so that they could be sung either in four parts or by one person while accompanied with a lute. The lute could be played by the singer or by another person. He also included an "invention for two to playe upon one Lute." This collection, *The First Booke of Songes or Ayres of Foure Partes with Tableture for the Lute*, included an introductory letter from Marenzio. This book was highly successful and was reprinted at least four times.

The next year, Dowland's reputation was enhanced when he was included in a published list of famous English musicians. He also received an invitation to return and accept a post from one of the noblemen he had known in Germany. Dowland did leave England again, but this time he went to Denmark, where in 1598 he became a lutenist at the court of King Christian IV. Dowland's pay was generous—he was one of the highest paid members of the Danish royal household. Dowland put out a second book of "ayres" dedicated to his wife, but his bad luck followed him overseas. Apparently, while Dowland was having the manuscript published by a Danish firm, his wife contracted to have it published in England.

In March 1603, Queen Elizabeth died, and in July of that year Dowland returned to England for about a year. He seems to have gone back and forth from England to Denmark for the next few years. He ended up in England, in deep financial trouble. Dowland became a bitter and resentful person, even though during this time playing the lute was as common as playing a guitar is today, and his music was published and very popular.

In 1612, long after Elizabeth's death, Dowland finally got from James I the appointment he had longed for. He became one of the king's lutes that October. His success continued, and he soon became the recipient of many honors and tributes. He lived long enough to be part of the funeral consort that played for James I's funeral in May of 1625. Dowland died early in 1626.

Contemporary accounts of Dowland's personality vary, but the evidence suggests a man with mood swings—"up" sometimes and intensely "down" at other times. Dowland did write cheerful tunes, but his best works are deeply sad. Two of his most famous songs, for instance, are "Flow, My Teares, Flow" and "In darknesse let mee dwell." Dowland was revered by his fellow musicians for his music compositions, but even more for his lute playing. A contemporary poet, Richard Barnfield, wrote of Dowland:

> Dowland to thee is deare, whose heavenly touch
> Upon the Lute doeth ravishe humaine sense.[23]

Dowland's songs continue to be sung, both as part-songs and as arrangements for voice and guitar. Many of his lute works have also been transcribed for guitar and are staples of the classical guitar literature.

THOMAS MORLEY (1576–1602)

Thomas Morley was born in Norwich, England. His father was a brewer and may also have worked at the local cathedral.[24] Thomas was probably a member of the chorus there. He must have lived elsewhere at some time, however, since he is known to have studied music with William Byrd. In 1588, he received a bachelor of music degree from Oxford University.[25] He also married around this time, although little is known about his wife except that her name was Susan.[26] In the early 1590s, Morley was hired as the organist in St. Paul's Church in London—a very prestigious honor—and Queen Elizabeth began to be aware of this up-and-coming musician, notably at an entertainment for the monarch in 1591.[27]

During the late 1580s and early 1590s, Morley came into contact with Renaissance music from mainland Europe, and he was very taken with the Italian style of writing. He also may have become mixed up in some Catholic-Protestant intrigues. Morley had apparently converted to Protestantism, and then "reconciled"—or reconverted—back to Catholicism. Thus, he was under some suspicion from both sides. A report from a Catholic double agent writing to his boss reveals what must have been a terrifying ordeal for Morley:

> Ther is one Morley that playeth on the organes in poules [i.e., St. Paul's] that was with me in my house. He seemed here to be a good Catholicke and was reconsiled, but not withstanding suspecting his behavoir I entercepted letters. . . . Whereby I discovered enoughe to have hanged him. Nevertheles he shewing with teares of great repentaunce, and asking on his knees forgiveness, I was content to let him goe. I here [hear] (that) since his coming thether [i.e., back to England] he hath played the promoter and apprehendeth [aids in the capture of] Catholickes.[28]

After Morley became Protestant again, his "reward" from the crown seems to have been a post as a Gentleman of the Chapel Royal in 1592. This began Morley's most productive musical period. He also seems to have married again, this time to a woman named Margaret with whom he had three children, two of whom survived their infancy.[29] During this time, Morley was living in the same parish as William Shakespeare, and it is likely that the two men knew one another. In Morley's *First Booke of Ayres*, published in 1600, he set to music the Shakespeare text from Act V, Scene III of *As You Like It*, "It was a Lover and his Lass."

In 1596, the Tallis/Byrd publishing monopoly expired, and the queen granted Morley the patent. An astute businessman, Morley decided to downplay the less profitable items and instead publish psalters—songbooks of psalms, rhymed and put into singable meters. Unfortunately, Morley's health was bad. He resigned from the Chapel Royal by 1602, and, although there is some controversy over the year of his death, he most likely died early in October 1602. Morley died a highly respected musician, well liked by his peers. Included in a book of airs by Thomas Weelkes is a six-part *Lament* dedicated to Morley entitled "Death has deprived me of my dearest friend."[30]

This composer of some of the most cheerful music in English history was the first to compose music for an Anglican funeral service. His funeral anthems are four-part choral homophony but with a "sensitive feeling for word accent and melodic line."[31] He also wrote Anglican anthems for one Great service, a worship service using elaborately written music, and for one Short service, a worship service using less elaborate music. He also wrote Verse anthems for Anglican worship services. In a Verse anthem, the choir sings one verse and a soloist (or small group of soloists) sings the next one. The verses continue to alternate until the end of the work. Morley is known for taking expressive techniques from his secular works and putting them into his religious works. He was not above using madrigalian word painting to express text, such as putting "the proud are scattered" on a rush of fast notes and "the meek are exalted" on the highest notes in a work.[32]

Morley is most remembered for his madrigals, which took the Italian madrigal craze, "translated" it into English music, and steered the English madrigal to its highest achievements. When "Elizabethan madrigals" are mentioned, it is Morley's madrigals, "balletts," and "canzonets" that immediately spring to mind. Although he owed much to his Italian counterparts, Morley's madrigal music is distinct from that of its predecessors. He was master of the lighter madrigal and the composer of some of the most popular tunes in the English language. In fact, his work mixes genres so that it is difficult to tell where, for instance, the dividing line is between his canzonets and his madrigals.

The popularity of Morley's madrigals has a great deal to do with the sunny, upbeat spirit of his works. Such works as "My bonny lass she smileth" and "Now is the Month of Maying" helped propel Morley to the forefront of the Elizabethan list of madrigal composers. Besides their character, Morley's madrigals (and canzonets and balletts) have well-defined rhythms and a propelling drive. Morley's works are accessible to amateur performers as well as to professionals. His skill was such that his music seems as natural as air. His works became the epitome of Elizabethan music—light, airy, and still the darling of madrigal societies worldwide.

As a publisher, Morley is personally responsible for publishing nine volumes of various types of secular song within a seven-year period. This added up to about 200 works available to the Elizabethan public—and to musicians of today. Six of the nine volumes were made up entirely of his own compositions. All this music was published in the 1590s. His last publication came out in 1601, and he died the following year.

Another of Morley's major legacies was his music instruction book entitled *A Plaine and Easie Introduction to Practicall Musicke*, published in 1597 and dedicated to William Byrd. The book is a scholar's gold mine of explanations for how music of Morley's time is to be performed.

THOMAS TALLIS (ca. 1505–1585)

Thomas Tallis was born in England, but no one knows exactly where. His career spanned four rulers and many religious and political upheavals. Yet he managed to weather all the storms, deal with the wildly differing personalities of his royal employers and their religious and musical tastes, and die honored by all who knew him.

The first year that can definitely be traced to him is 1532, when he is listed as an organist of the Catholic Benedictine Priory of Dover, England. Then he evidently moved to London, since his name shows up on the 1537–1538 payroll of a London church.[33] Actually, he may already have been working for the royal family at this time. In a petition that he wrote to Queen Elizabeth dated 1577, Tallis wrote that he "served the Queen and her ancestors almost fortie years."[34] If true, this would mean that he had been working two jobs in London since 1537.

In 1538, Tallis began working for Waltham Abbey, also in London. The church had three organs "of various sizes" and a men-and-boys choir. He is listed as a singer but probably also shared organ-playing duties. When Henry VIII established the Church of England as the country's official faith and dissolved the Catholic abbeys in 1540, Tallis—along with many other church musicians—was out of a job. He left with 20 shillings wages and 20 shillings "reward" to show for his work.[35]

Tallis quickly rebounded with work in Canterbury Cathedral, the leading church of the new religion, where he is listed as a lay clerk from 1541 to 1542. At this point, being a lay clerk meant you were a musician of some sort employed by a church; it didn't matter whether that church was Catholic or Protestant. Clerks were generally singers but could also play the organ or compose. It was uncommon for one person to be named the organist, for organ playing was usually shared among the clerks. Clerk/composers thought of themselves as craftsmen, not artists. Instead of selling their wares to customers, they crafted music in the service of the church. Much as cobblers made shoes, clerk/composers made music for anyone who hired them. Much as people today who produce advertisements may not actually use the product, Catholic composers could set the text for Protestant hymns. This is how someone such as Tallis (and later, William Byrd) could work for two opposing religions as long as they did not bring their personal beliefs into their jobs.

Tallis's name shows up as a paid employee for the private royal chapel in 1545, listed as a "Gentleman of the Chapel Royal." But as stated earlier, he may have been working for the court as early as 1537 and probably had been serving in the Chapel Royal full-time as early as 1543. Once there, Thomas Tallis found his niche. It is believed that he served his kings and queens as both a composer and an organist. Having already spent some years writing for the Catholic Church, he now wrote Protestant music for the Church of England through the remainder of Henry VIII's reign. As the new religion solidified, he wrote music for the official English liturgy throughout Edward VI's reign.

After Edward VI's death (and the extremely short reign of Lady Jane Grey) Queen Mary ascended to the throne, and the Catholic Church was reinstated in England. Queen Mary thought very highly of Tallis. In fact, he was her favorite composer, and whenever a state occasion needed music, Tallis was automatically asked to provide it. For this queen, Tallis wrote large-scale works of the type that Mary remembered from her youth. For instance, during her rule, Tallis wrote a seven-voiced Mass entitled "Puer natus est nobis." The title, "Unto Us a Child Is Born," may have referred to the belief that the queen was expecting a child.[36]

By the time Elizabeth became queen, Tallis had been an established musician in the Chapel Royal for quite some time. The new queen also thought highly of him and his work. Even though Elizabeth was officially Protestant, she asked for church music set to both English and Latin texts. She never banished Latin as a language of religion, though it was not commonly used outside of the court's private chapel. Queen Elizabeth did not ask for as much church music as her predecessors, and not all the music she asked for was for church use. So besides being retained as an employee of the Chapel Royal, Tallis also wrote (or arranged) secular works for organ, a small amount of which has survived. Most of it is in a collection of keyboard works known as the *Mulliner Book*.

In 1552, Tallis married a woman named Joan. It was a love match, and they were married for 33 years, until Tallis's death. They had no children. In 1572 Tallis was joined in the Chapel Royal by another soon-to-be-famous Catholic musician—William Byrd. Tallis and Byrd formed a friendship, even though Byrd was a generation younger. In fact, Tallis became godfather to one of Byrd's children.[37]

The two composers petitioned the queen for an additional source of income, and in January 1575 she responded with the offer of an exclusive license to print and publish all the music in England for the next 21 years. Later that year, the new Tallis/Byrd printing monopoly turned out its first product—*Cantiones Sacrae* (Sacred Songs), a collection of motets in Latin by the two composers. A motet is a religious polyphonic (several melody lines of equal importance sung simultaneously) vocal composition with Latin words, but not words from church liturgy. Each composer contributed 17 works to this collection, in honor of Queen Elizabeth reaching the seventeenth year of her reign. This venture was not the success it should have been. Apparently, overhead outweighed income, and in only two years the Tallis/Byrd team had to petition the queen for some rental property to offset their losses. Fortunately, she responded positively.[38]

Tallis died in 1585 and was buried in the parish churchyard of Greenwich, England. His wife lived for four more years in their house there. William Byrd was executor for Tallis's will. Tallis willed some money to the Greenwich church for the poor. He willed his music-printing monopoly shares to Byrd's son, knowing that Byrd would actually be the beneficiary in his son's minority and hoping that Byrd's son would inherit the monopoly later. Tallis also left some money to the Chapel Royal for his musical friends to have a feast in his honor.[39]

Tallis's longevity under so many changes of rule and through so many changes in composition styles is evidence not only of the excellence of his work, but also to his being a quiet man who stayed out of controversies. His epitaph on a brass plate inside the church in Greenwich praised him for his "honest vertuous lyff" and for serving four royal personages "with grete prayse."[40]

Although Tallis did compose some instrumental music (for keyboards and viols) and some secular vocal music, he is known mostly for his religious vocal works. Of his Catholic pieces, Tallis's most impressive achievement is his motet "Spem in Alium," which has eight five-part choirs singing a total of 40 independent contrapuntal parts. Later, Tallis wrote Anglican hymns in which the challenge was to take the homo-phonic, syllabic settings of text and infuse them with emotional and musical substance. Tallis wrote music for Anglican Church services, in-cluding a Short service. He wrote English anthems as well as adaptations of Latin motets that were reworked into English anthems. The anthems Tallis wrote for Queen Elizabeth's chapel are more ornate than those written for general use. Overall, Tallis is renowned for his intelligent handling of complex contrapuntal devices and inventive harmonies with-out interrupting the essential beauty of his work.

CHRISTOPHER TYE (ca. 1505–1573)

A contemporary of Thomas Tallis, Christopher Tye was a talented composer who helped formulate music for the Church of England in its infancy. After receiving his bachelor of music degree in Cambridge, he became a "lay clerk" at King's College where he composed music and taught choirboys. Tye left King's College sometime before 1539. In 1541 he was named master of the choristers at the Cathedral of Ely and, later, organist of the same cathedral.[41] Tye was introduced to court after this time and came into the favor of Edward VI who called him "our music's lecturer."

Records are scattered about his career through Mary's reign, but as a Catholic he must have been in favor. Tye received his doctorate of music from Cambridge in 1545, and in 1548 he received another doctorate of music from Oxford. Tye became a priest in 1560. The new queen, Eliz-abeth, however, did not choose her musicians by their religious beliefs, and so Tye sometimes played organ for her private chapel. As he grew older, Tye's personality soured and not even a queen could get the best of him, as this anecdote relates:

> Dr. Tye was a peevish and humoursome [temperamental] man, especially in his latter dayes, and sometimes playing on ye organ in ye chapel of qu. Elizab. Wh[ich] contained much musick but little delight to the ear, she would send ye verger to tell him yt [that] he play'd out of tune: whereupon he sent word yt her eares were out of Tune.[42]

Much of Tye's work has been lost. If he wrote any organ music, for instance, none has survived. Only about half of his Latin church music remains, and nothing written for Ely Cathedral has survived. Apparently, he played viol (a stringed instrument played with a bow) in court ensembles and composed many works for viol consort (a group of viols playing together).

Tye's legacy is in his Anglican music. During the latter part of Henry VIII's reign, the King's best composers were John Taverner, Christopher Tye, and Thomas Tallis. Of these, Tye set the standard for the new church. Though he was himself a Catholic, it was Tye who taught Edward VI about music, and it was Tye who became the "father of the English anthem,"[43] developing an expressive style of anthem influential to both his contemporaries and following generations. As one scholar wrote, "Music, which received a grievous wound in England at the dissolution of abbeys, was greatly beholden to him [Tye] for her recovery."[44]

THOMAS WEELKES (ca. 1576–1623)

Although Thomas Weelkes's birth date is unknown, he was baptized in 1576 in Elsted, England. Weelkes was just a child when the craze for madrigals hit England in 1588, and he began writing them at a young age. His first volume of madrigals, *Madrigals to 3, 4, 5 and 6 voyces*, was published in 1597. In 1598, he was hired as a private musician to Edward Darcye, who was a highly placed courtier. That same year, Weelkes became the organist at Winchester College, where he stayed for the next four years (until late 1602) and wrote some of his finest madrigals. In 1601, while still in his 20s, Weelkes was so well known that he was invited to contribute to a musical collection of works entitled *Triumphs of Oriana*, published by Thomas Morley. He also published three volumes of madrigals between 1597 and 1600.

In 1602, Weelkes received a bachelor of music degree from New College, Oxford, and joined the music staff of Chichester Cathedral. In early 1603, Weelkes married a woman from a wealthy Chichester family. This may have been a "shotgun wedding": Weelkes' first child was baptized just four months after the marriage.

Weelkes settled into his job at Chichester Cathedral. Apparently, the church had a lot of trouble with its musicians in general. A crisis developed when a strict Cathedral choirmaster followed a more easygoing predecessor. An overbearing taskmaster, the new choirmaster began issuing "admonishments"—written scoldings—for offensive behavior and also issuing fines taken from choir members' salaries. He began by decreeing that "the vicars choral and other singing-men of this Cathedral Church are very negligent in their service and duties."[45] Choir members were harassed and threatened for absenteeism, for "unreverend" gestures or "unseemly" talking in church, and for visiting alehouses. Three strikes and the chorister was out of a job. Possibly because they were under such insulting strictures, choir members failed to shape up. Instead, they practically dared the authorities to take action, and church officials hesitated to fire most of their choir. Weelkes, already plagued with a messy personal life, was now often in trouble on his job. But to be fair, so were many of his fellow workers.

In his fourth and last volume of madrigals, which came out in 1608, Weelkes described himself as a Gentleman of the Chapel Royal (although he may have been stretching the truth because he doesn't show up on the payroll anywhere around that time). Apparently, his personal reputation preceded him, and he never achieved a position at the royal court.[46] As time went on, Weelkes's behavior went from bad to worse. He was an alcoholic and became verbally abusive when drunk. By 1616, the authorities of Chichester Cathedral reported him to the bishop as "noted and famed for a comon drunckard and notorious swearer & blasphemer."[47]

Rather than take this "wakeup call" to heart, Weelkes slid even further down the bottle. A report from 1619 said that he, "very often came . . . disguised eyther from the Taverne or Ale house into the quire as is much to be lamented, for in those humoures he will bothe curse & sweare most dreadfully, & so profane the service of God . . . and though he hath bene often tymes admonished . . . to refrayne theis humors and reform hym selfe, yett he daylye continuse the same, & is rather worse than better therein."[48] In other words, he would sneak into a tavern and then show up to sing in the choir or play the organ drunk, abusive, and cursing throughout the service, apparently loud enough to be heard by people other than those closest to him.

In 1622, Weelkes's wife died. He continued working erratically as an organist and spending a lot of time at a friend's house in London. He died 13 months after his wife, in 1623, and was buried in St. Bride's, Fleet Street, London.

If William Byrd was the grand old man of madrigals, Thomas Weelkes was its prodigy. Weelkes was only 21 or 22 years old when he published his first madrigal set, *Madrigals to 3, 4, 5, and 6 voyces* in 1597. Ahead of his peers, this is only the second time in England that a published volume used the word "madrigal" in its title. He was also the first to indicate that his madrigals were fit either for voices or for any combination of voice and instruments. Almost all of the madrigals inside are some of the best ever written. Scholars consider "Cease, sorrows, now" one of the finest three-voiced English madrigals in existence. Even so, Weelkes had the humility to apologize for daring to publish works in his "unripened years."[49]

In 1598, Weelkes published *Balletts and Madrigals to five voices*. Six out of the total 24 works are madrigals, one is an elegy, and the rest are balletts. In the elegy, Weelkes uses the device of setting a major and a minor third together simultaneously (a G# against a G-natural) to indicate pain. This sort of daring is a hallmark of Weelkes's imaginative spirit.

Weelkes's publication, *Madrigals of 5 and 6 parts* (1600), was divided into two sets: a set of 10 five-voiced madrigals and a set of 10 six-voiced madrigals. As one scholar observed, "from the point of view of dramatic treatment and force of emotional expression, Weelkes' work in these two Sets stands alone in English madrigal literature."[50] One madrigal, "O Care, thou wilt despatch me" has been called one of the finest madrigals in existence—and Weelkes was still in his mid-20s at the time. Weelkes's last published work contained no madrigals. *Ayeres or Phantasticke Spirites for three voices* are lighter works and not of the same quality as his earlier compositions. After that, he published no more works.

Despite his erratic life and the fact that Morley's music is more often heard today, Weelkes's music continues to be sung by madrigal societies worldwide. Even so, Weelkes's alcoholism cost him more than a string of admonishments. As one historian puts it, "we have to recognise that he was a disappointment—a composer with the makings of greatness, but who failed lamentably to fulfil the . . . expectations aroused by his . . . early achievements."[51]

THOMAS WHYTHORNE (1528–1596)

Thomas Whythorne was born in Ilminster, England. He went to school in Oxford at Magdalen College, after which he went to work for English dramatist John Heywood as a "servant and scholar."[52] Later, he worked for a widowed noblewoman as a servingman and music tutor. The situation was uncomfortable. Apparently, Whythorne was in a sexual harrassment situation in which his (female) employer made unwanted advances.

When Queen Mary rose to the throne, Whythorne's employer lost her fortune in the upheaval and Whythorne was out of a job. Deciding it was time to see something of the Continent, he left for the European mainland. Returning to England in 1555, Whythorne became a music tutor for several noble houses, including the daughter of the aggressively love-lorn widow he had served some years before. He continued serving as a tutor in music and in other fields, and even as an accountant for one noble house, until 1565, when he decided to "make it" in music alone.

Whythorne remembered how popular madrigals had been in his Italian travels, and he felt that writing some madrigals suitable for English amateur musicians would be the shortest route to fame. So in 1571, he published *Songes for Three, Fower, and Five Voyces*. In 1590, he published another book of music entitled *Duos, or Songs for Two voices*. This was arranged for either two voices, or a voice and an instrument, or two instruments. Although they were a popular success, Whythorne's efforts were panned by critics. Kinder souls noted that while Whythorne's tunes were perhaps not of the high quality of those by William Byrd, they did not "merit the contempt that has been heaped upon them."[53]

Whythorne's book, *Songes for Three, Fower, and Five Voyces*, is the only book of English secular vocal music published between that of Wynken de Worde's in 1530 and William Byrd's part song book *Psalmes, Sonets, and Songs* in 1588. Whythorne's works are considered a forerunner of the "proper" Elizabethan madrigal, and as such he has a place as a pioneer of English part-song.[54]

Even though Whythorne is remembered as a composer, lutenist, and keyboard player, it is not for these things that he is famous. In 1955, scholars discovered an autobiography that Whythorne had written about his own life and career. This book is full of details about the training and life of an Elizabethan musician. It also provides intimate details of noble life, from the perspectives of both the master and servant. And, at least equally interesting, it is written in a phonetic spelling—Whythorne's self-styled "new orthografye." Because his stated aim was to "write words as they be sounded in speech,"[55] his work, published in 1960, is also the delight of people interested in the history of speech patterns.

Thomas Whythorne died in 1596, in London. Though not the greatest musician, he has become an incredible window through which the modern musician can view his world.

JOHN WILBYE (1574–1638)

John Wilbye, the third son of a tanner, was born in Norfolk, England. Nothing is known of his early musical education other than that his father apparently played the lute, for John inherited the instrument when his father died. In 1598, Wilbye became a domestic musician for one of England's wealthiest and most influential families, the Kytsons (see page 80). This family was well-supplied with both music books and instruments,

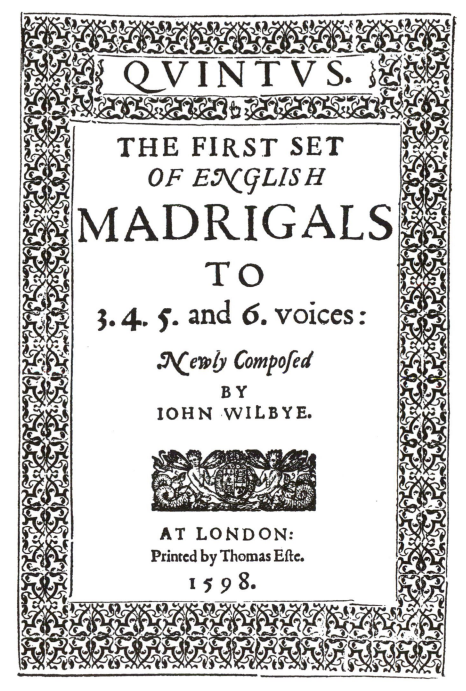

Figure 14. Frontispiece to John Wilbye's part book: Part five to the madrigals with five and six voices.

and expected their musicians to be the best. Wilbye did not disappoint. He was a loyal employee to the Kytsons for 28 years.

When Lady Kytson died in 1626, the estate broke up and Wilbye, who had never married, spent the last 10 years of his life in the service of Lady Kytson's youngest daughter. As a sign of her respect and personal favor, the late Lady Kytson had bequeathed to her faithful musician "a substantial bequest of furniture and furnishings."[56]

As a domestic musician who was not connected to the church, Wilbye's output is intended for secular use—including religiously tinged devotional songs. Wilbye's madrigals are considered some of the best ever written. His *First Set of Madrigals* was published in 1598 and was dedicated to one of the Kytson family. Wilbye published two collections—one in 1598 and the other in 1609, which cannot properly be called Elizabethan since Queen Elizabeth died in 1603. Wilbye handled textures anywhere from three to six voices. He enjoyed the polyphonic web of counterpoint and used less homophonic texture than other madrigal composers. He is especially admired for his ability to express the subtlety of text through a wide range of emotions, moving from joy to grief in a single seamless work.

NOTES

1. I. Holst, *Byrd*, from a series entitled *The Great Composers* (New York: Praeger Publishers, 1972), p. 19.

2. Ibid., p. 21.

3. E.H. Fellowes, *William Byrd* (London: Oxford University Press, 1948), p. 2.

4. J. Pulver, *A Biographical Dictionary of Old English Music* (London: Kegan Paul, Trench, Trubnert Co., 1927), p. 82.

5. Ibid., 83.

6. J. Kerman, "William Byrd," in *The New Grove Dictionary of Music and Musicians*, vol. 3 (London: Macmillan Publishers, 1980), p. 540.

7. Holst, p. 53.

8. Ibid.

9. Ibid.

10. Ibid., p. 55.

11. Ibid., pp. 55–56.

12. Pulver, p. 86.

13. Holst, p. 37.

14. Ibid., p. 64.

15. Ibid., pp. 66–67.

16. Pulver, p. 85.

17. E.F. Rimbault (ed.), *The Old Cheque-Book, or Book of Remembrance of The Chapel Royal from 1561 to 1744* (New York: Da Capo Press, 1966), p. 58.

18. D. Poulton, *John Dowland* (2nd ed.) (Berkeley and Los Angeles: University of California Press, 1982), p. 29.

19. Pulver, p. 143.

20. Ibid.

21. Poulton, p. 39.

22. Poulton, pp. 43–44.

23. Pulver, p. 146.

24. Philip Brett, "Thomas Morley," in *The New Grove Dictionary of Music and Musicians*, vol. 12 (London: Macmillan Publishers, 1980), p. 579.

25. Ibid., p. 330.

26. Ibid., p. 331.

27. Ibid., p. 330.

28. Brett, p. 579.

29. Pulver, p. 331.

30. Ibid., p. 329.

31. P. Le Huray, *Music and the Reformation in England 1549–1660* (New York: Oxford University Press, 1967), pp. 247–248.

32. Ibid.

33. P. Doe, "Thomas Tallis," in *The New Grove Dictionary of Music and Musicians*, vol. 18 (London: Macmillan Publishers, 1980), p. 541.

34. Pulver, p. 447.

35. Ibid., p. 446.

36. Doe, p. 543.

37. Pulver, p. 447.

38. Ibid.

39. Ibid.

40. Ibid.

41. Ibid., p. 471.

42. Ibid., p. 469.

43. H. Raynor, *Music in England* (Plymouth: Clarke, Doble & Brendon, 1980), p. 50.

44. Ibid., p. 49.

45. D. Brown, *Thomas Weelkes* (New York: Frederick A. Praeger, 1969), p. 34.

46. Ibid., p. 205.

47. Ibid., p. 41.

48. Ibid., p. 43.

49. F.H. Fellowes, *The English Madrigal Composers* (London: Oxford University Press, 1950), p. 192.

50. Ibid.

51. Brown, p. 205.
52. T. Whythorne, *The Autobiography of Thomas Whythorne, Modern Spelling Edition* (J.M. Osborne, ed.)(London: Oxford University Press, 1962), p. 6.
53. Pulver, p. 489.
54. Fellowes (1950), p. 34.
55. Whythorne, p. lvi.
56. D. Brown, *Wilbye*, from the series *Oxford Studies of Composers*, No. 11 (London: Oxford University Press, 1974), p. 9.

REFERENCES

Brett, P. "Thomas Morley." *The New Grove Dictionary of Music and Musicians* (Vol. 12, pp. 579–585). London: Macmillan Publishers, 1980.

Brown, D. *Thomas Weelkes*. New York: Frederick A. Praeger, 1969.

Brown, D. *Wilbye* (from the series *Oxford Studies of Composers*, No. 11). London: Oxford University Press, 1974.

Doe, P. *Tallis* (from the series *Oxford Studies of Composers*, No. 4). London: Oxford University Press, 1968.

Doe, P. "Thomas Tallis." *The New Grove Dictionary of Music and Musicians* (Vol. 18, pp. 541–548). London: Macmillan Publishers, 1980.

Doe, P. "Christopher Tye." *The New Grove Dictionary of Music and Musicians* (Vol. 19, pp. 297–300). London: Macmillan Publishers, 1980.

Fellowes, E.H. *William Byrd*. London: Oxford University Press, 1948.

Fellowes, E.H. *The English Madrigal Composers*. London: Oxford University Press, 1950.

Holst, I. *Byrd* (from the series *The Great Composers*). New York: Praeger Publishers, 1972.

Kerman, J. "William Byrd." *The New Grove Dictionary of Music and Musicians* (Vol. 3, pp. 537–552). London: Macmillan Publishers, 1980.

Kerman, J. *The Masses and Motets of William Byrd*. London: Faber & Faber, 1981.

Le Huray, P. *Music and the Reformation in England 1549–1660*. New York: Oxford University Press, 1967.

Poulton, D. "John Dowland." *The New Grove Dictionary of Music and Musicians* (Vol. 5, pp. 593–597). London: Macmillan Publishers, 1980.

Poulton, D. *John Dowland*. Berkeley: University of California Press, 1982.

Pulver, J. *A Biographical Dictionary of Old English Music*. London: Kegan Paul, Trench, Trubner, & Co., 1927.

Raynor, H. *Music in England*. Plymouth: Clarke, Doble & Brendon, 1980.

Rimbault, E.F. (ed.). *The Old Cheque-Book, or Book of Remembrance of The Chapel Royal from 1561 to 1744*. New York: Da Capo Press, 1966.

Whythorne, T. *The Autobiography of Thomas Whythorne, Modern Spelling Edition* (J.M. Osborne, ed.). London: Oxford University Press, 1962.

Appendix
Other Elizabethan Composers

MICHAEL CAVENDISH (1565?–1628)

Cavendish did not publish a book of madrigals or canzonets, but he did have a 1598 book of lutenist aires published. Scholars consider his work second only to John Dowland's. Cavendish has a madrigal entitled "Come, gentle swains" included in *Triumphs of Oriana*.[1]

JOHN FARMER (1565?–1605)

Farmer's 1599 set of *English Madrigals: To Foure Voices* has been described as "delightful," "melodious and attractive" and "charming." His religious work appears in *The Whole Booke of Psalmes*.[2] His madrigal, "Fair nymph I heard one telling," appears in *Triumphs of Oriana*.

GILES FARNABY (1560?–1600?)

Farnaby's 1598 publication entitled "Canzonets to Fowre Voyces with a Song of eight parts" contains works that may be more properly called light madrigals. Farnaby is also remembered as a fine technical writer and a composer who used more complex and daring harmonies than most other English madrigal composers, even though some scholars feel that his complex rhythms sometimes mar otherwise fine works.[3]

GEORGE KIRBYE (1565?–1634)

Kirbye had one book published in 1597, entitled *The first set of English Madrigalls to 4, 5, and 6 voices*. Known for his fine technical writing, Kirbye was better with quieter emotions. His works such as "Ah, sweet, alas, when first I saw" or "Sleep now, my Muse" show a sensitive nature and perceptive intelligence to his texts. Kirby's contribution to *Triumphs of Oriana* is a madrigal entitled "Bright Phoebus greets most clearly."[4]

JOHN MUNDY (1560?–1630)

Mundy's work, *Songs and Psalmes composed into 3, 4, and 5 parts for the use and delight of all such as either love or learne Musicke*, was published in 1594. Among its 30 works are five or six madrigals. Known as a rather conventional composer, Mundy has a five-voiced madrigal entitled "Lightly whipped she o'er the dales" in *Triumphs of Oriana*.[5]

WILLIAM MUNDY (ca. 1555–1630)

William Mundy began his church career as a boy singer. Eventually, he became a Gentleman of the Chapel Royal. Mundy wrote his music in both Latin and English. His church music styles include old-style Latin polyphony, French-style imitative works, and chordal homophonic English works.

NATHANIEL PATRICK (1560?–1595)

Nathaniel Patrick is a "lost" madrigal composer. The enormously long title of his 1597 work is *Songes of Sundrye Natures whereof some are Divine, some are Madrigalles and the rest Psalms and Hymnes in Latin composed for 5 and 6 voyces and one for 8 voyces by Nathanaell Pattrick sometyme Master of the children of the Cathedrall Church of Worcester and organist of the same*. Patrick died at a relatively young age, and his work came out after his death. Although scholars know of this work, the actual music is no longer in existence.[6]

JOHN SHEPHERD (ca. 1515–1558)

John Shepherd was both master of the choristers at Magdalen College, Oxford, and a Gentleman of the Chapel Royal. He wrote five complete

Masses, as well as 33 Anglican psalms and several anthems for the Anglican Church.

"LOST" ELIZABETHAN CHURCH COMPOSERS

Several composer-musicians are known to have written music for Anglican churches, but none of it survives. John Merbecke (ca. 1510–1585), Richard Edwards (1524–1566), William Hunnis, John Redford (ca. 1485–1547), Philip ap Rhys, and William Blitheman (ca. 1525–1591) fall into this category.

NOTES

1. E.H. Fellowes, *The English Madrigal Composers* (London: Oxford University Press, 1950), p. 236.
2. Ibid., p. 240.
3. Ibid., p. 233.
4. Ibid., p. 226.
5. Ibid., p. 224.
6. Ibid., p. 231.

REFERENCES

Fellowes, E.H. *The English Madrigal Composers*. London: Oxford University Press, 1950.

Raynor, H. *Music in England*. Plymouth: Clarke, Doble & Brendon, 1980.

Glossary

Accidental: a sharp, flat, or natural sign not otherwise indicated in the key signature.

Affable: friendly; courteous.

Anglicize: to give an English form to.

Anthem: a musical composition, usually set to words from the Bible.

Apprentice: someone learning a trade by working for a master for a fixed amount of time.

Atonality: the lack of a tonal center.

Audition: a test, or hearing of an actor or musician.

Ayre/air: a solo song with lute accompaniment. Also known as a lute song.

Ballad: a poetic story set to music.

Balletts: a vocal ensemble work that usually includes nonsense syllables, such as fa-la-la.

Baritone: male voice range roughly between the higher tenor range and the lower bass range.

Bar line: vertical line on a musical staff separating the measures.

Bas instrument: in the Renaissance, an instrument with low volume, meant for indoor use.

Bass: in vocal music, the lowest voice range.

Bellows: mechanical device to take in and expel air.

Bore: a passageway by which air passes through an instrument.

Broken consort: in the Renaissance era, a grouping of dissimilar instruments.

Burden: a recurring line following each stanza (of a carol), often in Latin.

Burlesque: satire or parody of a usually serious subject.

Canzonettes: a secular vocal work for three to five voices.

Castrato: males castrated as youths to keep their singing voices unnaturally high.

Choir: organized body of singers, especially in a church.

Chromaticism: a style of composition using notes outside the normal notation system.

Clef sign: symbol placed on a musical staff indicating note pitches.

Conical bore: a bore that is wider at one end than at the other.

Consort: in the Renaissance era, a grouping of instruments from the same family. Also known as Whole consort.

Counter-melody: a second melody fashioned to be played with another, primary melody.

Counterpoint: in music, one melody line against another to create a single fabric of music; polyphony.

Course: in the Renaissance, a pair of strings on a stringed instrument.

Cylindrical bore: a bore that is the same size throughout its length.

Descant: a counterpoint above the basic melody.

Ditty: Elizabethan word for song.

Duet: two instruments playing the same piece at the same time.

Duple: in music, tempo divided into twos; 2/4 or 4/4, for example.

Elevation: in dancing, the ability to leap.

Etiquette: rules for polite behavior; manners.

Fipple: a mouthpiece that automatically splits the airstream over another opening.

Flags: a hook fixed on the top of a note stem to indicate a particular rhythm.

Font: the particular typeface used during printing.

Frets: raised lines across the fingerboards of certain stringed instruments that mark the position for stopping the strings to produce a particular note.

Frottola: a form of popular secular vocal music in Renaissance Italy.

Fundamental: the acoustic effect produced by a single vibration; the lowest tone possible at any given point on an instrument.

Furies: mythological beings who wreaked vengeance on mortals.

Galliard: dance music played in triple time at a moderately fast tempo.

Glissando: the execution of rapid scales by a sliding movement.

Guild: an association of merchants or artisans; forerunner of the union.

Half-step: smallest interval between two notes in Western music.

Harmonic series: the fundamental tone and its overtones at any given point on an instrument; the overtone series is fundamental, octave, fifth, fourth, and so on.

Harpsichord: a keyboard instrument widely used from the sixteenth to the eighteenth centuries.

Haut instrument: in the Renaissance, an instrument with a loud volume, meant for outdoor use.

Hexameter: in poetry, a line of verse containing six metrical feet.

Jigg: a short comedic play, usually involving singing and dancing, often performed following a serious or tragic play.

Key jacks: a long piece of wood in a keyboard instrument that connects the key to the plectrum, enabling the plectrum to pluck a string when a player strikes a key.

Key signature: sharps or flats following the clef sign at the beginning of each staff, which apply to specific tones whenever they occur.

Lament: a melody with text expressing grief, sorrow, or regret.

Madrigal: an Italian song form also known as songs, sonets, canzonets, or ayres.

Major scale: a series of single notes moving up or down in steps, in a particular order of half- and whole steps (the order of steps is: whole, whole, half, whole whole whole half).

Mandora: a variant type of lute.

Masque: an elaborate dramatic and musical performance popular in England.

Minor scale: consisting of several different varieties, but all beginning with a whole step followed by a half-step, as opposed to the major scale's two whole steps.

Minstrel: a musician who makes a living singing and reciting poetry.

Mixed consort: see *Broken consort.*

Motet: a polyphonic vocal composition of a sacred nature, usually unaccompanied.

Mouth hole: a lateral orifice in which a stream of air is directed against the opposite lower edge of a hole drilled in the mouthpiece of a flute.

Nomenclature: terminology.

Note head: shaped form at the end of a note stem, usually round or diamond-shaped.

Note stem: a line protruding from a note head.

Octave: any tone with twice the frequency of any other tone.

Organ manual: keyboard of an organ.

Pandora: a variant type of lute, or possibly of guitar.

Part-book: a printed music book containing one individual part of a multivoiced work.

Patron: a person or institution that financially supports musicians or commissions their music.

Peer: a person who is an equal to another person in some way.

Pipe (musical): a term for any type of flute.

Plectrum: a small piece of horn, tortoise-shell, wood, ivory, metal, and the like, used for playing.

Points of imitation: part writing device whereby a phrase in one voice is repeated by another.

Polyphonic: music involving the combination of two or more independent melody lines.

Pricksong: a song written down, not passed along by oral tradition.

Privy: Elizabethan word for private.

Psalme: another word for church hymn, generally with words adapted from the Book of Psalms.

Psalter: a book of English verse paraphrases of the psalms, intended to be sung.

Quill: one of the large, strong flight or tail feathers of a bird, fashioned into a plectrum or writing instrument.

Rest: a moment of silence in music.

Satire: the use of sarcasm, irony, or wit in exposing abuses or follies; ridicule.

Secular: not under control of the church; worldly.

Solfeggio: the use of syllables for the tones of a major scale.

Solmization: the use of syllables as names for the tones of a major scale.

Solo: executed by a single voice or instrument.

Sonnet: a type of poem usually containing 14 lines.

Soprano: the highest voice in the SATB (soprano, alto, tenor, bass) vocal grouping.

Sound post: in violins, a small piece of pine wood fixed between the table and the back which conveys sound vibrations of the table to the back of the instrument.

Stable of musicians: a group of musicians belonging to a certain patron.

Staff: a system of lines and spaces indicating musical notes and their relation to one another.

Stanza: the division of a poem into a certain number of lines.

Suite: in music, a form of instrumental composition consisting of a series of dance forms.

Tablature: a type of music writing suitable for one type of instrument, particularly the lute.

Through-composed: a song in which each stanza has music different from the other stanzas.

Time signature: sign placed at the beginning of a work of music to indicate its time or meter.

Tone holes: holes in an instrument which vary its pitch by covering and uncovering them.

Treble clef: a symbol placed on a musical staff indicating higher pitches on its staff lines and spaces, as opposed to notes on a staff line with a Bass clef.

Trill: rapid alternation between a given note and the note above it.

Triple: in music, a tempo divisible by threes; for instance, 3/4 or 6/4.

Venue: means of getting to an object.

Vernacular: language of the people of a region.

Verse anthem: a type of hymn sung in the Church of England.

Viol: early bowed stringed instruments of varying sizes.

Violin bridge: the wooden support on the instrument table across which its strings are stretched.

Virginals: an English term for the harpsichord, or variants of that instrument.

Waits: English musicians acting as night watchmen, sounding the hours with their instruments; later applied to musicians grouped together into town bands.

Whole consort: see *Consort.*

Whole step: the distance of two half-steps between notes.

Index

About the Author

SUZANNE LORD is Assistant Professor of Flute and Music History at Southern Illinois University, Carbondale.